The Obama Doctrine

THE OBAMA DOCTRINE

American Grand Strategy Today

COLIN DUECK

OXFORD
UNIVERSITY PRESS

UNIVERSITY PRESS

Oxford University Press is a department of the University of
Oxford. It furthers the University's objective of excellence in research,
scholarship, and education by publishing worldwide.

Oxford   New York
Auckland   Cape Town   Dar es Salaam   Hong Kong   Karachi
Kuala Lumpur   Madrid   Melbourne   Mexico City   Nairobi
New Delhi   Shanghai   Taipei   Toronto

With offices in
Argentina   Austria   Brazil   Chile   Czech Republic   France   Greece
Guatemala   Hungary   Italy   Japan   Poland   Portugal   Singapore
South Korea   Switzerland   Thailand   Turkey   Ukraine   Vietnam

Oxford is a registered trademark of Oxford University Press
in the UK and certain other countries.

Published in the United States of America by
Oxford University Press
198 Madison Avenue, New York, NY 10016

Cataloging-in-Publication data is on file at the Library of Congress
ISBN 978-0-19-020262-0

9 8 7 6 5 4 3 2 1
Printed in the United States of America
on acid-free paper

*This book is dedicated to
my wife Kirsten and our son Jack*

CONTENTS

ACKNOWLEDGMENTS

Since 2008, my understanding of American foreign policy has been enriched by discussions, interviews, panels, debates, and conversations with a diverse group of people whose opinions I respect—even when we do not always agree. An incomplete list of such people would have to include Elliot Abrams, David Adesnik, A. T. Alden, Robert Art, Michael Barone, Peter Beinart, Peter Berkowitz, Dan Blumenthal, John Bolton, Hal Brands, Christopher Bright, Shawn Brimley, Ted Bromund, Chris Brose, Ian Brzezinski, Mark Brzezinski, Jonathan Burks, Jim Carafano, Eliot Cohen, Bridge Colby, Ryan Crocker, Tom Davis, Daniel Deudney, Tom Donnelly, Michael Doran, Daniel Drezner, Mackenzie Eaglen, Nicholas Eberstadt, Eric Edelman, Drew Erdmann, Peter Feaver, Zhu Feng, Jamie Fly, Aaron Friedberg, David Frum, Francis Fukuyama, John Gaddis, Adam Garfinkle, Michael Gerson, James Goldgeier, Fred Greenstein, Jakub Grygiel, Nick Gvosdev, Richard Haass, Mary Habeck, Stephen Hadley, Jacob Heilbrunn, Charles Hill, John Hillen, Kim Holmes, Brian Hook, Michael Horowitz, Will Inboden, Fred Kagan, Robert Karem, Mark Katz, Zachary Keck, Charles Kesler, Greg Koblentz, Andrew Krepinevich, Sarah Kreps, Bill Kristol, Matt Kroenig, Charles Kupchan, James Kurth, Jim Lacey, Mark Lagon, Chris Layne, Daniel Leger, Paul Lettow, Robert Lieber, Tod Lindberg, Fred Logevall, Becky Lollar, Rich Lowry, Alan Luxenberg, Tom

Mahnken, Peter Mandaville, Dan Markey, John Maurer, Walter McDougall, Eric McGlinchey, Bryan McGrath, John McIntyre, Wess Mitchell, Mitch Muncy, Joshua Muravchik, Chuck Myers, Henry Nau, Hung Nguyen, Grover Norquist, Michael O'Hanlon, Meghan O'Sullivan, Mac Owens, Danielle Pletka, Ionut Popescu, Chris Preble, Jeremy Rabkin, Mitchell Reiss, Stanley Renshon, Joe Riley, Stephen Rosen, Robert Ross, Joshua Rovner, Mark Royce, Paul Saunders, Nadia Schadlow, Kori Schake, Gary Schmitt, Jim Shinn, Dmitri Simes, Kiron Skinner, Marion Smith, Henry Sokolski, Matt Spalding, Jeremi Suri, Ray Takeyh, Jim Talent, Jim Thomas, Trevor Thrall, Peter Trubowitz, Ming Wan, Vin Weber, George Will, William Wohlforth, Joe Wood, Leet Wood, Dov Zakheim, Roger Zakheim, Robert Zarate, and Philip Zelikow. My thanks to all of them. In the end, the arguments contained in these pages—and the responsibility for them—are mine alone.

It has been a genuine pleasure to work with editor David McBride, Sarah Rosenthal, and the staff of Oxford University Press on this book. My sincere thanks to them all.

Portions of various chapters are drawn and revised from my own articles in *Claremont Review of Books*, *Orbis*, and *Ricochet*. My thanks to the editors and publishers of those journals and websites for permission to reprint these sections.

Portions of different chapters are revised and reprinted from the following sources—*Orbis* 50:2, Colin Dueck, "Strategies for Managing Rogue States," 223–41, copyright 2006, with permission from Elsevier (chapters 1 and 2); "The Accommodator: Obama's Foreign Policy," by Colin Dueck, in *Policy Review* 169 (October–November 2011) with the permission of the publisher, Hoover Institution Press. Copyright 2011 by the Board of Trustees of Leland Stanford Junior University (chapters 1 and 2); *Claremont Review of Books*, Winter 2011–2012, Colin Dueck, "How Wars End" (chapter 2); *Ricochet*, February

21, 2014, Colin Dueck, "Ukrainian Unrest and Obama's Failed Reset" (chapters 2 and 4); and *Foreign Affairs* online, January 29, 2014. Copyright 2014 by the Council on Foreign Relations, Inc., at www.foreignaffairs.com (chapter 4).

Thanks also for permission to reprint from the former editor of *Policy Review*, Tod Lindberg. That journal is missed.

Special thanks to Pris Regan, who as chair of George Mason University's Department of Public and International Affairs between 2010 and 2014 provided friendship and support essential to the writing of this work. Pris also played a crucial role in the formation of George Mason's new School of Policy, Government, and International Affairs, in which we are both now faculty.

Introduction

Every modern American president has a foreign policy doctrine. We know of the Truman doctrine, the Carter doctrine, the Reagan doctrine, and the Bush doctrine. They are encapsulations of a president's foreign policy strategy—for better or worse.

What is the Obama doctrine? The flexible quality of the current president's foreign policy has encouraged an unusual range of theories as to its nature. Since Barack Obama first ran for the White House, and in the intervening years, various commentators have identified the following as central elements of the Obama doctrine:

- Engagement (Robert Singh)
- Leading from behind (Ryan Lizza)
- Drone strikes (David Rohde)
- A kinder, gentler empire (Robert Weiss)
- A lack of genuine strategic thinking (Leslie Gelb)[1]

The variety of these interpretations—together with the fact that all of them contain at least some plausibility—points to the shifting, ambiguous quality of American foreign policy under Obama. Perhaps the most plausible theory from the above list is the one offered by Leslie Gelb, president emeritus at the Council on Foreign Relations: that because Obama does not think in genuinely strategic terms internationally, there really is no Obama doctrine at all. Certainly this meshes with the view of many of the US president's critics.

If the definition of a grand strategy is that it imposes a rigorous coherence between ends and means on a country's international behavior over a wide range of specific regional cases, then it must be conceded that for the most part President Obama imposes no such rigor on US foreign policy. In fact, as I detail later in this book, the president's foreign policies have often been characterized by a striking disconnect between ends and means, as between words and actions.

Still, some of Obama's critics misread him in saying that he has no strategy whatsoever. If we define grand strategy a little more loosely, and perhaps more realistically, then we see that President Obama does indeed have a kind of implicit grand strategy, and that he has pursued it quite consistently since entering the Oval Office, whatever the twists and turns. That strategy, I suggest, is one of *overarching American retrenchment and accommodation internationally, in large part to allow the president to focus on securing liberal policy legacies at home.*

To expand on this definition: overseas, President Obama has emphasized US retrenchment and accommodation, using a hybrid approach that in certain cases combines with containment, engagement, assertion, integration, and even occasional—as in Libya—regime change. The strategic mixture pursued by Obama puts special emphasis on international gestures of goodwill, combined with the gradual retrenchment of America's military presence abroad. This approach fits not only with the president's sincere foreign policy convictions, but with his very ambitious domestic purposes. Obama's belief has long been that there needs to be a greater focus on domestic priorities than during the Bush years, and in particular on the possibility of achieving progressive domestic policy legacies. His preference therefore is to retrench America's military presence overseas, accommodate international rivalries, and focus on transformational domestic goals.

One value added of this definition is that it incorporates domestic policy and political priorities—as governments do—into the consideration of foreign policy strategy. In itself, this is not necessarily scandalous. US presidents are among other things practical politicians, and practical politicians understand that domestic political support must be built and sustained for even the most high-minded initiatives overseas. Foreign policy may be subject to domestic political considerations in other ways as well. Public opinion exerts pressure on decision-makers; interest groups have their say; presidents, candidates, and members of Congress look to win election or re-election; and political parties clash over office and objectives. Some of these considerations may veer into the less admirable, but they are obviously central within the American political system, and American foreign policy is neither made nor understood in ignorance of them. I do not say that Obama is the first president to factor domestic political priorities into his foreign policy approach—far from it. Nor do I question his sincere belief in the correctness of both his domestic and international priorities. What I argue, specifically, is that at the end of the day, Obama's highest priorities are domestic, and that this has had a powerful effect on his foreign policy choices.

The sources I use to describe and analyze the Obama doctrine—both its goals and its consequences—are mostly sympathetic to the president and many of his overarching assumptions. I also detail existing Republican criticisms of his foreign policy: in fact, readers will find an entire chapter on the subject. But in terms of first assessing the goals and consequences of

Obama's foreign policy approach, the clear majority of citations are from sources more often supportive of the president than not. This includes, for example, journalistic reports, books and articles appreciative of the Obama administration's intentions; chronicles from leading newspapers such as the *Guardian, New York Times,* and *Washington Post,* not known for conservative politics; and published accounts from those who have worked on international and military issues for the president. They are all public record. The fact that these accounts provide in total a rather harsh assessment of the president's foreign policy achievements, despite their frequent sympathy with his overarching ideas, should make them all the more credible to the objective reader.

I also place heavy reliance on the president's speeches, comments, writings, and addresses for evidence of his foreign policy strategy. This is only appropriate. In a way, the heart of the Obama doctrine has been hiding in plain sight, since the president has been clear from the very beginning about his most treasured priorities. He has said, in his own words, that he looks to "transform this nation," "end wars," and focus on "nation-building right here at home."[2] And he has certainly tried to do so, according to his own lights.

It might be asked—and numerous intelligent observers have asked—whether such a thing as a foreign policy strategy is even possible, especially given the complexities of international relations, not to mention the American political system today.[3] Indeed, no less an authority than former president Bill Clinton once confided his view that when it came to grand strategy, presidents just "made it up as they went along."[4] Certainly, Clinton would be in a good position to know whether or not that was true. President Obama, for his part, has said, "I don't really even need George Kennan right now," referring to the intellectual architect of America's Cold War containment strategy.[5] But this statement should not necessarily be interpreted as modesty on the part of the current president. Rather, it may indicate a profound confidence: namely, that Obama already knows what he wants to do.

The international, political, and bureaucratic obstacles to any coherent US national security policy are obviously massive. Even at the best of times, the making of American grand strategy is an immensely complicated, contentious, and messy process, characterized by regular surprises, pushback, infighting, and incremental adjustments.[6] Given both the nature of the American polity, and the nature of strategy itself, we can hardly expect anything else. The formation of US grand strategy was complicated and contentious when the aforementioned George Kennan answered to Secretary of State George Marshall at a pivotal moment in American diplomatic history under President Harry Truman.[7] If this was true for them in their day, how much more true must it be for us. So if we define grand strategy—wrongly—as simply a prefabricated plan, carried out to the letter against all resistance, then clearly no president and probably no world leader has ever had such a strategy, nor ever will. But if we adopt a less stringent definition, we see that all presidents necessarily make choices and decisions in relation to US foreign and national security policy, based at least partially upon their own preexisting assumptions. Even a president's refusal to make a clear decision on some leading international or military issue is itself a choice, with material consequences.

A grand strategy assumes certain national goals, ends, or interests. It identifies existing challenges or threats to those interests. And it selects and recommends the particular policy instruments or means by which challenges are met and national goals pursued. Strategies may not be entirely coherent, preplanned, or well coordinated—in fact, they frequently are not. But the inescapable nature of limited resources, difficult choices, and strategic trade-offs in a country's foreign and defense policy means that decisions regarding grand strategy are both implicit and inevitable. The issue in judging any president's foreign policy is not whether he can avoid difficult strategic choices; he cannot. The real issue is the accuracy, fitness, and coherence of his strategic choices, however vague or implicit.[8]

In chapter 1, I describe some of the leading and perennial options in American grand strategy, including containment, regime change, engagement, integration, accommodation, retrenchment, and nonintervention. I offer a definition of grand strategy, and place special emphasis on the common US practice of mixed or hybrid strategies. This is followed by a brief analysis of some typical interactions between international strategy and domestic political considerations. I then make a case for how to think about Obama's place in American party politics, centering, as he himself does, on his domestic policy ambitions.

President Obama is frequently described by sympathetic observers as essentially moderate, practical, and nonideological in terms of his approach to public policy. In terms of his personal manner and tactical approach, Obama really is generally calm, flexible, and pragmatic. Yet those qualities are employed, in his view, toward a higher purpose—to bring about transformative changes to America's domestic life in a liberal or progressive direction. Since Obama's greatest ambitions are within the domestic policy arena, he is very reluctant to risk them through international or military policies that might shatter his center-left coalition. The president therefore keeps the final strategic decisions in his own hands, in consultation with a tight inner circle of White House advisers. The resulting paradox is a highly centralized decision-making process in which clear and internally coherent foreign policy decisions are often delayed or avoided, in order to minimize domestic political risk.

Again, this is not to deny that Obama simultaneously believes his foreign policies serve US international as well as global interests. No doubt he believes all of that. The question that naturally follows is whether the Obama doctrine has actually worked as intended. That question in turn can be broken down into two initial components: is the Obama doctrine working internationally? And is it working domestically? Chapters 2 and 3 address those twin concerns.

Insofar as the purpose of Obama's grand strategy has been to retrench America's strategic presence overseas without undue risk to basic US interests, and to encourage new patterns of international cooperation through diplomatic accommodations, then it must be said that on balance the Obama doctrine is not working. The president's core assumptions regarding international affairs are sincere and well intentioned, but frequently unrealistic. Wedded as Obama is to these assumptions, he has never fully appreciated the possible risks, costs, and downsides of US retrenchment and accommodation. What international successes he has secured have generally come from going against type. Moreover, the practical implementation of stated US policies overseas has often been weak under Obama. In one case after another, the president has simply refused to impose a serious coherence on specific regional or functional US policies abroad. Leading international actors including the governments of China, Russia, and Iran, along with Islamist militants in the Arab world, have naturally interpreted the current trend as one of US disengagement, creating a power vacuum that they are happy to fill. This is the unintended legacy of the Obama doctrine overseas, detailed in chapter 2.

In domestic political terms, the Obama doctrine has had more success in achieving some of the president's basic goals. After all, if a key concern inside the White House has been to prevent international military entanglements from derailing either the president's domestic policy agenda or his re-election, then it must be said: mission accomplished. During Obama's first term, whatever substantial problems there were with his foreign policy, he gave the public much of what it wanted: namely, a staggered withdrawal of American troops from Iraq and Afghanistan, avoidance of major new ground interventions, and an end to Osama Bin Laden. The last of these, in particular, allowed him to run for re-election in 2012 as an incumbent president with a clear political edge on foreign policy issues—a remarkable reversal of traditional partisan advantages. Of course, congressional Republicans put up staunch opposition to many of Obama's domestic policies from the very beginning; he has not been able to achieve everything he desired. No president ever has. But by any reasonable standard, the Obama years have seen dramatic and sweeping policy changes in a liberal direction on a whole host of issues including healthcare, financial regulation, and same-sex marriage, just to name a few—and in no significant case have they been held hostage to diplomatic or military controversies overseas. In that specific sense, the Obama doctrine has achieved its purpose, at least up until now.

One controversy looking toward the presidential election of 2016 is whether the political pattern from 2012 will hold. There are multiple signs it may not. Early in his second term, as the public observed Obama's handling of new international crises over Syria, Ukraine, and Iraq, his approval ratings on foreign policy issues dropped precipitously. In a sense, the rather disengaged international approach from his first term came back to haunt him. Yet despite tactical adjustments, there was little sign of any fundamental rethinking on his part. On the contrary, he remained committed to his overall approach. If Obama is both an unpopular president, and specifically an unpopular foreign policy president, come 2016, this will inevitably pose a serious problem for the Democratic Party's next presidential nominee, whatever position he or she takes on the issues.

None of this to say that Republicans will automatically take advantage of growing popular discomfort with Obama's foreign policy. For one thing, the GOP has recently been divided over international issues to an extent not seen since the early 1950s. Obama's presidency has witnessed the rise of a vocal, newly influential faction of libertarian and conservative noninterventionists, best represented by Senator Rand Paul (R-KY) and by think tanks such as the Cato Institute. Republican noninterventionists favor a new US strategy of deep retrenchment, including strict avoidance of foreign wars, cuts in defense spending, cuts in foreign aid, and cuts in America's military presence, bases, and alliance commitments overseas. For the first time since Senator Robert Taft of Ohio last ran for president in 1952, it is entirely possible that a noninterventionist might capture the GOP's presidential nomination. Obviously this would represent a historic challenge to traditional party tendencies on foreign policy issues, and if successful politically, to America's posture abroad.

What observers from outside the GOP often fail to appreciate, however, is that among Republican conservatives the roots of a more hawkish approach toward national security issues run very deep—well beyond the precincts of neoconservative intellectuals. Even now, the majority of conservatives and Republicans do not actually support any comprehensive disengagement or profound retrenchment of US military power overseas. In fact, for all practical purposes most GOP conservatives concur on aggressive counterterrorism, robust military spending, a firm line toward adversaries such as Iran, support for core US alliances, and a more muscular foreign policy approach than the one pursued by President Obama. Republican conservatives remain, of all American political constituencies, rather hawkish on national security issues. This means that while a noninterventionist could conceivably win the GOP nomination, so too could a more hawkish candidate. Nor is it obvious that a noninterventionist would necessarily perform better in a general election—more likely, the opposite.

In chapter 4, I sketch current debates within the GOP over foreign policy issues; delineate the various leading factions; and analyze the political strengths, limitations, bases of support, and policy convictions of each group in detail, referring to leading personalities and institutions as well as to extensive polling data from the Obama era. Then I discuss some possible implications for Republican Party foreign policy stands looking toward the presidential primaries and general election of 2016.

One advantage of this close analysis is the identification of a distinct conservative group caught between the GOP's neoisolationists and its most forceful security hawks. I call this third grouping the Republican Party's conservative nationalists. Conservative nationalists are skeptical regarding foreign aid, nation-building, and multilateral humanitarian interventions—especially as handled by President Obama—but continue to favor strong national defenses and an unyielding stance toward US adversaries overseas. A crucial factor in the coming Republican presidential primaries will be the direction these nationalists take. The GOP's nationalists have grown deeply skeptical of foreign interventions under Obama, but they are still quite hawkish on a range of national security issues, and as it turns out, Tea Party supporters tend to be conservative nationalists rather than strict noninterventionists. This is just one illustration of the way in which a simplistic dichotomy of Republicans as either neoconservative or isolationist is positively unhelpful and misleading.

In chapter 5, I shift to policy recommendations, centering on an international strategy of conservative American realism. A robust, conservative, and specifically American realism would exercise a stabilizing forward presence in Europe and Asia, while applying what I call "strategies of pressure" against US adversaries and competitors overseas. I show what such a strategy might look like in relation to China, Russia, Iran, and al-Qaeda, and why it is both viable and necessary internationally. I explain how this approach would differ from those of both Barack Obama and George W. Bush, and address related and valid concerns over the need to bring American deficit spending under control. In domestic political terms, my argument is that a foreign policy stance informed by robust conservative realism can help bridge the gap between most of the Republican Party's current factions while winning over some Democrats and independents—but that those who would dismantle America's forward strategic presence since World War II can and must be refuted.[9]

Conservatives need to learn a number of lessons from the past decade, but the answer is not to relapse into a narrow isolationism. In the end, within the American political system the pursuit of a serious, sustained foreign policy strategy is very much up to the president. The last two chapters of this book provide Republicans—and anyone interested in where Republicans may be headed—with analysis, predictions, and recommendations surrounding the political viability and international merits of several possible GOP foreign policy stands, looking toward 2016 and beyond.

1

Barack Obama and American Grand Strategy

In June 2011, President Obama announced the beginning of US troop withdrawals from Afghanistan, saying "the tide of war is receding." Specifically, he indicated that over 30,000 troops would come home by September 2012. Militarily, the announcement made little sense. If US forces in Afghanistan were central to the struggle against al-Qaeda, as the president had said more than once, then why withdraw so many of them so quickly? The answer requires factoring in domestic political considerations. In the approving words of David Corn, Washington bureau chief of *Mother Jones*:

Obama, his aides believed, was in a sound place; he was ending the wars in Iraq and Afghanistan—even if too slowly for some—without having to worry that large portions of the voting public would perceive him as weak on national security ... "We could shrug off the far Right," a senior administration official said. "And to the far Left we could say we share the goal of ending the war. This was a good spot." His counterterrorism strategy was not aimed at grand geostrategic initiatives ... And his political desire was to conclude the Afghanistan war without being seen as opposed to the war. The overarching message was that the 9/11 era was over.[1]

American grand strategy under Barack Obama emphasizes international retrenchment and accommodation, in order to allow the president to focus on securing liberal policy legacies at home. Like other US presidents, Obama pursues a mixed or hybrid approach toward questions of grand strategy, using elements of containment in some cases, and regime change in others. But the distinctive strategic mixture preferred by Obama places special emphasis on gestures of international goodwill, led by American example, and on the incremental retrenchment of US military commitments overseas. This approach, in turn, fits not only with Obama's genuine foreign policy convictions, but with his very ambitious domestic policy goals. Obama is careful and pragmatic tactically and stylistically, but his overarching goals are exceptionally bold—to "transform this nation," as he puts it, and leave behind a historic policy legacy of progressive, liberal reforms. Since his greatest ambitions are in the domestic policy arena, he is loathe to risk them through international strategic entanglements that might also fracture his center-left domestic coalition. Obama's main emphasis overseas is therefore upon gradually scaling back America's strategic footprint, in order to focus on what he calls "nation-building right here at home."

Grand Strategies in the American Experience

A grand strategy is a calculated relationship on the part of a country's leaders of ends and means in the face of potential international opponents. Any grand strategy does several things. First, it specifies certain national goals, ends, or interests. Second, it identifies existing challenges or threats to those interests. Third, it selects and recommends the particular policy instruments or means by which challenges are met and national goals pursued. These policy instruments might include, for example, diplomatic commitments; military intervention; foreign aid; and economic sanctions. A grand strategy is therefore a kind of conceptual road map, describing how to identify, prioritize, and match national resources to national interests against potential threats. Such strategies may not be entirely coherent, preplanned, or well coordinated—in fact, they frequently are not. But the inescapable nature of limited resources, hard choices, and strategic trade-offs in a country's foreign and defense policies means that decisions regarding grand strategy are both implicit and inevitable.[2]

A viable strategy must ensure that ends and means are well matched. Commitments, for example, should not exceed capabilities. Yet strategy also recognizes that our targets are—unlike, say, sculpture—animate objects, with the ability to respond, make choices, and fight back. Consequently, effective foreign policy strategists should and do strike a fine balance. On the one hand, they need to know what they want. On the other, they must be flexible as to how exactly they pursue it, given the inevitable surprises resulting from pushback by other actors within the international system.

What are the basic strategic alternatives open to the United States, in relation to its international opponents? The options can be simplified into a range of fundamental grand strategy types.

A strategy of *retrenchment* looks for ways to reduce a country's international and military costs and commitments. This might be done by cutting defense spending, withdrawing from certain alliance obligations, scaling back on strategic deployments abroad, reducing international expenditures, or all of the above.[3] Retrenchment does not necessarily avoid strategic entanglements altogether, but the desired direction is certainly one of lowered cost and reduced commitment. This tends to be especially appealing during periods of fiscal constraint and austerity, or in the wake of a sense of international overextension. The Nixon administration, for example, engaged in a significant measure of strategic retrenchment during the early 1970s, in the wake of the Vietnam War. Retrenchment may be implemented competently or incompetently; it does not always work as planned. In particular, the desire to reduce costs may actually trigger increased strategic and international risks that eventually impose even greater costs. As one of the leading realist scholars of international relations, Robert Gilpin, points out: "Retrenchment by its very nature is an indication of relative weakness and declining power, and thus retrenchment can have a deteriorating effect on relations with allies and rivals ... Rivals are stimulated to 'close in,' and frequently they precipitate a conflict in the process." For this reason, while Gilpin agrees that strategic retrenchment can sometimes work, he describes it as a "hazardous course," involving serious risk.[4]

Containment involves balancing, drawing lines, and creating geopolitical counterweights around the perimeter of a given opponent, often through military commitments to allies, but also through economic and diplomatic support. It is essentially a defensive strategy, in that the aim is to prevent expansion, deter aggression, and deny hostile gains. The utility of this strategy is not limited to only one historical era; US presidents both before and after the Cold War attempted versions of containment against a range of international opponents. Theodore Roosevelt, Woodrow Wilson, and Franklin Roosevelt, for example, each tried, in his own way, to contain German expansion short of US military intervention. The Clinton administration, in the 1990s, attempted to contain both Iraq and Iran. But of course the most well-known use of this strategy historically was the containment of the Soviet Union. In a sense anti-Soviet containment was traditional balance of power policy, creating diplomatic and military counterweights against a potential aggressor. The early Cold War version, however, had certain features that do not always follow from a desire to simply counterbalance. Under traditional balance of power diplomacy, opponents often engage in straightforward negotiations, even as they try to outmaneuver one another. But under early Cold War containment, as best articulated by US diplomat George Kennan, further negotiations were viewed as essentially futile and counterproductive due to the nature of Stalin's regime. Washington abjured significant diplomacy with the USSR, and tried to quarantine it instead, in the hopes that the Soviet Communist system would eventually mellow or collapse.[5] This was an important distinction. Containment can sometimes be combined with negotiations, under the right circumstances. Still, any strategy of containment requires patience, strength, and vigilance in order to take effect.

Regime change or *rollback* is a strategy aimed at the overthrow of a hostile government. This is the most assertive of the strategies discussed, and it can be implemented directly or indirectly. American policies of regime change generally aim at the replacement of an unfriendly government with a friendly one. Such strategies long predate the administration of George W. Bush, and will no doubt continue to be used, as they were, for example, by Barack Obama in relation to Libya, George H. W. Bush in relation to Panama, and Dwight Eisenhower in relation to Guatemala and Iran. Direct rollback entails the use of every policy tool up to full-scale war in order to achieve the toppling of a given regime. Indirect rollback involves covert action along with intense military, economic, and diplomatic pressure, with the goal of precipitating an opponent's collapse. Indirect rollback can also be combined with elements of containment. The United States experimented with such combinations during its Cold War struggle with the Soviet Union. One of George Kennan's great insights in 1946–1947 was that the USSR—unlike Hitler's Germany—was not actually inclined to risk war.[6] This distinction made anti-Soviet containment possible. Yet the costs and frustrations of Cold War containment sometimes left a more assertive strategy of regime change, rollback, or "liberation" rather appealing by comparison.[7] Direct anti-Communist rollback was in fact tried against North Korea in the fall of 1950, but was rejected in relation to China and the Soviet Union. Only under Ronald Reagan in the 1980s did Washington hit upon a version of indirect rollback combined with containment that served the US national interest. Rollback and regime change are essentially what military historian Hans Delbruck called "strategies of annihilation," rather than "strategies of exhaustion."[8] As such, they fit with an American preference for immediate and decisive results. Regime change has the one great advantage that when it works, it removes the existing threat altogether. But this advantage comes with great potential costs and risks. When strategies of regime change or rollback fail—as, for example, in 1961 against Cuba in the Bay of Pigs—they tend to fail spectacularly. And naturally a declared policy of regime change complicates diplomacy with the target state, and may even invite preemptive attack, without actually removing the existing threat.

Foreign policy analysts often speak of strategies of *engagement*, but the term is used to refer to some very distinct strategic alternatives, with contrasting core assumptions that should be clearly differentiated.

Engagement as *integration* is a strategy by which patterns of economic interdependence, political liberalization, and membership in international institutions are encouraged and expected to nudge potentially hostile, autocratic regimes in a friendlier, more cooperative, and democratic direction.[9] The classical US

Open Door policy toward China might be seen in this tradition. Integration is a common American strategic approach toward adversaries as well as allies, rooted in classical liberal assumptions about the nature of international politics. Some observers, for example, saw US detente with the Soviet bloc during the 1970s as just this sort of strategy. In the long term, there is evidence that elements of detente such as human rights provisions within the 1975 Helsinki accords helped to encourage seeds of dissent and thereby undermine Communist rule in Eastern Europe. In the short term, however, there is also considerable evidence that increased economic and institutional contact with the West actually helped prop up Communist regimes such as East Germany's.[10] The power of transnational contact to corrode authoritarian rule is often overestimated within the Western world. At the very least, the path by which such liberalization occurs is frequently more uneven, haphazard, and violent than liberal theory might suggest.

Engagement as *bargaining* rests on very different assumptions. A bargaining approach toward a potential opponent makes no claims about liberal democratic progress internationally, but simply involves the mutual exchange of interests and concessions, through negotiation, compromise, promises, and sometimes threats. Strictly speaking, bargaining is not a strategy in itself, but may be combined with other strategies, or may be avoided altogether. Observers often call upon the United States to engage its adversaries or "try diplomacy," when what they mean in essence is negotiate. To negotiate, in turn, is to bargain. But clearly a great deal depends on the nature of the precise bargain on offer—in other words, the particular terms available from the other side. The purpose of grand strategy is to advance concrete national interests. If a US adversary is willing to come to an agreement, however limited, that promotes those interests, then diplomatic efforts should be embraced. Otherwise, we ought to recognize that diplomacy is not an end in itself, and that it can even be used by skillful opponents to blunt or delay the advancement of American goals.[11]

A strategy of *accommodation* involves unilateral (i.e., one-way) concessions in an attempt to alter or satiate the aggressive demands, intentions, and ambitions of a potential opponent. This is distinct from simple bargaining, which entails mutual, simultaneous concessions without any expectation of changing the other actor's intentions. Efforts at accommodation typically begin with a one-sided concession toward the target state—some costly gesture of goodwill—in the hope of triggering a subsequent process of mutual restraint, conciliation, and possibly friendship. The risk of exploitation is deliberate, in order to be convincing.[12] Accommodation is not an uncommon strategy in international relations, when faced with potential threats or demands, and in the abstract it can sometimes work. The case of Britain's diplomatic accommodation of the United States, beginning in the 1890s, is often taken as an historical example of success. But the risks of any such strategy are obviously great. Since concrete concessions are made by one side only, there is nothing to stop the target state from pocketing its gains and moving on to the next demand.[13] If an opponent's intentions remain fundamentally hostile and unchanged, then efforts at accommodation only add to that opponent's power, and may even be taken as a sign of weakness, without removing the basic sources of conflict and tension. Strategies of accommodation are sometimes called *appeasement*, and the underlying logic is essentially the same.[14]

A strategy of *offshore balancing* is the preferred alternative of several leading foreign policy realists within the academy, including Christopher Layne, John Mearsheimer, Robert Pape, and Stephen Walt.[15] Under offshore balancing, the United States would still try to ensure that no one country dominates

Europe, Northeast Asia, or the Persian Gulf. But it would make others assume the main burden, and rely on local powers to balance one another, while stationing US military forces over the horizon—either offshore or within the United States. Under this strategy, America would maintain reduced land forces; rely on its relative military advantages at sea and in the air; embrace sharp reductions in the size of its army and marines; avoid counterinsurgency operations or peripheral interventions; and abstain from international projects involving the military occupation or governance of developing countries. According to their advocates, all of these strategic adjustments would mean much less expense. US armed forces would come onshore only once it appeared that regional powers could not maintain the balance themselves against a would-be hegemon. American troops would then exit and go back over the horizon, with the threat checked.[16] For the most part, the United States would avoid foreign wars, capitalize on its insular position, disband existing alliance commitments in Europe and East Asia, abandon the pursuit of American preponderance or hegemony overseas, and cut defense spending to about 2% of GDP.[17] Advocates of offshore balancing suggest that such a strategy was in fact the norm for most of US history, and that it worked perfectly well during that time. They argue that removing the sense of an American threat would reduce the need for other powers to develop weapons of mass destruction. They further suggest that offshore balancing would undercut support for anti-American terrorism, in that an extensive US troop presence overseas is itself a leading cause of terrorist attacks against the United States.[18] Finally, according to Mearsheimer, a strategy of offshore balancing would permit the United States to "pay for important domestic programs," curb America's "unlawful behavior abroad," and "tame our fearsome national security state."[19]

A strict posture of *nonintervention* goes beyond retrenchment to avoid international or strategic commitments and entanglements altogether, whether as threat or inducement. This avoidance, prevention, or dismantling of military, economic, and diplomatic commitments is also sometimes called *anti-intervention, nonentanglement,* or *disentanglement.* Properly understood, such a strategy is neither hawkish nor conciliatory, since it involves the use of neither sticks nor carrots to achieve the desired goals.[20] Nonintervention can be an appealing stance for maritime democratic powers such as the United States, both culturally and geopolitically. Arguably, it was America's strategic baseline for most of its history, at least with regard to Europe and mainland Asia. The United States, of course, tried to avoid involvement in both world wars, only to discover that it had vital interests at stake. And while America adopted a much more forward presence internationally during the 1940s, efforts at and perceptions of nonintervention in specific cases have in fact continued to characterize US grand strategy. In 1950, for example, North Korea attacked south under the mistaken impression that Washington would not intervene. Iraq's Saddam Hussein made a similar mistake in 1990 with regard to Kuwait. If true nonintervention were an option for the United States, these misperceptions would not matter. Certainly, the United States is not obliged to intervene in every case of international conflict; in circumstances where interests are limited, threats are modest, and the costs outweigh the benefits, nonintervention may be a perfectly good option. But at the overarching level, Americans typically believe that a more open, liberal, democratic international order is in the interest of the United States. This order is not self-sustaining. It requires protection, which a general strategy of nonintervention does not provide. When America adopts a posture of nonintervention, naturally this empowers authoritarian regimes to pursue their own international ambitions, and robs the

United States of its ability to influence potential conflicts overseas. Since the United States often finds itself drawn into such conflicts in any case, out of the pull of its own national interests, the initial impression of American disentanglement only encourages instability and war in the meantime. For these reasons, over the long term, a strategy of nonintervention can be the most costly and risky of all.[21]

When considering the above strategic options, keep in mind that the United States has never actually followed only one of them at a time, even within a single presidential administration. The norm instead has been *hybrid strategies*, which vary by time and place, and combine the advantages (or disadvantages) of pure strategic types such as integration and containment. In fact, hybrid strategies have been ubiquitous in American history, and have altered more by emphasis and degree than by absolute contrast. It is commonly suggested that the United States pursued strategic nonintervention before 1941, containment during the Cold War, and regime change under George W. Bush. But in reality, American strategy during each of these periods was a hybrid or mixture of multiple options. Regime change, for example, was pursued by American presidents in numerous cases overseas, long before George W. Bush; the real question has always been its relative prominence, implementation, and scope. Cold War US presidents pursued not only containment, but also integration, regime change, and bargaining, depending on the region and the moment. And well before the Japanese attack on Pearl Harbor in 1941, the United States was actively involved in international affairs, pursuing limited strategies of containment, bargaining, regime change, and above all integration, in addition to nonintervention. The continuities in American grand strategy over time are therefore at least as striking as the differences. And one such continuity is that individual presidents have frequently been given remarkable leeway to define and pursue hybrid strategies in ways that can lead to either dramatic failure or striking success.[22]

Since the practice of grand strategy involves building and maintaining policy tools of varying cost and expense to society at large, inevitably there is a domestic political component to it. The mobilization and extraction of national resources to meet international challenges can hardly be taken for granted as a constant. For one thing, various political factions within the country or even within a single political party may have sincere, principled disagreements over what the national interest actually is. Moreover, key constituencies of leading domestic political coalitions may have a powerful interest for or against some feature of a given international strategy. Presidents are commanders-in-chief and heads of state, but they are also party leaders and politicians—and often savvy ones—who head particular domestic coalitions with specific interests and preferences across a wide range of policy issues. As such, they typically seek not only to act upon their own beliefs regarding international affairs, but to also achieve domestic policy goals, reward party loyalists, win re-election, and secure a lasting historical legacy. The party coalitions that presidents lead each differ in terms of their readiness to invest national resources and attention into various tools of grand strategy. As leaders and managers of distinct partisan coalitions, presidents therefore differ widely in terms of the political capital they are willing to expend in pursuit of costly international strategies.

It is sometimes suggested, by both scholars and general observers, that presidents engage in aggressive foreign policies in order to secure electoral success or reward some narrow group of domestic political supporters. According to this school of thought, the political incentives for hawkish foreign policy behavior then leave the country overextended, strategically. But in a democratic system like that of the United States, the opposite is at least as likely: that presidents may underreact to international threats or challenges, and leave the country strategically underextended, as it were, because of domestic political pressures or constraints, including the policy preferences of dominant party coalitions. Certain grand strategies, even if sensible from a strictly international perspective, may entail economic expenses and domestic political risks that are simply unacceptable to a given president or supporting coalition. The practical implementation of grand strategy should consequently be viewed, as it no doubt is inside the White House, as a running series of trade-offs between international risks and domestic political ones—trade-offs to which various presidents will respond differently, depending upon their own particular policy convictions and coalition interests.[23]

Since President Obama's greatest policy goals are actually within the domestic arena, we need to take a moment to consider those goals, together with his current role in patterns of US party politics. This will subsequently allow us to turn back again to Obama's foreign policy goals, having placed them—as he does—in their domestic American context.

Obama's Place in American Politics

President Obama is often described by sympathetic observers as essentially moderate, pragmatic, and nonideological in terms of his approach to public policy. He certainly views himself this way, and stylistically as well as tactically the perception carries a great deal of truth.[24] It is, however, dramatically incomplete, and indeed Obama's own self-image, words, and actions also provide much evidence that in overarching terms he is not literally in the middle or equidistant between the major ideological tendencies of American political development. On the contrary, in the great and recurring debate within this country between conservatives on the one hand, and liberals or progressives on the other, he hopes for and works toward liberal policy legacies; leads a distinctly progressive Democratic Party coalition; and is in some ways one of the more impressive such leaders that party has had in many years.[25]

Political scientists have shown that to a remarkable extent, most votes in the US Congress can be organized and depicted along a single ideological continuum. This continuum is best described as ranging from liberal, to moderate, to conservative, where the biggest issue is that of the government's proper role in the economy.[26] The two great political parties in the United States have not always lined up neatly on either side of this issue; there have been conservative Democrats historically, especially in the South, as well as liberal Republicans. But in recent decades, voters as well as political officials have increasingly sorted themselves into each party along ideological lines, with economic liberals voting Democrat, and economic conservatives voting Republican. This has encouraged a process known as polarization, whereby the elected leaders of the two parties overlap less and less in ideological terms. Moreover, partisan polarization on economic issues has been supplemented by partisan polarization on social and cultural matters.[27] Especially since the 1960s, on a wide range of social issues including civil rights, abortion, crime, and the implementation of traditional moral norms, Republican officials have become more consistently conservative, while Democratic officials have become more consistently liberal. To be sure, there are still millions of moderate American voters who fall between the most commonly stated positions of the two major parties on both economic and social matters. Millions more are cross-pressured, agreeing with one party on certain issues but not on others.[28] Yet the parties themselves are truly polarized today ideologically, as much as at any time over the past century, with the GOP as a clearly conservative-leaning party, and the Democrats as a liberal-leaning one. And while presidents in one sense represent all Americans, they also represent and are expected to represent the policy preferences of the party coalition of which they are the head.

Every impactful president has been, among other things, a party leader, working to achieve the broad goals of one party coalition or ideological tendency rather than another. For example, the major waves of liberal and progressive legislation within the United States over the past century have all come under Democratic presidents, notably Woodrow Wilson, Franklin Roosevelt, and Lyndon Johnson. Conservatives have often played the role of trying to slow down, contain, and if possible roll back such waves of liberal legislation, a role they have played with at best mixed success. Only rarely, as under Ronald Reagan, have American conservatives found a president who truly nudged the country in a rightward direction.[29] But one thing all four of the above presidents had in common, whether Democratic or Republican, is that they triggered fierce ideological opposition, precisely because they were understood to be working toward historic policy changes supported by either liberals or conservatives but not both. Another thing they each had in common is that they sometimes left ideological purists on their own side dissatisfied, for the simple reason that being an ideological purist and being president are practically incompatible. Successful presidents often tack and weave politically, precisely in order to accomplish long-term principled goals. Those rare presidents like FDR and Reagan, who leave behind powerful and enduring legacies in terms of policy accomplishments, governmental priorities, and partisan alignments, are described by the leading scholar of presidential politics Stephen Skowronek as "reconstructive" presidents.[30] An equally good term would be "transformational." Not all presidents seek to be transformational, and even fewer actually succeed.

One starting point for understanding Obama's presidency is that he looks for it to be a transformational one. In fact, he has frequently reiterated his ambition to "transform this nation."[31] Moreover he is far from indifferent to the broad policy content of such a transformation. He does not look, for example, to be a transformational president pushing the country in a conservative direction. He looks to be a transformational president on behalf of broadly liberal or progressive goals. His comments comparing Reagan's presidency with that of Bill Clinton are instructive in this regard. Ideologically, Obama was certainly more sympathetic to Clinton's policy agenda than to Reagan's. But Obama gives credit to the latter figure, saying: "I think Ronald Reagan changed the trajectory of America . . . in a way that Bill Clinton did not."[32] That is to say, Obama respects Reagan for being a highly consequential president, even if he disagrees with the basic direction Reagan took. Indeed, one of Obama's chief criticisms of the Clinton years is that Democrats—including Clinton himself—seemed to have given up on the possibilities for more sweeping policy changes, intimidated as they were by the strength of Republican conservatism in the country at large. Still, Obama does not hold Clinton entirely responsible for this period of liberal Democratic weakness or timidity; he recognizes that the moment must be ripe, in order for transformational leadership to have a chance.[33] What happened by 2008–2009, according to Obama's own account, was not only the arrival of a potentially transformative president—namely himself—but also the arrival of a ripe moment, due to pent-up popular demand along with the apparent failures of the Bush years.

Obama has often benefited politically from his calm, careful demeanor, even though it is sometimes mistaken for a lack of core conviction. His personality and decision-making style are described quite accurately as cerebral, detached, and even-tempered. He likes to gather a range of information, hear various points of view, keep his options open, and take his time in making a decision. He furthermore sees the discursive process as inherently beneficial, and enjoys positioning himself rhetorically between what he typically describes as false extremes.[34] All of these qualities frequently lead observers to call him moderate, pragmatic, or even conservative, which in turn encourages the impression that he is somehow highly enigmatic or paradoxical given his obvious progressive sympathies. But there is really no great puzzle here; personality and decision-making style are simply not the same things as overarching policy goals.

Obama's personal background, rhetorical skills, and political talents are truly interesting and unusual, but his basic policy beliefs are and have long been quite conventionally liberal. During his four years as a US senator, for example, Obama compiled a lifetime approval rating of approximately 90% from the liberal Americans for Democratic Action, and less than 10% from the American Conservative Union.[35] This was a fairly good indication of his core convictions. A genuine moderate, within the context of US politics, would have compiled a rating of about 50% from both groups. Numerous public opinion polls from 2008 onward demonstrate that the median American voter also perceives Obama as a rather liberal, center-left figure—not "extreme" left, admittedly, but also not really in the middle. In 2008, more voters actually viewed themselves as closer to the GOP's center-right presidential nominee John McCain, ideologically, than to Barack Obama.[36] The very same pattern repeated in 2012, in relation to Mitt Romney.[37] Yet a majority of Americans voted for Obama both times, for other reasons. Obama clearly views himself as opposed to any rigid ideology.[38] But in practice, on major US public policy issues, he usually ends up agreeing far more with the liberal position than the conservative one. The way he maintains his self-image as free from ideology, in his own words, is that "the arguments of liberals are more often grounded in reason and fact."[39] That is to say, for Obama there is no contradiction between being a liberal or a progressive on the one hand, and being nonideological on the other, since liberal policy conclusions tend to be objectively true. To be sure, this is a fascinating way of squaring that particular circle. Nevertheless it is hard to take seriously any depiction of him as someone truly in the middle of the American political spectrum as it actually exists today.

Like most consequential presidents, Obama taps into very broadly held beliefs in this country regarding the American creed, while making his own distinct case as to the proper implications of that creed. Specifically, he argues with considerable rhetorical power that the progressive cause, the American cause, and sheer common sense are all really one and the same. Take three of his leading speeches on the subject: December 2011 in Kansas, September 2012 at the Democratic Party's national convention, and January 2013 in his second inaugural address. In these addresses, Obama celebrates what he calls the American dream—defined mainly as economic security, prosperity, and opportunity for the average citizen—while arguing that "fair play" along with the needs of a modern economy require regular and urgent government action to protect that very same dream. After a quick nod in the direction of "rugged individualism," he proceeds to dismiss conservative beliefs regarding government's proper role in the economy as cynical, uncaring, outdated, and impractical. The contrast he therefore offers is between "two fundamentally different visions," one in which inequalities are redressed and "everyone does their fair share," and the other in which "you're on your own." Finally, he ties the overall argument into a sense of civic patriotism and "American values."[40] This is heady stuff, especially for liberals, who for decades sought a Democratic Party leader capable of making such a link between US nationalism and progressive ideals. Of course, it is not the only way of interpreting American values or the American creed. US conservatives, for their part, view that creed as essentially an injunction to limited government and individual liberty, rather than to what Obama calls "collective action" to redress inequality. But it is precisely the genius of transformational presidents, if they are successful, to leave as commonsensical what was once controversial—and all with reference to the unifying force of the nation's core values.[41]

Obama believes and has long believed in an expansive role for the federal government to promote social justice, reduce inequalities, and counter abuses in the private sector. He looks for big, bold policy changes toward that end. As he sometimes reminds his White House staff, in an unsubtle dig at the policy modesty of the Clinton years, "we're not here to do school uniforms."[42] Yet Obama is also very much focused on what he calls "getting stuff done." In other words, he is a politician, not a pristine saint or martyr. He is well aware of the distinction between the ideal and the achievable; has no objection to making incremental progress toward his goals; and willingly takes half a loaf instead of none. This is the sense in which he is accurately described as practical. In terms of his personal manner and tactical approach, Obama really is calm, flexible, and pragmatic. Yet those qualities, for him, are employed in the end toward a higher purpose, and that purpose is to bring about transformative changes to America's social, economic, and political life in a progressive or liberal direction. Accounts by sympathetic journalists tend to paint a similar picture. For the forty-fourth US president, the policy specifics are negotiable, but the core priorities, progressive convictions, and soaring ambitions are not.[43]

The actual policy record of the Obama years provides considerable evidence for the sheer scale of this president's transformative and progressive agenda. The 111th Congress alone passed legislation in 2009–2010 amounting to one of the great waves of liberal policy reforms in recent generations.[44] This included, notably, the 2009 economic stimulus package, which spent more money in absolute terms than FDR's New Deal; sweeping regulatory reforms of the US financial system; and above all, the 2010 Affordable Care Act, a historic and dramatic overhaul of American healthcare. No doubt Obama was sincere in his initially stated desire to work together with willing Republicans in achieving these public policy goals, but given that GOP conservatives disagreed in principle with the efficacy, scope, and even constitutionality of Obama's reform agenda, it is hardly surprising that they refused to cooperate in the achievement of it. Indeed the 2010 congressional midterms indicated, whether or not progressives cared to admit it, that the median American voter felt the Democrats were overreaching politically and legislatively.[45] The president spent much of 2011 locked in budgetary trench warfare with congressional Republicans, only to emerge the following year with a combative defense of his record and achievements as well as of core progressive values. Having campaigned for re-election on an unusually direct stance of liberal social and economic populism, Obama and his base of supporters felt vindicated by the solidly winning result. A one-term president can easily be interpreted as a failure, but a president serving out two full terms with a clear progressive policy legacy is something America has not really seen since FDR.[46] To be sure, congressional Republicans managed to block much of what Obama wanted during his second term. Still, the underlying attempt at ambitious, progressive policy reforms interwoven with tactical concessions and adjustments continued. On a wide range of issues including energy, banking, the environment, healthcare, education, gun control, immigration, taxation, and gay rights, Obama has encouraged, pursued, and often accomplished truly sweeping liberal policy changes since first being elected to the White House. Overall, he has governed with an eye on securing his place historically as one of the country's great progressive presidents.[47]

Obama's Grand Strategy

Where does Obama's foreign policy fit into all this? What is his grand strategy overseas? Readers will have noted that the previous section made no mention of international affairs. This is no coincidence. The point is precisely that Obama's first priority is not foreign policy, but domestic. To a greater extent than most presidents since World War II, he simply devotes less time, political capital, and intellectual energy to international priorities as opposed to domestic ones. This is hardly to say that Obama has no deeply held beliefs regarding world politics. On the contrary, he does, and more will be said about them in a moment. But for him, at the end of the day, international strategies are subordinate to domestic considerations—specifically, to his domestic policy agenda. That agenda, as we have just indicated, is not simply to win elections—which he would view as rather unambitious—but to safeguard and advance significant liberal or progressive policy legacies.

Under Obama, foreign policy is viewed very much in the light of whether it furthers, protects, or risks key components of his domestic agenda. As the *Economist* observed in December 2012: "Mr. Obama and his team believe that his outstanding task is to secure a domestic legacy. Their fear is that foreign entanglements may threaten that goal."[48] In itself, this is not necessarily scandalous; domestic factors always interact with international ones in the formation of grand strategy, and decisions regarding that interaction must rest on value judgments as well as estimates of utility. But obviously this has multiple and important implications for American grand strategy. In Obama's case, the implications are as follows. First, it means that national resources must be shifted in relative terms from security spending to domestic social and economic spending—a shift clearly visible in federal budgets since 2009. Second, it means steering clear of partisan political fights over national security that might detract from Obama's political capital. And third, it means that potentially costly new international entanglements must for the most part be avoided. Sometimes these three imperatives are in tension with one another. For example, during the autumn of 2009, Obama was tempted to begin winding down America's military engagement in Afghanistan, yet at the same time wanted to avoid appearing weak on national security. So he settled on an approach that called for temporary US escalation in Afghanistan, resolved by subsequent disengagement beginning in July 2011. That approach was hardly optimal militarily, but it was the least bad policy in domestic political terms given his overarching priorities.[49] This pattern has been repeated many times during his presidency. Obama's evident concern is that foreign commitments and heated national security debates might detract time, money, and attention from his very ambitious domestic reform agenda. The main implication of this concern when it comes to US grand strategy is an overarching emphasis on international accommodation and retrenchment, tempered by the desire to preempt criticism from Republicans.

The domestic political arguments for international accommodation and retrenchment are matched and reinforced, in Obama's mind, by a genuine principled case for a more modest and conciliatory American stance abroad. By all appearances Obama sincerely believes, and has said repeatedly over the years, that the United States should be more accommodating toward potential adversaries and rivals overseas—accommodating of their interests, their perspectives, and their wishes. The reason is that through accommodation, these potential rivals can be turned, if not into friends, then at least into something other than adversaries. At least this is what Obama believes. He can certainly be cold-blooded when making short-term or tactical calculations in relation to clear, existing US enemies. After all this is the president who hunted down Osama bin Laden, went to war over Libya, and escalated the use of unmanned drone strikes—basically targeted killings—against suspected terrorists in multiple countries. As the president made clear in his 2009 Nobel Prize acceptance speech, he is no strict pacifist: "the instruments of war do have a role to play in preserving the peace ... war is sometimes necessary."[50]

At heart, however, Obama does not really believe that conflict is at the essence of world politics. On the contrary, he believes that genuine and overarching international cooperation is possible, if apparent adversaries can learn to listen to and accommodate one another. Moreover he has a very specific and characteristic formula for promoting such cooperation—a style he seems to have first fully developed as a community organizer in Chicago. It is not through traditional American mechanisms such as the bold promotion of democracy or economic interdependence overseas. Rather, it is through the mutual accommodation of interests, led by American example. What this means is that in the case of partially adversarial or even hostile relationships with other countries, the United States reaches out and makes some gesture or concession or accommodation, in the expectation of reciprocal concession. In such cases, "American leadership" or "leading by example" means essentially taking the lead in making concessions. Similarly, in the case of friendly or allied relationships, the United States under Obama frequently proposes new regimens or collective concessions—sometimes on the part of allies, sometimes on the part of the United States—in order to catalyze broad processes of international accommodation on issues such as arms control, counterterrorism, or climate change. Either way, the expectation is one of mounting agreement, reduced conflict, and increased cooperation internationally, based upon mutual accommodation, and sparked by American example.

For Obama, this sincere emphasis on international accommodation dovetails with a conviction that strategic retrenchment is very much in the US national interest. It is not simply that Obama's domestic political base wants to see a shift from guns to butter, or from international military priorities to domestic ones. He himself wants to see the same shift, and he has in fact implemented a certain retrenchment of US military power and geopolitical reach during his time in office. Overall—with some important exceptions—he has looked to cut costs, minimize commitments, avoid new military interventions, and scale back on America's strategic footprint abroad. Obama believes that a modest strategic retrenchment can and already has freed up national energy and resources to revive the US economy and pursue progressive domestic reforms, or as he frequently puts it, "nation-building here at home."[51]

As with most presidents, US grand strategy under Obama is a hybrid or mixture of numerous alternatives, varying by time and place. Just as it would be a mistake to caricature US strategy under George W. Bush as simply one of regime change, so too it would be a mistake to oversimplify Obama's actual strategic practices. There are certainly clear elements of strategic types other than accommodation and retrenchment under this administration.

Containment, for example, is emphasized in relation to North Korea and to a lesser degree toward Iran. Even Obama's policy toward China has elements of containment. Regime change or rollback was the final alternative pursued against Gaddafi's Libya in 2011, and one might say that Obama has pursued an assertive strategy of rollback against the core of al-Qaeda. Integration through diplomatic contact and membership in international institutions is a stated American goal with regard to both China and Russia. Bargaining has also clearly been used as a technique by the Obama administration in relation to these same two great powers. Even nonintervention has been a kind of tacit US strategy in some cases recently, as in parts of Africa. Overall, however—and especially in comparison to his immediate predecessor—Obama's main emphasis when it comes to grand strategy has been on international accommodation and retrenchment. The real issue is whether his strategy has worked.

Sympathetic observers often suggested that the problem with Obama's grand strategy was the disconnect between its international and its domestic political effectiveness. The Obama doctrine—so the argument went—was realistic and sophisticated about the limits of US power, but did not play well domestically, where voters prefer what one presidential adviser called a "John Wayne" kind of figure.[52] Actually, the truth for several years was very nearly the opposite. Major parts of Obama's grand strategy—especially the aspect of incremental retrenchment—played relatively well with the general public inside the United States, allowing him to win re-election along with numerous domestic policy victories. Internationally, however, it simply did not work as advertised. There was indeed a disconnect here, but it was between the Obama doctrine's ineffectiveness internationally and its political effectiveness at home.

If the goal of US accommodation and retrenchment was to strengthen America's position abroad and encourage potential adversaries to accommodate the United States, then it has to be said the strategy did not work. US retrenchment under Obama combined with his particular style of foreign policy leadership allowed numerous threats to germinate internationally, carrying serious long-term consequences. However, for years many of those threats were insufficiently vivid to grab the general public's attention within the United States. So if, as I have suggested, a major goal of US accommodation and retrenchment was to allow President Obama to secure progressive policy legacies, win domestic political victories, and preserve the strength of his center-left coalition, then it must be conceded that—during his first term, at least—the strategy worked fairly well. Obama in fact prevented complicated and violent conflicts within Afghanistan, Libya, Iraq, Syria, and East Asia from derailing his domestic agenda. Meanwhile, he achieved potentially transformative domestic reforms in a progressive or liberal direction, over healthcare, financial regulation, and gay rights, to name only a few leading issue areas. And of course he won re-election—the ultimate domestic political test.

Insofar as one of the key features of the Obama doctrine was a light footprint overseas, this was not a bad fit with the preferences of the median American voter. Obama's mixture of aggressive strikes against al-Qaeda combined with an avoidance of "boots on the ground" was a fair reflection of how much of congressional and popular opinion felt about US foreign policy, in the wake of major wars in Iraq and Afghanistan and a major recession. In fact, this particular mixture of international strategies put Republicans in a difficult position, forcing them to criticize Obama either as doing too little abroad—not an especially popular sentiment with the general public—or as doing too much, which most leading Republicans understood was simply not true. Obama consequently did something in his 2012 re-election campaign that no Democrat had done since 1964: he made foreign policy a winning issue for Democrats. In strictly partisan political terms, this was an impressive achievement. The question then became what price would be paid internationally due to the way he had handled American grand strategy.

2

International Accommodation and Retrenchment

In March 2009, Secretary of State Hillary Clinton presented her Russian counterpart a red plastic button with the word "reset" emblazoned on it. The button was supposed to symbolize a sincere effort by the incoming Obama administration to restart US-Russian relations on a more positive footing. The translation of the word "reset" into Russian, however, was mistaken.[1] As it turns out, many of the assumptions behind Obama's well-intentioned desire to restart relations with Vladimir Putin's Russia were also in error. Multiple efforts to accommodate Russian security concerns—over missile defense, NATO expansion, human rights, the fate of post-Soviet states, and nuclear arms control, just to name a few leading issues—did not alter Putin's international direction. On the contrary, five years after the red reset button was presented, Putin's forces seized control of the Crimean peninsula from Ukraine, and began to wage a covert war against that country, out of a determination to keep it within Russia's sphere of influence. President Obama announced that Putin did not understand twenty-first-century international realities. But in some ways, Putin understood them better than Obama.

In terms of concrete US interests, there has been very limited payoff from President Obama's emphasis on accommodation and retrenchment abroad. In those cases where Obama has had genuine international success, such success has often followed precisely by emphasizing strategies of containment or even rollback. The problems, risks, downsides, and potential long-term costs of US retrenchment, accommodation, and offshore balancing have not been well understood or fully appreciated within the United States either by journalistic coverage or by most academic commentary. In essence, when it comes to numerous international security challenges, Obama has kicked a number of cans down the road, and has typically refused to impose any serious coherence on specific regional or functional policies such as the Asia pivot, America's Afghan withdrawal, or US counterterrorist practices. Overseas, as I show in one case after another, the Obama doctrine is simply not working very well.

Obama's Incoming Strategy

When Barack Obama initially ran for president in 2007–2008, he laid out a number of key foreign policy priorities and assumptions, most of which were reiterated during his first year in the White House, informing a range of US international initiatives in 2009. These early statements and initiatives amounted to an implicit but significant adjustment in American grand strategy, though he rarely framed it that way. Indeed the roots of Obama's international policy convictions long predated his run for the presidency. By his own account, several years spent as a boy in Indonesia had a powerful personal impact, persuading him, for example, that moderate political Islam was a real possibility and that his own international childhood gave him special insight into world affairs unavailable to most Americans.[2] As a college student, Obama was highly critical of existing US foreign policies, especially under Ronald Reagan. During the 1980s, he decried the Cold War arms race, wrote in favor of nuclear disarmament, called for disinvestment from South Africa, and in the words of the *New Yorker's* Ryan Lizza, "gravitated toward conventionally left-leaning positions."[3] While Obama's understanding of international politics obviously developed much further after his college days, it is unlikely that these early convictions ever became entirely irrelevant. In his 2006 memoir, *The Audacity of Hope*, Obama made clear his belief that the United States had a lot to make up for in terms of its foreign policy behavior historically, including the following practices:

> Our tendency to view nations and conflicts through the prism of the Cold War; our tireless promotion of American-style capitalism and multinational corporations; the tolerance and occasional encouragement of tyranny, corruption, and environmental degradation when it served our interests ... In other words, our record is mixed.[4]

Obama's first really significant foreign policy stance in terms of its eventual political impact was his 2002 speech as an Illinois state senator against the prospect of war in Iraq. In that speech, Obama stated his belief that such a war was deliberately intended by the Bush administration to distract the country from domestic economic problems:

> What I am opposed to is the attempt by political hacks like Karl Rove to distract us from a rise in the uninsured, a rise in the poverty rate, a drop in the median income—to distract us from corporate scandals and a stock market that has just gone through the worst month since the Great Depression. That's what I'm opposed to.[5]

This was one of the defining speeches that would ultimately help carry Obama to the 2008 Democratic presidential nomination, against opponents who had taken no such early stance against the war in Iraq. The Illinois senator's foreign policy and national security assumptions were widely articulated through a range of position statements and campaign addresses in 2007–2008. As a candidate for the White House, Obama laid out a variety of proposed changes to US international security policies, all of which informed a number of significant presidential addresses and governmental initiatives issued in 2009. These proposed changes and initiatives included:

- Scaling back numerous elements of the Bush administration's "war on terror" relating to the imprisonment, interrogation, surveillance, capture, and/or killing of suspected terrorists: "we reject as false the choice between our safety and our ideals."[6]
- Pressing forward the Israeli-Palestinian peace process, notably by asking Israelis to halt any further settlements in the West Bank, and by working with Syria diplomatically
- American diplomatic outreach to the Muslim world, "based upon mutual interest and mutual respect"[7]
- A renewed US focus on combating the core of al-Qaeda and its allies in Afghanistan[8]
- Nuclear abolition as the clearly declared policy of the United States, bolstered by multiple American initiatives relating to nuclear arms control and nonproliferation[9]
- Direct diplomacy and US outreach to adversaries, including rogue state leaders in Iran and North Korea: "we will extend a hand if you are willing to unclench your fist."[10]
- Putting US-Russian relations on a more cordial and cooperative footing to address a range of common concerns[11]

- US strategic reassurance of and cooperation with China, to the same end[12]
- A rejection of "balance of power" or "containment" policies as outdated and irrelevant to the twenty-first century[13]
- Ending the war in Iraq, "responsibly"[14]
- Toning down the Bush administration's "freedom agenda" in the Middle East and elsewhere
- A more light-footed, cautious, multilateral, and low-cost approach toward US military interventions overseas
- A shift in US national security priorities toward new concerns such as poverty, genocide, economic development, disease, globalization, and women's issues[15]
- A special injunction to "save this planet" by taking the lead on climate change[16]
- A greater use of international organizations, "soft power," "smart power," and techniques of global governance to solve collective action problems worldwide[17]
- An overarching shift in emphasis from international military toward domestic socioeconomic concerns, visible, for example, in new patterns of federal spending, presidential attention, and policy prioritization
- Restoring America's moral standing, its "force of example," and its reputation internationally through the above initiatives[18]

To an unusual extent, even factoring in the succession of an unpopular chief executive by a leader from the other party, all of these proposed changes were accompanied by a vocal self-definition in constant antipathy toward the preceding president: anything but Bush. The proposed policy changes were further accompanied by a very strong highlight—especially in 2008 and early 2009—on the rhetorical skills, personal background, charisma, and international appeal of Obama as a single individual. Whether or not he believed every bit of his own exceptional press, there does seem to have been a powerful assumption with Obama and his most dedicated supporters that the man's unprecedented autobiography and personal qualities might help unlock benign transformations not only in US foreign policy but in international relations more generally.

Obama did not propose as an incoming president to dismantle America's leading role in world affairs. In fact, he called for "visionary leadership" to restore and renew that role, on the premise that US national security and well-being depended upon the security and well-being of the rest of the world.[19] Yet this rejection of pure disentanglement hardly amounted to its polar opposite. In terms of the strategic archetypes laid out in chapter 1, Obama—like most presidents—proposed in 2008–2009 to use a mixture of foreign policy tools and approaches. For example, with regard to what he called al-Qaeda's "core" along the Pakistani-Afghan border, Obama in effect promised a strategy of rollback, tempered by reforms in US practices relating to counterterrorist surveillance, detention, and interrogation. The incoming president also seemed to embrace certain components of strategic engagement, including a willingness to internationally integrate and bargain with US adversaries or competitors in Moscow, Beijing, Pyongyang, and Tehran. (US trade policy under Obama is discussed in chapter 5.) The most striking change in American strategic assumptions from the Bush era, however, was a strong emphasis on international accommodation and retrenchment by the United States. Obama himself was quite clear on this point: he did not propose simply to sit down and bargain hard with existing US adversaries. On the contrary, he repeatedly suggested that open-minded diplomacy, compromise, and mutual dialogue, sparked by American example under his personal leadership, might trigger broad changes in the demands, intentions, and ambitions of superficially hostile foreign actors—the essential premise of a strategy of accommodation. He also made it very clear that while he did not aim to dismantle America's international presence, he would certainly look for ways to reduce US military costs and commitments overseas—a form of strategic retrenchment. In other words, this would be a hybrid strategy with special emphasis on international accommodation and retrenchment, and the ultimate purpose of that new strategy—as Obama also made clear—was not only to encourage a more cooperative and peaceful international order, but to permit a fresh domestic focus on liberal or progressive policy reforms within the United States.

It has now been several years since Obama entered the White House—plenty of time to assess the effectiveness of his foreign policy strategy. And it must be said that in important respects his strategy of international accommodation and retrenchment has failed. American accommodation and retrenchment have not triggered significantly greater international cooperation. To some extent, of course, Obama has been constrained in the implementation of his strategy by domestic political criticism or pushback on many of these issues. Yet the failures appear to involve international pushback and mistaken conceptions as well.

Let's look at how Obama's grand strategy has played out in relation to five leading areas of concern: (1) counterterrorism; (2) nuclear proliferation, including North Korea and Iran; (3), great power competitors, namely China and Russia; (4) the Arab world; and (5) the relationship between US alliance commitments, defense spending, and the new American posture overseas.

Counterterrorism

On the issue of terrorism, Obama made clear his expectation upon becoming president that a series of significant American and allied gestures would help to ease transnational counterterror efforts, while undercutting support within the Muslim world for groups like al-Qaeda. The United States, Obama said, would withdraw militarily from Iraq; "end the use of torture"; close detention facilities at Guantánamo Bay; engage in public outreach toward Muslims worldwide; and press for a peace agreement between Israel and the Palestinians, on the assumption that such measures in combination would help to undercut anti-American feeling internationally. In the case of Israel, it was not so much the United States but the Israelis themselves who were expected to help kickstart peace negotiations by imposing a freeze on the construction of new Jewish settlements in the West Bank and Jerusalem. To be sure, Obama promised from the very beginning to take the fight to the core of al-Qaeda in Pakistan and Afghanistan. But his overall tone, compared to that of the Bush administration, was much more accommodating toward international criticism of US counterterrorist practices. Indeed Obama made it abundantly clear, especially when first running for president in 2007–2008, that he agreed with much of this international criticism, and viewed the Bush administration itself as a major source of America's foreign policy problems. On the issue of counterterrorism, as on others, Obama stated repeatedly that the United States had lost much of its international reputation and moral standing under George W. Bush, and that a different set of policies as well as a different leader could regain that standing and reputation with a more conciliatory approach. Obama himself would be especially well suited to this role, his supporters suggested, not only because of his status as the first African American president, but also because of his international background, his charisma, and his proven ability to bring people together across cultural, ethnic, and political divides. In essence, the incoming president indicated that he wanted to accommodate international criticism of previous counterterrorism policies, along with Muslim opinion overseas, while containing and rolling back the core of al-Qaeda.

After Obama became president, it soon became clear there would be more continuity than change in US Counterterrorist policies. Part of this was because the new president and his aides were now reading the same daily threat reports that George W. Bush once read. Part of it was because the second-term Bush administration had already revised multiple counterterrorism practices, under intense pressure from Congress, interest groups, and the nation's courts. Part of the reason for continuity was simply the sheer technical and political difficulty of altering existing policies on a range of thorny and complicated matters relating to the surveillance, detention, rendition, targeting, and interrogation of suspected terrorists, combined with only a limited determination to do so on the part of the new president. In any case, Obama made some significant policy modifications and narrowed the scope of counterterror efforts in certain areas, while actually expanding them in others, such as US drone strikes in Pakistan and Yemen.[20] In the end, his implicit counterterrorism strategy ended up as a hybrid one, with strong components of rollback and containment as well as accommodation and retrenchment. The president's greatest success in this area, and a very considerable one, was the American raid against Osama bin Laden's secret compound in May 2011. The White House subsequently used this success to account for further US strategic retrenchment, notably in Afghanistan, on the grounds that al-Qaeda was now on its last legs. In other words, the president's overarching aspiration remained one of scaling back inherited wars, including the one on terrorism.

Running for re-election in 2012, Obama claimed that "Al Qaeda is on the path to defeat."[21] The president's basic argument—as expressed, for example, in a May 2013 address at the National Defense University—was that while "local militias or extremists" may attack "soft targets," the "core Al Qaeda is a shell of its former self."[22] This rather understated the extent of the danger. In fact, during the first three years of the Arab Spring (2011–2013), leading affiliates of al-Qaeda and like-minded groups took advantage of weakened governments throughout North Africa and the Middle East to stage some remarkable advances.[23] Al-Qaeda in Iraq (AQI), reorganized under the name of the Islamic State of Iraq and Syria (ISIS), staged a violent resurgence during 2012–2013, aided by the absence of American forces inside Iraq. ISIS also began to play a leading role in the armed rebellion against Syrian dictator Bashar al-Assad, as did the newly formed Jabhat al-Nusra (JAN), formally recognized as an al-Qaeda affiliate in 2013. Indeed the Syrian civil war became a magnet for thousands of jihadist fighters from around the world, turning it into a homeland security concern for the United States and its European allies.

In North Africa, across a vast region including Algeria, Mali, Niger, and Libya, al-Qaeda in the Islamic Maghreb (AQIM) expanded its operations dramatically after 2011, as did associated jihadist groups such as Libya's Ansar al-Sharia. It was Ansar al-Sharia that attacked the United States consulate in Benghazi on September 11, 2012, in a premeditated and heavily armed assault that killed four Americans including US ambassador Christopher Stevens. Islamist terrorists and militias took advantage of Mu'ammar Gaddafi's 2011 overthrow and the weakness of Libya's successor government to transfer weapons and fighters throughout the region.

In Egypt, jihadist militants worked with Bedouin tribesmen to use the Sinai Peninsula as a base of operations during the Muslim

Brotherhood's period in office during 2012–2013. In Yemen, al-Qaeda in the Arabian Peninsula (AQAP) fought an unstable US-backed government and encouraged repeated terrorist attacks inside the United States, typically using radicalized American citizens in touch with AQAP. This included, for example, the December 2009 "underwear bomber," who attempted to crash a Northwest Airlines flight carrying almost three hundred people, along with the November 2009 attack by Nidal Malik Hasan on a US army post in Fort Hood, Texas, killing thirteen Americans and wounding thirty others. Attempted terrorist attacks by AQAP throughout the Middle East and inside the United States have continued in subsequent years.

In Somalia, al-Qaeda affiliate al-Shabab fought a back-and-forth struggle with the US-backed Somali government, staging attacks in Kenya as well. In Nigeria, Boko Haram continued terrorist operations in its effort to establish strict Islamic law. The same was true for the Islamic Emirate of the Caucasus, al-Qaeda's affiliate in the Russian provinces of Chechnya and Dagestan. Finally, in Pakistan, the original core of al-Qaeda continued to operate under bin Laden's successor Ayman al-Zawahiri, decimated since 2002 by US military pressure, but still playing an important supportive role for allies around the world. Al-Zawahiri's group remained embedded within a network of sympathetic forces in the region, and looked to rebuild following America's troop withdrawal from Afghanistan.

President Obama tended to emphasize sharp distinctions between local militias, lone-wolf terrorists, regional affiliates, and a wrecked al-Qaeda core, in order to argue that on balance "Al Qaeda is on the run." In doing so, however, he overstated his own counterterrorism successes, and understated the continuing nature of the threat. Al-Qaeda is a transnational and decentralized network of jihadist terrorists capable of collaborating with one another as well as with other radical Islamists, tribal leaders, and organized criminals in specific regional contexts. The fact that al-Qaeda's local affiliates often act with considerable autonomy does not lessen their common determination to launch terrorist attacks and expunge Western influence from the Muslim world. Viewed as a single loose and resilient network, al-Qaeda is arguably stronger today than before, demonstrating fresh momentum across North Africa and possibly Afghanistan as US forces withdraw. By no means is al-Qaeda close to being defeated at the hands of the United States.[24]

An equally disturbing scenario is that groups even more brutal and aggressive than al-Qaeda seize the mantle of international leadership over jihadist terrorism. In the summer of 2014, this seemed like a genuine possibility, as the Islamic State of Iraq and Syria (ISIS) rose to fresh prominence. Under its leader, Abu Bakr al-Baghdadi, ISIS flourished inside the conditions of Syria's civil war, fighting against the Assad government, moderate rebels, and Jabhat al-Nusra all at the same time. So aggressive was ISIS that al-Qaeda's central leader Zawahiri disowned the group early in 2014. Baghdadi responded by taking advantage of the Iraqi government's deep unpopularity among Sunni Arabs. He allied with local tribal leaders along with Sunni militants to launch a series of rapid advances across the northwest of Iraq. No longer buttressed by American bases, and torn by sectarian division, Iraq's army collapsed with stunning speed. The country appeared to collapse into three independent entities: a Kurdish north, a Shiite-dominated rump government in the southeast, and a newly announced Islamic caliphate led by Baghdadi in Iraq's Sunni Arab triangle. The fact that this new jihadist state in Iraq's northwest also controlled large parts of Syria, and furthermore threatened the kingdom of Jordan, made its existence still more alarming. Baghdadi and his allies could legitimately claim not only to have seized control of an impressive expanse of territory, population, and plunder, but also to have at least temporarily erased the postcolonial boundaries written by Sykes-Picot almost a century earlier. This raised the very real likelihood that ISIS might now replace al-Qaeda as the single most dynamic, assertive, and appealing group of transnational jihadists from the perspective of potential new recruits. Such intraterrorist competition might well be appealing from an American point of view, provided the various groups actually weakened one another. But the corresponding danger was that in trying to outbid themselves for support, ISIS and al-Qaeda might try to ratchet up spectacular attacks on Western targets, leaving the United States and its allies once again in the crossfire. Indeed numerous leading US officials stated publicly in 2014 that both ISIS and Jabhat al-Nusra had to be viewed as terrorist threats to the American homeland. That summer, President Obama therefore authorized sending several hundred US military advisers to support the government of Iraq, along with limited airstrikes against ISIS, but he was clearly reluctant to do much more.[25]

On the whole, the accommodationist elements within Obama's initial counterterrorism approach have not really worked as expected. Within most Muslim countries, the United States remains roughly as unpopular under Obama as it was under Bush.[26] Most of Obama's early proposals on detention and interrogation have been dialed back at least partway, the end result of which has been considerable confusion. To be sure, the finding and killing of Osama bin Laden in the spring of 2011 was a great success, but that very success was due to the fact that in this particular case Obama ignored multilateral pieties throughout the operation. The strike against bin Laden's secret compound was a unilateral American military operation launched inside of Pakistan without the permission of that country, based upon intelligence gathered aggressively over a period of years dating back to the Bush administration, and without excessive concern for legalistic objections. On the other hand, there is no indication that those sympathetic to violent jihadists are especially impressed by Obama's personality or by his halting efforts to pressure Israel while partially reforming US detention and interrogation of suspected terrorists. Attempted homegrown attacks by radicalized Islamists within the United States have only increased since 2009. Nobody can reasonably say that Obama is primarily responsible for these attempts, but it is just as unreasonable to suggest that support for terrorism between 2001 and 2008 was primarily due to the policies of George W. Bush. The point is that anti-American terrorists plot their attacks without being appeased by particular US policy concessions or presidents. The radical Islamist hatred of American influence goes well beyond specific administrations, and it is profoundly solipsistic to think otherwise.

In terms of overall American resources committed to counterterrorism by the Obama administration, the single greatest theater in the struggle against al-Qaeda has been in Afghanistan. With regard to that country, Obama has pursued a hybrid policy of rollback against al-Qaeda, engagement with the Afghan government, and military intervention plus attempted negotiation in relation to the Taliban—all intermixed with growing US retrenchment after 2011.

On first running for president in 2007–2008, Obama made renewed US counterterrorism and military efforts in Afghanistan central to his foreign policy platform, arguing that President Bush had neglected that vital theater by focusing on Iraq. Within weeks of entering the White House, Obama authorized some 20,000 additional US troops to Afghanistan. The mission declared by the president was to "disrupt, dismantle, and defeat Al Qaeda" in its Afghan base through a new American effort against the Taliban.[27]

It soon became obvious that existing US troop levels were not adequate to fulfill the stated mission. Obama was forced to conduct a second and more contentious round of deliberations during the autumn of 2009 over what to do next. His leading military advisers, supported by CIA director Leon Panetta, argued for 40,000 or at the very least 30,000 more US troops for Afghanistan. Secretaries Clinton and Gates also leaned toward this position. On the other side, Vice President Biden, White House advisers including David Axelrod and Rahm Emanuel, the American ambassador to Kabul, Karl Eikenberry, and congressional Democrats such as Speaker Nancy Pelosi were deeply wary of such an escalated military presence. Biden, in particular, argued for diplomatic outreach toward the Taliban, a more limited US military commitment, and increased reliance on long-distance airstrikes against terrorist camps by unmanned aerial vehicles or drones. Looming behind this debate was the concern of many congressional Democrats that US military escalation in Afghanistan might endanger domestic priorities such as healthcare, just as Vietnam had wrecked Lyndon Johnson's domestic reform agenda several decades earlier. Obama's final decision, announced in December 2009, was to escalate militarily while indicating strict limits to that escalation. Specifically, he authorized another 33,000 troops to Afghanistan, but in a gesture intended to reassure skeptics, simultaneously announced that US troops would start to come home in July 2011 subject to conditions on the ground.[28] The risk of this approach within Afghanistan, of course, was that the Taliban could simply wait out the United States, if they knew ahead of time exactly when the Americans would be leaving. In the meantime, US soldiers and marines hammered Taliban forces effectively, robbing them of valuable numbers, space, and morale.[29]

On June 22, 2011, Obama took to the airwaves to announce the beginning of US troop withdrawals from Afghanistan. He declared that the United States would remove 5,000 troops from that country immediately, another 5,000 by the end of 2011, and then a further 23,000 by September 2012.[30] Everyone had expected some sort of token withdrawal, but the overall size and pace of the announced disengagement came as a surprise to many defense experts, whether Democrat or Republican. If Afghanistan was strategically vital to US counterterrorism efforts, as Obama himself had said repeatedly, then why walk away from combat operations just when the Taliban were reeling? Still, Obama and his political advisers were determined to run on a re-election platform emphasizing the conclusion of "Bush's wars." By 2011, the US war in Afghanistan was increasingly unpopular at home. Obama was under particular pressure from Democratic Party leaders in Congress to begin extensive American troop withdrawals.[31] The killing of Osama bin Laden that spring allowed the administration to claim that here was a case of mission accomplished. The overarching concern was to have all US troops from the autumn 2009 Afghan surge visibly on their way stateside well before November 2012. Secretary of Defense Robert Gates recorded his impressions from 2011: "The president doesn't trust his commanders, can't stand Karzai, doesn't believe in his own strategy, and doesn't consider the war to be his. For him, it's all about getting out."[32]

Attempted diplomatic accommodation of the Taliban—confident and hostile as that group was toward the United States—turned out to be quite fruitless. The great question during Obama's second term was whether the United States would retain a serious commitment to Afghanistan. Certainly, there was an American interest in doing so. The United States invested a great deal of blood and treasure in Afghanistan over a decade and more, in response to 9/11. The chief purpose of this investment, as articulated by both Barack Obama and George W. Bush, was to prevent al-Qaeda from again using Afghan territory as a safe haven for terror operations against the United States and its allies. American combat efforts in Afghanistan, however unpopular with US public opinion over time, helped accomplish this purpose. Al-Qaeda's central base within Afghanistan was devastated after the US invasion of 2001, and never really recovered. Obama's troop surge of 2009–2010 also did considerable good, by setting the Taliban back on its heels while Afghan military and security forces improved. Nevertheless, it was misleading for the president to suggest beginning in 2011 that the war was nearing its completion. On the contrary, attacks by the Taliban and the even more radical Haqqani network against Afghan government forces looked likely to mount as American combat units departed. This was exactly why a significant base presence by the United States in Afghanistan, including several thousand American troops, was so important—to help the Afghan government resist the Taliban, the Haqqani, and al-Qaeda, through continued US military training, advice, and counterterrorism.[33] At times, President Obama publicly recognized this. At other times, he seemed uninterested in any extensive continuing American commitment. The mixed signals emanating from the White House were as disturbing to US allies as they were encouraging to the Taliban and its associates. To be sure, Afghanistan's President Karzai was often an exceptionally difficult partner for the United States. Still, doubts regarding the solidity of Obama's commitment to Afghanistan were not entirely groundless. Fortunately, Karzai's successor, Ashraf Ghani, favored a continuing American base presence in his country.[34]

Nuclear Weapons and Rogue States

President Obama has demonstrated a long-standing interest in the concept of nuclear disarmament. In March 1983, as an undergraduate student at Columbia University, he wrote an article for the student weekly *Sundial* called "Breaking the War Mentality" in which he voiced his revulsion against what he called the "Cold War militarism" of "military-industrial interests" with their "billion dollar erector sets," and argued for the reduction or elimination of nuclear weapons.[35] Of course, Obama has come a very long way since then, but his attraction to nuclear abolition still exists—it is an issue of special interest to him.[36]

Under Obama's leadership, the United States has followed a nuclear nonproliferation policy that assumes that if the United States takes the initiative by making important concessions on nuclear weapons, the rest of the world will follow. This is an excellent example of his overarching strategy of international accommodation and retrenchment, pursued with incremental flexibility and a little hard bargaining. The president has announced that worldwide nuclear abolition is the goal of his administration, and that the United States will take concrete steps of its own toward that end. He has overseen a Nuclear Weapons Posture Review, declaring that the United States will neither develop new nuclear warheads nor use nuclear weapons against chemical or biological attacks from any nonnuclear weapons state in compliance with the Non-Proliferation Treaty (NPT). He has pressed for and signed the New START Treaty with Moscow, which reduces Russian and American arsenals to some 1,550 nuclear warheads and 700 delivery vehicles each. He has urged the ratification of the Comprehensive Test Ban Treaty. He has overseen a Nuclear Security Summit in Washington, DC, in an attempt to encourage the safekeeping of nuclear materials internationally. He has called for a global treaty to verifiably end production of fissile materials. He has tried in all sincerity to engage Iran diplomatically on the issue of its nuclear weapons program. All of these policy components are intended to be part of an interlocking approach toward nuclear nonproliferation. Obama's assumption—as he clarified most notably in an April 2009 address in Prague—is that if the United States pursues nuclear arms control treaties, reduces the role of these weapons in its defense strategy, cuts its own arsenal, and urges others to do the same, then momentum can be built not only toward the nonproliferation but also toward the worldwide abolition of nuclear weapons. As he hastened to add in that Prague speech: "I'm not naive." But he went on to insist that when it comes to the goal of nuclear abolition, we "must ignore the voices" of skepticism, and instead say, "Yes, we can."[37] This overarching preference for nuclear retrenchment and accommodation was reiterated in a June 2013 address in Berlin.[38]

It would be unreasonable to judge the results of Obama's nuclear nonproliferation policies simply by asking whether these terrible weapons have been abolished since his inauguration. Nobody expected that. The more reasonable question would be to ask whether his nuclear nonproliferation policies have on balance promoted US national security interests and international stability since 2009, and whether the declared policy of nuclear abolition is actually helpful or realistic. Here the answer unfortunately is no. To begin with, there is little reason to believe that any other existing nuclear weapons state, apart from possibly Great Britain, is remotely serious about giving up its entire nuclear arsenal. Nor are the British exactly the ones America would most like to see disarmed. Russia, despite reductions over the past quarter-century, views nuclear weapons as essential to its security and status as a great power. China, India, Pakistan, Israel, and France continue to enhance and upgrade their own nuclear arsenals. The government of North Korea tested nuclear weapons in 2009 and 2013, in open defiance of Obama's position, and the government of Iran gives every indication of working energetically toward nuclear weapons capacity. All of this is because most existing and aspiring nuclear weapons states do not develop the bomb primarily on the basis of whether the United States is cutting back its nuclear arsenal. They build and maintain the bomb for reasons to do with their own geopolitical orientation, status seeking, and security concerns.[39]

There is very little evidence to suggest that any other countries will engage in nuclear abstention or reversal because of Obama's well-intentioned changes and concessions in America's nuclear weapons posture. Indeed, these nuclear policy changes might unintentionally weaken US deterrence stands in critical regions, even as the need for such deterrence grows. An Iranian nuclear weapon could very well encourage Turkey, Egypt, or Saudi Arabia to acquire or develop nuclear weapons of its own.[40] The same set of concerns might lead Japan, South Korea, and others within the Asia-Pacific region to build nuclear weapons eventually if North Korea's arsenal is not rolled back. Meanwhile, Obama's stated goal of global zero does nothing concretely to prevent either North Korea or Iran from moving forward with its own nuclear weapons programs. So if anything, an American position that deliberately downplays the role of nuclear weapons in US commitments to allies overseas might encourage those same allies to look to their own devices, and either accommodate US adversaries, or develop the bomb—perhaps both. The final outcome—a world with *more* nuclear weapons states—would then be the very opposite of the one intended by Obama.[41] The best that can be said of the president's declared commitment to American nuclear abolition is that he has done relatively little to implement it.

In the case of US strategy toward Iran, Obama started out with aspirations for engagement and accommodation, introduced elements of a containment strategy after an initial rebuff from Tehran, and then cycled back toward accommodation after the election of Iran's new president, Hassan Rouhani, in 2013. The process began in 2009 with a dramatic attempt by Obama at diplomatic outreach, in which he called for fruitful, direct negotiations over Tehran's nuclear program. He sent letters to Iran's Supreme Leader, the Ayatollah Ali Khamenei, and recorded a video message to the Iranian people in the apparent expectation this would help kick-start the process of mutual conciliation. The response of Iran's political leaders was largely hostile and suspicious. In June of that same year, Iranian elections commonly viewed as fraudulent sparked widespread protests that were put down with brute force by the regime's security services. Continuing to hope for diplomatic progress over the nuclear issue, Obama's response to this crackdown was relatively mild. Desultory negotiations went on for several years between Iran and the "P5 + 1" (the five permanent United Nations Security Council members, plus Germany), without resolution.[42] Obama therefore proceeded simultaneously along a parallel track of more assertive measures against Iran, to give his diplomatic efforts some bite. First, the United States ramped up energy-related and financial sanctions against Tehran—sometimes unilaterally, sometimes in cooperation with the United Nations or American allies. Numerous unilateral sanctions were further imposed by the US Congress over initial objections from the White House. Second, in cooperation with the Israelis, Obama maintained a covert campaign of cyber sabotage—Operation Olympic Games—to infiltrate and disrupt Iran's nuclear weapons program. These covert actions, sanctions, and diplomacy all built on similar efforts from Bush's second term, and in combination over time they had some real impact. Operation Olympic Games shut down hundreds of Iranian centrifuges and may have set back Tehran's nuclear program by a year or two.[43] International sanctions against Iran, though incomplete, imposed considerable damage on that nation's economy. It was within this context that the Iranian people elected Hassan Rouhani, a seasoned and polished negotiator, as their new

president in June 2013 on a promise to lift sanctions through diplomacy. In a series of early statements surrounding the nuclear
issue, Rouhani struck a more conciliatory tone. Obama was
clearly eager to work with this new interlocutor, and serious negotiations over Iran's nuclear program now began in earnest. In
November 2013, Iran and the P5+1 reached an interim agreement
by which some international sanctions were lifted in exchange
for a temporary freeze on limited components of Tehran's nuclear program. The central question was whether Iran would
agree in later rounds of diplomacy to abide by existing UN resolutions and verifiably dismantle its nuclear weapons program.
There continued to be good reason for skepticism on this point.
Rouhani's mandate after all, both from his election and from
Iran's Supreme Leader, was to win reduced sanctions, not to give
up Tehran's nuclear program.

President Obama has declared repeatedly that the United States
will not accept Iranian possession of the bomb, but there are multiple stages of nascent, latent, and virtual nuclear weapons capability through which nations progress before they actually test the
bomb, and this is exactly the progress Iran is currently making. In
the abstract, if the United States could secure a deal that actually dismantles Iranian nuclear weapons capability—namely, one
that stops Iran's uranium enrichment, halts its reprocessing, shuts
down its key nuclear weapons facilities, and ships out its enriched
uranium and centrifuges, all under truly complete inspections
with the full cooperation of the Iranian government—then such a
deal would be worth taking. We know what such a process would
resemble: something like South Africa's approach to its own nuclear weapons program at the fall of apartheid. Yet there is no indication that the government of Iran is interested in these sorts of
terms, under Rouhani or anyone else. The risk as nuclear negotiations proceed, therefore, is that the United States will accept a deal

that dismantles international economic and diplomatic pressure on Iran while legitimizing and keeping that country's nascent nuclear weapons capabilities largely in place. Having removed international pressure, the government of Iran would then be free to circumvent any agreement and build a nuclear weapon in a relatively short time at its own discretion. As the Rand Corporation's Gregory Jones put it in a paper for the Nonproliferation Policy Education Center:

> If the P5+1 should be so foolish as to agree to allow Iran to keep its current enrichment facilities, then Iran will have legitimized these facilities and its ability to quickly produce the HEU [highly enriched uranium] for nuclear weapons whenever it decides to do so. The only negotiated solution that would prevent Iran from quickly being able to produce HEU would be for Iran to permanently shut down its enrichment facilities and export its stockpiles of enriched uranium. By saying that the P5+1 must accept continuing continued Iranian uranium enrichment, advocates of a negotiated solution are essentially admitting that no satisfactory negotiated solution is possible.[44]

This might be described as the North Korean model of nonproliferation. Nor is this risk so far-fetched: as the International Atomic Energy Agency (IAEA) has repeatedly declared, Iran already stands in violation of numerous existing treaties and agreements related to nuclear nonproliferation. Indeed Iran has never even admitted that it has a nuclear weapons program. On the whole, its approach seems rather closer to that of North Korea than to the South African model. Meanwhile, any impression of a possible US-Iranian agreement over the heads of American allies in the region is naturally deeply unnerving to those allies. Indeed, the Obama administration's discussion of a possible nuclear deal has been strangely detached from reference to persistent patterns in Iranian foreign policy under its current regime. The Islamic Republic of Iran remains visibly and profoundly hostile toward the United States and the international order that it heads. Since 2009 alone, Tehran has repeatedly backed terrorist attacks within the Middle East and beyond; militarily and financially aided Hamas, Hezbollah, and Syria's Assad, notably through Iraq; worked on its ballistic missile as well as its nuclear weapons capabilities; supported militant insurgents in Iraq and Afghanistan who have attacked and killed American troops in those countries; and plotted assassination on US soil. The mainstream Iranian feeling, moreover, is that Iran is and deserves to be the predominant major power within the Persian Gulf region, and that its nuclear program is basically nonnegotiable as a matter of national pride, security, and identity. It would be wonderful if Rouhani represented a fundamental shift in these broad patterns and priorities, but so far there is really no sign that he does.[45]

With regard to North Korea, Obama made it clear on running for president and after his inauguration that he welcomed direct negotiations with Pyongyang in order to resolve the nuclear issue. He offered wide economic and diplomatic benefits to North Korea under the promise of a new round of talks, and played down any previous US aspirations for "regime change."[46] The response of the North Korean government was extremely hostile. In fact, it had already backtracked on a prior agreement reached with the Bush administration under the "Six-Party Talks" (North Korea, South Korea, Russia, Japan, China, and the United States). In 2009, soon after Obama's diplomatic outreach, Pyongyang pulled out of the Six-Party Talks, tested a nuclear device, and essentially declared itself a nuclear weapons state. In 2010, it revealed secret uranium enrichment facilities, torpedoed a South Korean warship, and bombarded a South Korean island, killing a number of civilians and marines in the process. In 2012—now under a new hereditary leader, Kim Jong-un—North Korea hinted at a desire to negotiate for assistance, then blasted away any such prospect by testing a number of long-range missiles. In early 2013, it conducted another nuclear weapons test, cut off communications with Seoul, and warned of the imminent outbreak of war. These various provocations were typically accompanied by blood-curdling threats against the United States and its allies. The North Korean pattern of attempted threats, unreliability, and extortion was already so clear during Obama's first year in office that even a US administration deeply committed to engagement lost interest in being blackmailed. As Secretary of Defense Robert Gates put it at the time, "I'm tired of buying the same horse twice." Obama therefore settled on a policy of "strategic patience," whereby the United States would contain North Korea, consult with regional allies, pursue existing sanctions, and indicate a continued willingness to talk, but only if Pyongyang first lived up to its existing commitments under prior international agreements.[47] This particular policy had much to recommend it. Still, North Korea's government, its various money-laundering schemes, and its nuclear weapons status all in combination remained a grave danger in Northeast Asia and beyond. Insofar as President Obama had any success in managing this threat, it was through a strategy of containment, not accommodation.

Great Power Competitors

The next category of concern, including major authoritarian powers that pursue a mixture of rivalry and cooperation with America, includes China and Russia. These governments continue to view the United States under Obama as a strategic threat to their stature and integrity, but they pursue some cooperation with Washington in areas such as trade and arms control while simultaneously pursuing geopolitical competition with the United States. Their common interests with Washington are more extensive, and their hostility toward the United States less profound, than is the case with Iran or North Korea. Nevertheless the governments of China and Russia, like most governments overseas, are largely indifferent to Obama's personal charms. They are interested in whether he concedes to their interests and priorities, not in his personal background as such, or in any vision he might have for a more liberal international order. In cases where Obama gives Moscow or Beijing most of what they want, as he did, for instance, in the 2009–2010 New START negotiations with Russia, then naturally they are happy to accept the concession, and even to offer a modest quid pro quo. But in cases where he offers accommodating or hopeful gestures, yet runs up against the perceived vital national interests of either power, then they simply decline to offer any reciprocal and proportionate accommodation. Neither power, for example, has any intention of surrendering its nuclear arsenal, no matter what Obama says or does in relation to his goal of nuclear zero. Nor has either power offered genuinely full cooperation with regard to Iranian or North Korean nuclear proliferation. Chinese and Russian leaders are not especially impressed by Obama. If anything, they are encouraged by the implication of long-term US strategic withdrawal under his leadership, because it leaves them stronger within their own neighborhoods. In this case, as in many others, American strategic disengagement is not interpreted as transformational benevolence, but as a sign of weakness.

In the case of Russia, the Obama administration pursued a strategy of engagement and accommodation, with little payoff in the end for distinctly American interests. When first running for the White House, Obama suggested that President Bush had been too confrontational toward Moscow, and that relations needed to improve. Russia's invasion of neighboring Georgia in August 2008 threatened that concept, leaving Russian troops in occupation of separatist republics in South Ossetia and Abkhazia. But after necessary condemnations of the invasion itself, Obama quietly drew the conclusion that the war had been as much the fault of Georgia and the Bush administration, as of the Russians.[48] Obama entered the White House carrying a special emphasis on nuclear arms control with Moscow, both for its own sake and in the expectation this might have spinoff effects with regard to nuclear nonproliferation in other countries. He also had particular hopes for cooperative diplomacy with Russia's then-president, Dmitry Medvedev. Under a fresh US policy commonly known as the "reset," Obama set out to accommodate Russian concerns over a wide variety of issues. In September 2009, he scaled back planned NATO missile defenses for Poland and the Czech Republic. He toned down democratization and human rights as major issues in US-Russian relations, delinking them from negotiations over security concerns. He eased Moscow's accession into the World Trade Organization, to help encourage international trade and investment for Russia. He downplayed prospects for NATO's expansion into Georgia or Ukraine. Indeed when Ukrainians elected a new, pro-Russian president in 2010—Viktor Yanukovych—Obama made clear the United States had no objection. More broadly, Obama refused to see the necessity of any intense competition with Moscow for influence within former Soviet republics in Central Asia, the Caucasus, or Eastern Europe. The basic purpose of this more conciliatory American approach was not only to secure Russian cooperation on specific issues such as nuclear arms control, Iran, and Afghanistan, but to kick-start a broader process of cooperation between the two powers. In the words of Jeffrey Mankoff, a leading Russia expert at the Center for Strategic and International Studies, the Obama administration's premise was that

> By working together over a gradually expanding range of issues, the two sides would build up trust and the habit of cooperation, which would over time broaden the range of common interests and change the two sides' expectations . . . If he could reduce tensions by addressing Moscow's major criticisms of U.S. policy, Obama hoped to gain Russian cooperation in addressing the worsening situation in Afghanistan and Washington's mounting confrontation with Iran over Tehran's nuclear program . . . For Washington, arms control was attractive because of Obama's stated commitment to eventually eliminating nuclear weapons and his desire to convince other states to abjure developing them . . . With the reset, the Obama administration has sought to effectively end the post–Cold War period in which the geopolitical alignments of Russia and its neighbors are a prize to be won . . . even if their leaders define those interests to include remaining in Russia's orbit, as [Ukraine's] Yanukovych has done.[49]

The White House contends that the reset succeeded in accomplishing these goals, but in fact any direct payoff for US national interests resulting from a more accommodating approach has been quite minimal. The more common pattern has been that Russia has offered strictly limited cooperation in ways that suit its own interests in any case, while simultaneously pressing its advantages relative to the United States. In relation to the Afghan conflict, Moscow did agree to allow US forces transit across Russian airspace on their way into Afghanistan. Yet this seems to have been mainly because of Russian fears of the Taliban, not because of US concessions in other areas. On Iran's nuclear program, Moscow offered initial approval for certain limited UN Security Council sanctions. Over time, however, Russia resumed its more familiar role as a major obstacle to strengthened sanctions against Tehran. The 2010 New START agreement is often held up as a considerable success of the Russia reset. But again, in practical terms, what New START accomplished was to lock in the number of American nuclear weapons on par with Moscow, at a slightly lower level the cash-strapped Russians could actually afford. Naturally this was attractive to Russia, which seeks to bolster any lingering form of military equality with the United States, but why it was essential to American national security interests is not entirely obvious. Current US satellite technology can provide impressive insights into Russian nuclear capabilities, with or without a formal arms control treaty. Moreover the Russians made very clear in their preamble to New START Moscow's continuing opposition to US missile defenses, as an implicit price to be paid for that agreement. Indeed while running for re-election in 2012, Obama assured Medvedev that "on all these issues, but particularly missile defense, this can be solved, but it's important for him [i.e., Putin] to give me space ... This is my last election. After my election I have more flexibility."[50] It is difficult to avoid the impression that either Obama views missile defense as a chip to be traded for Russian approval or thinks little of its value in the first place—perhaps both.

In truth, Medvedev's presidential tenure did not represent any fundamental break with the foreign policy and domestic regime built up by Vladimir Putin since 2000. Putin remained a dominating influence as prime minister—Batman to Medvedev's Robin, in the words of a leaked State Department cable[51]—and he formally returned as Russia's president in 2012. While running for that office, Putin laid out his vision of a new "Eurasian Union," in an ongoing effort to tie former Soviet republics closer to Moscow rather than to the European Union, China, or the United States.[52] Several of Russia's neighbors in the "Near Abroad" of Central Asia, the Caucasus, and Eastern Europe remained skeptical of any such association, or preferred to hedge their bets between the various major powers, but this was not for lack of effort on Putin's part. The Russian government utilized an imaginative variety of sticks and carrots—including financial, commercial, and security incentives, covert action, outright bribery, implicit military pressure, economic sanctions, cultural diplomacy, propaganda, and the manipulation of oil and gas prices and supplies—to nudge a number of former Soviet republics into closer association with Moscow, or at least away from the West. Belarus, Ukraine, Moldova, Georgia, Armenia, Kazakhstan, Tajikistan, and Kyrgyzstan seemed especially vulnerable to these techniques.[53]

In November 2013, under intense pressure from Moscow, Ukraine's president, Viktor Yanukovych, withdrew his country from negotiations over association with the European Union. The announcement sparked dismay among the many Ukrainians who looked for their nation to be something other than a decrepit Russian dependency. Widespread protests were met with a violent government crackdown, drawing international attention. In February 2014 Ukraine's parliament removed Yanukovych from office and established an interim pro-Western government. Within days, Russia responded with a deft, ruthless campaign of subversion against Ukraine, utilizing a combination of information warfare, cyberattacks, covert action, special operations, and conventional military forces, all rapidly deployed. Masked gunmen seized key locations in Crimea, followed by Russian troops. A referendum engineered by Moscow to tear Crimea from Ukraine produced the desired result. With de facto control over the Crimean peninsula, Putin announced its annexation by Russia. He then set about on a sustained effort to unsettle Ukraine's new government, encouraging pro-Russian separatists in the eastern part of the country to wreak havoc and demand their independence. Armed insurgents backed by Moscow fought back and forth with Ukrainian government troops. The insurgents even went so far as to shoot down a Malaysian civilian airliner loaded with European passengers. The main response to all of this from the United States and its European allies was to condemn Russian actions verbally and impose some limited economic sanctions on Moscow. The limited nature of these sanctions, while annoying to Russia, was sufficiently weak as to be almost a relief. The Ukraine crisis devolved into predictably fitful diplomacy, while Putin pocketed his new territorial gains. That same year, the Eurasian Economic Union was finally born, including Russia, Belarus, and Kazakhstan. Ukraine's central government now leaned very much against Putin, but for all practical purposes the country remained a battleground of Russian versus Western influence with Moscow pressing its case aggressively.[54]

Evidently, President Obama's attempted accommodation of Moscow's deep-seated security concerns starting in 2009 did not assuage those concerns, because a striking pattern during the Obama era has been Russia's persistent assertiveness relative to the United States. Under both Putin and Medvedev, and in spite of any US diplomatic reset, Moscow continued to work toward an exclusive Russian sphere of influence within the Near Abroad; object to virtually any existing US missile defense plans whatsoever; occupy portions of Georgia militarily; build up and modernize the Russian armed forces; provide technical support for Iran's nuclear program while blocking further UN sanctions against it; actively work against US military base negotiations in parts of Central Asia; and block any UN action against Syria's violent suppression of domestic opposition, while arming and supporting the Syrian government. Russia then forcibly dismantled a sovereign state, in Ukraine, annexing part of that country to itself. Putin further used this time to consolidate his authoritarian system at home and to crack down on extensive political protests that began in 2011. One key aspect of this crackdown—ironically, given Obama's obvious desire to stay out of Russia's internal affairs—was to essentially accuse the United States of plotting to overthrow Putin's government and dismantle the Russian nation through domestic political unrest. Late in 2012, Moscow expelled the United States Agency for International Development (USAID) on these grounds—an organization that had given over $2.6 billion in aid to Russia since the 1990s. Nevertheless, the following June in Berlin, Obama laid out his hopes for further progress in US-Russian nuclear arms negotiations, a prospect that excited little enthusiasm in Moscow. That very same month, when former National Security Agency contractor Edward Snowden revealed thousands of classified documents to the press and was indicted under the US Espionage Act, Russia agreed to grant him asylum in defiance of the United States. The obvious breakdown of the US-Russia reset by this point led Obama to cancel a planned summit with Putin, but beyond that Moscow faced few costs for its assertive intransigence. Indeed one might say that Putin secured what he could from the reset, and was prepared to move on without any pretense of friendly relations or even visible respect. The reset is dead, but no coherent US strategy toward Russia has replaced it—and wherever American influence retreated, from Central Asia across the Caucasus to the Middle East, Putin is happy to fill the gap.[55]

With regard to China, Obama has pursued a hybrid strategy that includes elements of engagement, integration, and accommodation on the one hand, and implicit containment, balancing, or deterrence on the other. The elements of balancing and deterrence grew more pronounced with the 2011 announcement of the administration's "pivot" to Asia, but the primary emphasis of Obama's China strategy has always been engagement.

On coming into office, Obama and his foreign policy team emphasized their desire to "avoid zero-sum thinking" in relation to China, a power they viewed as "already ascended."[56] The United States would reassure Beijing, welcome its rising influence, and look for cooperation over a range of issues including nonproliferation, climate change, international economics, and North Korea.[57] Secretary Clinton indicated early on that human rights concerns inside China would not prevent cooperation on other matters.[58] As in many parts of the world, the premise of Obama's approach was that if the United States reached out and engaged diplomatically, accommodating a number of Beijing's concerns, then China would reciprocate with cooperative behavior.

During the opening months of 2009, the Chinese government out of its own interest was largely supportive of US efforts to bolster existing international financial regimes.[59] But across a wider range of American concerns, Beijing offered little cooperation to the United States and in some cases outright hostility. On the issue of climate change, for example, the Obama administration went into the Copenhagen conference of December 2009 offering to make significant cuts in American carbon emissions, in the hope that this position would trigger similar concessions from Beijing. China's response was essentially a refusal to make any comparable reductions in absolute terms, and as environmentalists noted, the conference achieved virtually nothing of practical import.[60] On the issue of North Korea's repeated provocations and nuclear weapons program, the Chinese offered little assistance, anxious as they were that North Korea be propped up as a barrier to American influence.[61] On nuclear nonproliferation generally, Beijing showed no interest whatsoever in signing on to President

Obama's abolitionist agenda. On international economic issues, China continued to engage in mass-scale cyber theft against American companies. Most dramatically, in relation to a number of maritime territorial disputes within the East and South China Seas, assertive Chinese claims pushed up against the position of other countries including Vietnam, the Philippines, Taiwan, South Korea, and Japan, causing serious military tensions. Chinese vessels pressing their claims even collided occasionally with US surveillance ships. Beijing's aggressive behavior sufficiently alarmed China's neighbors that they began to approach Washington for reassurance regarding America's diplomatic and military commitments in the region. The nations worried by China's new assertiveness included not only traditional US allies such as Japan, Australia, the Philippines, South Korea, and Taiwan, but also Burma and Vietnam.[62]

Beijing's actions created the opportunity for an assertion of American diplomatic influence relative to China, and to its credit starting in 2010–2011 the Obama administration took that opportunity. Under a fresh course initially described as the "pivot to Asia," the administration strengthened US diplomatic ties in the region, introduced some modest new US Marine and Navy deployments to Australia and Singapore respectively, and indicated Washington's continued determination to play a key role in the Asia-Pacific.[63] However the president chooses to label it, the pivot amounts to a somewhat enhanced US deterrence, containment, or balancing of China's expanding power, and as such represents a useful strategic correction from 2009. Still, there remain serious questions about the pivot's implementation, consequences, and overall coherence. Beijing cannot be expected to welcome its own semicontainment, and indeed it does not. This makes it all the more important for American pronouncements surrounding the pivot to be backed up with credible material commitments, precisely to avoid any misunderstanding that might permit military escalation in a crisis situation. Yet even as the US government declares fresh interest in the Asia-Pacific, it has cut the US Navy—the armed service most responsible for giving the pivot some teeth in that part of the world. Nor do repeated budgetary crises and threatened government shutdowns in Washington reassure either friendly or rival Asian powers of America's capacity to remain a steady force within their region. The Obama administration declares its support for US allies in the Asia-Pacific, but at the same time frequently insists that it takes no position in territorial disputes between China and its neighbors. In practical terms, this tends to muddy the waters and raise the risk of deterrence failure.[64] In general, Obama has had more success with China when he supplements US engagement with a strong dose of counterbalancing and deterrence—and when Beijing is so assertive that it unintentionally drives regional powers into America's arms.[65]

The Arab Spring

Like many of the greatest foreign policy challenges that have faced previous American presidents, the Arab Spring was unexpected. On December 17, 2010, a Tunisian street vendor set himself on fire in protest against police treatment. This event catalyzed popular discontent over a wide range of political, social, and economic issues in relation to Tunisia's ruling president, who resigned four weeks later as a result. Seeing that existing governments could be toppled, mass demonstrations began to erupt out of similar causes throughout the Arab world—events that became known as the Arab Spring. Since Egypt had long been a key US ally, and arguably the leading Arab nation, developments in that country were of special significance. President Obama maintained a long-standing US policy of engagement and alliance with the Egyptian government of Hosni Mubarak until early in 2011, when Obama switched to calls for regime change by nonviolent methods. This was followed by attempted US engagement and accommodation of Egypt's Muslim Brotherhood, which lasted until its political collapse in 2013. All of these policies toward Egypt on Obama's part were also informed by powerful assumptions of American retrenchment and nonintervention. In the words of Vali Nasr, who worked at the State Department between 2009 and 2011:

> As the extraordinary events were unfolding, there was certitude of a sort in the White House. Obama remained intent upon leaving the Middle East, and he was not going to let himself be distanced from that mission by sudden eruptions of pro-democracy protests, teetering dictators, and looming civil wars. He did not know whether the Arab Spring would lead to ubiquitous democracy or a prolonged period of instability, but regardless, he was determined that America would not try to influence the outcome—not if that meant reversing course to get involved in the region . . . It was the right policy for a president who did not want to get any more involved than he absolutely had to with the problems of Egypt and the Middle East.[66]

When the Arab Spring first spread to Egypt, and toward the end of January 2011, mass protests began against Hosni Mubarak, for much the same reason as in Tunisia: namely, deep dissatisfaction with the status quo. The attention of international media was captured in particular by the dramatic spectacle of antigovernment demonstrators in Cairo's Tahrir Square, many of whom appeared young, progressive, courageous, photogenic, and familiar with Internet activism. Like numerous Americans suddenly watching these events unfold on television, President Obama sympathized and identified with the demonstrators. Convinced after observing several days of protests that Mubarak's days were numbered, Obama phoned the Egyptian president and asked him to step down from office, a position Obama repeated publicly on American television immediately afterward.[67] According to friendly accounts, such as that of James Mann, the call for Mubarak to step down was made by Obama and several of his leading White House advisers "on the fly," "without defining further what they meant or setting out in detail what they felt should happen next." Rather, the key reference point was autobiographical: "Just as they looked at themselves as a new generation, the Obamians viewed the events in Tunisia and Egypt as a sign of a new era."[68] In the words of a Brookings Institution study: "Obama was determined to be on the right side of history ... This was a historic moment for Obama, not just for the Egyptian people, signified by the linkage that he drew between their nonviolent revolution and the movements led by his heroes, Mahatma Gandhi and Martin Luther King."[69] Obama made the self-referential linkage more explicit again in a public address several days later.

US allies in the region were understandably shocked at Washington's sudden abandonment of Mubarak. As one of Obama's aides put it, the feeling among America's regional partners was: "Thirty years of friendship goes out the window in three days? What kind of friend is that?"[70] On February 11, under massive pressure from multiple directions, Mubarak resigned and fled Cairo. The Egyptian army assumed power through an interim transitional government and paved the way for open elections. That November, a plurality of votes and seats in nationwide parliamentary elections were won by the previously outlawed Muslim Brotherhood. This was followed by June 2012 presidential elections in which the winning candidate was Mohamed Morsi, also of the Muslim Brotherhood. President Obama was aware from early on of the possibility that the Muslim Brotherhood might assume power after Mubarak, but Obama was not especially disturbed by this. Assured by numerous advisers that the Brotherhood had moderated over the years—and in any case determined not to interfere in Egypt's electoral process—Obama was willing to take a chance on a Muslim Brotherhood government, engaging and supporting it financially and diplomatically, in the hopes that the practicalities of governance would nudge it in the right direction. As Vali Nasr describes it:

> The administration was also hoping that Egypt's Muslim Brothers would take a page from Turkey's experience and worry less about Islamist ideology than about improving governance and fixing the economy. American envoys met with Brotherhood members, and the White House even hosted a delegation from the group in April 2012 to discuss economic and political issues and future US-Egyptian ties. "They all had PhDs from American universities, and said all the right things," according to one person who attended the meetings. "It was easy to feel optimistic, but who knows."[71]

Multiple sympathetic accounts confirm that "the Obama administration rushed to forge a working relationship with the Muslim Brotherhood," and that President Obama in particular viewed a Brotherhood government in Cairo as a worthwhile bet.[72] In reality, this was an astonishing gamble to take. One of the explicit and foundational goals of Egypt's Muslim Brotherhood was and is to expunge the country of Western influence and establish strict Islamic law or "sharia." To be sure, there have long been many fascinating doctrinal disputes within the Brotherhood over how to reach that goal, in terms of timing, strategy, and method. Indeed Egypt's Islamic Jihad—which later merged into al-Qaeda—was born out of dissatisfaction with the Muslim Brotherhood's slower-paced approach. Al-Qaeda uses terrorist attacks against the "Far Enemy"—the United States—to undermine the "Near Enemy," namely secular and US-aligned governments within the Arab world. The Egyptian Muslim Brotherhood uses, when permitted, parliamentary and extraparliamentary means to accomplish much the same goal. Yet the two groups have a great deal in common philosophically, which is partly what makes them such rivals. Before winning elections in 2011–2012, numerous leaders of Egypt's Muslim Brotherhood announced their support for the killing of US troops in Iraq and Afghanistan; described the United States of America as an illegitimate "gang" deserving of attack; called for the violent destruction of Israel; and championed a highly noxious anti-Semitism.[73] Just to take one example of the latter tendency, in 2010 the Brotherhood's Mohamed Morsi—later to be president of Egypt—gave a number of speeches where he called on his fellow citizens to "nurse our children and our grandchildren on hatred" of "these bloodsuckers who attack the Palestinians, these warmongers, these descendants of apes and pigs."[74] Those kinds of sentiments are hardly unusual within the Brotherhood. On the contrary, they are and have long been quite common and conventional, which means they should probably be taken seriously as indicative of core beliefs.[75]

The Brotherhood also has a history that shows an increasingly sophisticated understanding of Western media and of the need to reassure it while continuing to articulate core convictions to a domestic Egyptian audience. Sometimes the disconnections between the Brotherhood's self-declared purposes and its massaging of Western opinion are so blatantly contradictory as to turn almost comical. When the American embassy in Cairo was assaulted by an angry mob on September 11, 2012, the

Brotherhood celebrated the attack in Arabic online, while taking care to condemn the same attack in English. US embassy staff had to remind the Brotherhood that some Americans can read Arabic.[76] This kind of attempted manipulation of Western sources is entirely typical of the Muslim Brotherhood over the years. Nevertheless, when representatives of the Brotherhood tried to reassure US officials, journalists, and academics of their "moderation" in 2011–2012, President Obama chose—as it were—to believe the English-language version, rather than the Arabic one.

Having seized—for the first time in its almost ninety-year history—key levers of power within the Egyptian state, the Muslim Brotherhood set out to take that country in an Islamist direction. Internationally, Morsi's government reached out to Tehran, distanced itself from the United States, and allowed for military aid to flow from Egypt to Hamas, the Muslim Brotherhood's violently anti-Israeli branch within the Gaza Strip. Egypt's Sinai became a chaotic base for insurgent Bedouin tribesmen and jihadist militants, the latter of whom attacked Israeli territory under the rubric of al-Qaeda in the Sinai Peninsula.[77] At the same time, Morsi reassured the United States that he would not tear up Egypt's peace treaty with Israel anytime soon; continued American aid to the new government in Cairo was simply too appealing. Domestically, the Brotherhood pushed through a variety of Islamist and authoritarian measures while showing itself to be incapable of running a modern economy. In the summer of 2013, millions of Egyptians consequently took to the streets in protest against the overreaching ideological agenda and sheer incompetence of Morsi's government. For the second time in less than three years, the Egyptian army stepped in to depose an unpopular regime and to manage an orderly transition. Obama was uncertain how to handle this latest development. Characteristically torn between apparent legal concerns and obvious regional US security interests, he decided to suspend some military aid to Cairo without cutting all of it or describing Morsi's overthrow as a coup, but by this time all parties in Egypt held the American president in contempt. Genuine Egyptian liberals together with the nation's army viewed Obama as a supporter of the Muslim Brotherhood, and of course the Brotherhood had never really been friendly to Obama or America in the first place.

Perhaps Mubarak's rule was bound to end, especially given his loss of support from the Egyptian military. Still, the course that never seems to have occurred to President Obama during these epochal events in the heart of the Arab world was to focus on supporting America's allies, such as they were, while refusing to assist self-declared US adversaries. Egypt has little historical experience with liberal democracy, and in any case Facebook activists were never going to run the country. In the absence of Mubarak, only two forces existed with the organization, weight, and numbers to exercise power: the country's army, and the Muslim Brotherhood. The army had made it clear for decades that while hardly a perfect ally, it was willing to cooperate with the United States on counterterrorism, peace with Israel, and the maintenance of a relatively pluralistic society. The Muslim Brotherhood, on the other hand, had made clear its rejection of all these things. Yet when the Arab Spring first spread to Egypt, Obama helped push a long-standing US ally out the door in a matter of days, with little planning or forethought as to what might come next, other than the stated assumption that liberal democratic forces would somehow emerge triumphant and that the historically anti-American Muslim Brotherhood would turn out to be a viable partner for the United States. Neither of these things turned out to be remotely true. There are indeed genuine liberals and genuine democrats inside Egypt, but they are a weak force politically and could use a little concrete assistance from the United States rather than American support of the Muslim Brotherhood. The best likely option for US interests and nascent democratic forces inside Egypt remains a relatively tolerant government, backed by the nation's army, allied to Washington, and nudging forward liberal political reforms in a gradual rather than unintentionally disastrous way.

In Libya, Obama adopted a policy of regime change in 2011, followed by a de facto policy of US disengagement and nonintervention. The combination was strategically incoherent and risked whatever gains were made by Mu'ammar Gaddafi's overthrow.

When the Arab Spring first spread to Libya early in 2011, President Obama grew concerned by Gaddafi's violent crackdown against antigovernment protests. In a rare confluence of calls for collective action, Britain and France together with the Arab League and the UN Security Council agreed that outside intervention against Gaddafi was welcome. Key figures within the Obama administration, including Secretary Clinton, UN ambassador Susan Rice, and foreign policy adviser Samantha Power persuaded the president that Libya's rebels were viable, and that this represented an opportunity to vindicate the principle of international humanitarian action in order to prevent atrocities against civilians.[78] Yet Obama was simultaneously determined to make US intervention in this case as light-footed as possible. Not only would there be no major American combat forces on the ground: US airpower would operate under severe limitations, on the premise of conformity to international legal standards. In other words, in Obama's mind, this would be no Iraq. After a nail-biting few months, Gaddafi's forces were eventually routed and he himself killed by an angry mob. While American weaponry, intelligence, refueling, and aerial support were vital to Gaddafi's overthrow, the Obama administration refused to describe the US military operation as a war, preferring to label it a "kinetic action" in which the United States was "leading from behind."[79] On these grounds, the president felt no need to receive congressional approval for American intervention in Libya.

On September 11, 2012, in a heavily armed and largely preplanned assault, several dozen men including members of the al-Qaeda-aligned Ansar al-Sharia attacked US diplomatic compounds within the Libyan city of Benghazi, killing US ambassador Christopher Stevens along with three other Americans. In the days immediately following the attack, the Obama administration described it as a spontaneous demonstration against an anti-Muslim video, suggesting that the video itself was a primary cause.[80] An independent panel later concluded that the attack had indeed been premeditated, and that embassy security was "grossly inadequate," but that there had been no deliberate wrongdoing by State Department officials.[81] In the midst of a US presidential election campaign, many Republicans suspected that the Obama administration had initially played down the possibility of an Islamist terrorist attack in Benghazi, for fear of how it might comport with claims of success in relation to al-Qaeda. During a forceful debate performance against GOP presidential candidate Mitt Romney, Obama managed to evade and fight back against this charge. Still, amid mutual accusations between the two parties over supposedly edited talking points, the broader picture with regard to public policy was largely missed: namely, that US follow-through on the 2011 Libyan operation was in fact profoundly and visibly weak.

Having toppled an admittedly nasty dictator, the United States had some obligation to help ensure a stable postwar transition in a friendly direction. Otherwise, the initial intervention made little sense strategically. In this specific sense, Libya was actually very much like Iraq. Yet after taking credit for Gaddafi's overthrow, President Obama's attention turned elsewhere, and he provided little support for Libya's nascent democratic authorities to stave off mounting violence and disorder. Arguably, the biggest beneficiaries of Gaddafi's toppling were the various militias, paramilitaries, and radical Islamist forces that swept over the country, making it a new haven for terrorism and organized crime. It was entirely understandable that under these circumstances Obama chose not to send major American ground forces into Libya—everyone had seen enough of that for a while. What was less understandable was the virtual lack of US diplomatic and political engagement, technical assistance, support, or training for Libyan government security services.[82] For an administration that prided itself on the skillful exercise of US soft power, there was very little of it in this case. Libya continued to spiral downward into failed-state status, with radical Islamists including al-Qaeda associates and affiliates picking up the pieces. No doubt, President Obama was determined to keep the American footprint in Libya very light. But if the president was not also determined to leave Libya a better place after US intervention than before it—both for American interests and for Libyans themselves—then it is not clear why the United States intervened in the first place.[83]

With regard to Syria, Obama pursued an initial policy of engagement and accommodation, followed after August 2011 by a stated American goal of regime change. Yet the de facto US policy remained largely one of nonintervention, and the various components of the administration's approach did not add up to a successful combination. On first entering the White House, President Obama hoped that Syria's dictator, Bashar al-Assad, might be helpful in brokering peace negotiations with Israel. For this reason, Obama initially tried to engage and accommodate Assad diplomatically, a process that yielded no significant results.[84] When the Arab Spring spread to Syria early in 2011, leading to peaceful antigovernment protests, Assad's regime replied by massacring innocent civilians. These attacks only encouraged more forceful protests, which soon developed into an armed rebellion with distinctly sectarian and region-wide implications.[85] In particular, the initial uprising turned into a brutally violent conflict between Syria's ruling Alawite minority and the nation's Sunni majority. It also turned into a proxy war between Sunni and Shia throughout the Middle East, as well as a multi-directional struggle for influence between al-Qaeda, Iran, Arab Gulf states, Russia, and—whether or not Obama fully appreciated it—American influence. In order to stay in power, Assad received vital military support from Russia, Iran, and Lebanon's Hezbollah. His opponents received much less, with the notable exception of Islamist rebels, who received considerable assistance from Sunni Gulf donors.

In August 2011, stung by the repeated spectacle of Syrian government atrocities against civilians, Obama embraced the goal of regime change, saying that "the time has come for President Assad to step aside." The United States simultaneously ratcheted up economic sanctions against Assad's regime, as well as humanitarian assistance to Syrian civilians.[86] Obama further indicated one year later that the use of chemical weapons by the Syrian government would constitute a "red line," triggering more forceful US military action.[87] He was very reluctant to go much further. His fear, specifically, was that American weapons sent to Syria's rebels might end up in the hands of jihadist forces, and that even a limited program of covert aid might lead inexorably to expanded US military intervention in Syria. Indeed the last thing Obama wanted running for re-election in 2012 was yet another complicated American military engagement in the Muslim world.[88] So for a variety of reasons, he continued to block significant covert US military support to Syria's rebels, even when leading advisers such as Secretary Clinton, Secretary of Defense Leon Panetta, and

CIA director David Petraeus all favored such support.[89] Obama's concern over the unintentional strengthening of al-Qaeda's Syrian associates, in particular, was certainly valid. Yet in one of the ironies that often characterize international relations, the very desire to avoid this specific outcome helped produce it. As Syria's civil war dragged on, radical Islamist forces such as Jabhat al-Nusra only grew stronger, gaining a reputation as the most ferocious, organized, and well-armed fighters inside the rebellion. In other words, US nonintervention in Syria did not weaken al-Qaeda's affiliates in that country. On the contrary, it allowed them to flourish.[90]

In August 2013, proof of Assad's large-scale use of chemical weapons against Syrian civilians left Obama little choice but to enforce his declared red line. The administration began to prepare, however reluctantly, for what Secretary of State John Kerry described as "unbelievably small" US airstrikes against the Syrian regime, on the understanding that their purpose was to punish Assad rather than to overthrow him.[91] At seemingly the last minute, an escape hatch opened in the form of a Russian offer to help broker the peaceful dismantling of Syria's chemical weapons arsenal. Obama leapt at the chance to avoid a military action he had never wanted in the first place. Under the Geneva agreement of September 2013, Assad agreed to hand over his chemical weapons for their supervised destruction under the eyes of the hitherto obscure Organization for the Prohibition of Chemical Weapons (OPCW). In the following months, the OPCW did heroic work with a very small staff in moving this process along, but one disturbing question among many was whether Assad had actually disclosed all of his chemical weapons stockpiles and facilities. There seemed good reason to suspect he might not have, as a dictator fighting for his life in the midst of a vicious civil war. In any case, the initial US goal laid out by Obama in the summer of 2011—that it was time for Assad to step aside—was largely forgotten, and left to the improbable realm of diplomatic negotiations between Syria's dictator and his opponents. In reality, since Assad and the rebels were now fighting over who would rule Syria, there was little to negotiate about. It was unclear whether Obama expected such negotiations to actually succeed. Meanwhile, the most extreme Islamist forces continued to secure territory and gain stature inside Syria, as other rebel groups such as the Free Syrian Army splintered and peeled off in despair at ever receiving US aid.[92]

By any reasonable standard, and judged on its own declared terms, President Obama's approach toward Syria was strategically incoherent. First, he announced that Assad must go. Then, over a period extending into years, he refused to take even the most modest action to give that announcement practical meaning. Nor was this disconnect between words and actions without real-world consequences. The major unintended beneficiaries—each in their own way—were Syrian Islamists, jihadists, Russia, Iran, and of course Assad. The major losers on the ground were the one group inside Syria that might have corresponded with US regional interests, namely, Assad's non-Islamist opponents. Yet it was precisely this group Obama refused to arm and support concretely, in spite of urgings from within his own cabinet. From the perspective of grand strategy, American policy toward Syria could not be judged as anything other than embarrassing. The only way it made sense is if Obama was simply determined at each step to avoid deepening US intervention, regardless of other factors, and most likely this was his guiding principle here. Indeed, it emerged shortly after the Geneva agreement that the White House had recently reviewed its Middle East policy and decided to re-emphasize diplomatic negotiations rather than any further US military actions in the region.[93] This emphasis was reiterated in Obama's September 2013 address to the United Nations, where he appeared to communicate the lack of any really vital interest in the Syrian conflict, calling it "someone else's civil war."[94] Still, in that case he should never have tied US credibility to specific political outcomes inside Syria, since the lesson drawn by allies and adversaries alike from this example was that commitments, red lines, and declarations issued by the United States and by the president specifically count for little when called upon. This is a terrible lesson for others to draw about the world's only superpower, and to believe that it has no serious international consequences is delusional.[95]

With regard to Iraq, Obama's approach was a hybrid of US engagement, retrenchment, and nonintervention, with the element of engagement fading dramatically in 2011–2012. As a presidential candidate in 2008, then-senator Obama gained a crucial edge among Democratic primary voters on his long-standing opposition to the war in Iraq. During that election campaign, candidate Obama promised to withdraw all US combat units from Iraq within sixteen months of his inauguration. President Bush's management of the Iraq war had indeed been fatefully overoptimistic and inadequate between 2003 and 2006. Bush eventually imposed a coherent strategy on the situation in the form of a 2007 US "surge" involving additional troops and counterinsurgency techniques—a strategy Obama opposed as senator. The surge left American interests and conditions in Iraq significantly improved by the time Obama entered the White House.[96] In one of its final foreign policy acts, the Bush administration further negotiated a three-year security agreement with Iraq, on the expectation it could be renewed by Bush's successor. Sectarian violence and American casualties in Iraq were both down dramatically by the beginning of 2009. As the US surge commander General David Petraeus made clear repeatedly, all of these gains were fragile, reversible, and dependent on Iraqi domestic political reconciliation backed by persistent American engagement. For this very reason, on first becoming president, Obama made the sensible decision to slow down his earlier plans for US military disengagement from Iraq, even at the cost of frustrating his liberal political base. In August 2010, the president declared a formal end to American combat operations in Iraq, but in reality a stabilizing US military presence continued.[97] The real turning point came in 2011. As it came time to renegotiate the Iraqi-US security agreement, multiple complications arose. One sticking point was the legal status of American troops in Iraq. Another issue was the number of those troops, along with their exact mission. The administration's stance was that the diplomatic initiative on these matters needed to come from Baghdad. In truth, Obama and his inner circle within the White House were unenthusiastic about keeping a large number of US troops overseas in the specific aftermath of a war they had never supported in the first place:

> U.S. military leaders had worried about the impact of a complete withdrawal from Iraq. But in political terms, making a clean break was much better for Obama than leaving some American troops in the country. Getting out of Iraq had been the central theme in the campaign that brought him to the White House. He had reaffirmed that commitment within weeks of taking office ... Obama was preparing to run for reelection in 2012. Any decision to extend the American troop presence there would be portrayed as a violation of these promises and of the "dumb-war" views on which Obama's career in national politics had been based.[98]

Iraq's prime minister, Nouri al-Maliki, for his part, was either unwilling or unable to give the Obama administration its desired assurances regarding continued legal immunity for US troops stationed in Iraq—especially given the small number of troops being discussed by the White House:

> Washington offered to leave behind 10,000 combat troops. Iraqis across the political spectrum thought that number showed a lack of seriousness and commitment, and even in Washington the chairman of the Joint Chiefs, Admiral Mullen, told the president it would "constitute high risk" . . . In effect, Washington confirmed what Iraqis suspected: America was not serious about Iraq, it was not committed to its security, and privately it was happy not to have to leave behind even the 10,000 troops it had offered.[99]

It is not clear whether a better-managed negotiation on the American side could have overcome these points of resistance, but certainly it would have been worth the effort. As status talks finally broke down between Baghdad and Washington, all US troops left Iraq in a rush toward the end of 2011. Sensitive to how this might be portrayed, and in any case genuinely happy to be done with Iraq, the White House chose to present an evident diplomatic-strategic failure as a successful vindication of Obama's longstanding promise to withdraw American forces. The claim that President Obama had kept his word to "end the war in Iraq" was made central to his 2012 re-election campaign.[100] Of course, he had not ended any war inside Iraq. On the contrary, he had inherited a reasonably improved American position in that country, and then exited from it hastily in the end, with predictably negative results for US security interests within the region. As anticipated by several of the president's Pentagon advisers, US disengagement from Iraq encouraged a number of very disturbing trends. Without a significant military presence on the ground—along with the intelligence capabilities this would have entailed—the United States was unable to help Baghdad combat resurgent jihadists in Iraq, reorganized as the Islamic State of Iraq and Syria. Radical Islamist terrorists thus staged a violent comeback inside Iraq between 2012 and 2014, asserting control over much of the country's northwest. Meanwhile, Iraqi prime minister Maliki continued to drift closer to Tehran diplomatically, for example in allowing Iranian overflights of weapons and supplies to Assad. Maliki also demonstrated increasingly authoritarian tendencies at home, cracking down on political opponents and alienating Iraq's Sunni minority. Sunni alienation only played into renewed sectarian violence. Perhaps many of these thorny problems were beyond America's ability to solve, and would have occurred regardless of any continued US presence. Certainly President Obama seemed to think so. But to some extent, the assumption of American powerlessness became self-fulfilling. Obama was hardly responsible for the initial invasion of Iraq—an invasion he had opposed quite consistently. Yet having become president of the United States in 2009, he necessarily assumed an obligation to preserve US foreign policy interests under conditions as they actually existed. In 2009–2010, he discharged this obligation responsibly in relation to Iraq and said explicitly that a continued US military presence was vital both to American interests and to prospects for a reasonably stable, democratic ally in Baghdad. He was right in saying that—which is exactly why the subsequent semivoluntary collapse of America's position in Iraq represented such a significant failure.[101]

US Allies, Defense Spending, and Offshore Balancing

In relation to America's traditional allies overseas, President Obama has pursued a policy of engagement, intermixed with growing US strategic retrenchment. This combination of mixed messages has disconcerted some long-standing US allies. Obama's tendency to search for diplomatic accommodation with Moscow, Beijing, and Tehran has also frequently unnerved American allies in Central and Eastern Europe, East Asia, and the Middle East, respectively.

On first becoming president, Obama made it clear that he looked to retrench strategically, reset US relations with Russia, reassure China, and reach out to Iran diplomatically. In several important instances, not always appreciated inside the United States, this emphasis on American retrenchment together with the accommodation of geopolitical adversaries was worrying to traditional US allies. In the autumn of 2009, for example, the Obama administration's decision to scale back missile defense plans for Poland and the Czech Republic—a decision communicated without much prior consultation—was interpreted in both those countries as resulting from a US desire to accommodate Russian objections. Insofar as this appeared to reflect a prioritization of Russian demands over the concerns of US treaty allies, naturally it was discouraging to those allied governments.[102] The administration would later recalibrate its missile defense plans to some extent, but a strong and not altogether positive impression had already been made in Warsaw and Prague regarding President Obama's instinctive preferences.

The same pattern repeated in other regions. In the Middle East, traditional US allies such as Israel, Saudi Arabia, and numerous Persian Gulf states were deeply dismayed by Obama's policies in relation to Egypt, Syria, and Iran. A series of presidential decisions to call for Mubarak's overthrow, pursue nuclear detente with Tehran, and essentially abandon Syria's rebels, led America's Middle East allies to wonder out loud whether the United States would support its allies in that part of the world. In

East Asia, the complaints were usually more subtle, but anxiety certainly existed as to whether Washington would stand by traditional alliance commitments, especially in an age of American defense cuts and partisan disagreement. Concerns over US constancy were exacerbated by the strangely cool, detached tone that President Obama initially set in relation to some core American allies such as Israel and Great Britain. To be sure, Obama was no isolationist; he did not simply dismantle the US alliance system built up since the 1940s and 1950s. On the contrary, he regularly referred to the need for its continuation and strengthening, and in some specific times and places such as the Asia pivot of 2011 there really was a bolstering of America's alliance ties, including fresh strategic deployments, joint military exercises, and productive diplomatic activity. But since these types of supportive words and actions existed alongside powerful material indicators of overarching US international retrenchment—together with repeated and widely heard presidential declarations that the time had come for Americans to focus on nation-building at home—there was frequent confusion abroad as to whether the United States was coming or going. Another way of putting it was that Obama usually (not always) said the right things in relation to traditional alliances, but the words were not always matched by concrete measures of support. Consequently there was a feeling of mixed messages received in allied capitals, and an unmistakable sense overseas that the United States was disengaging from much of its traditional role in the world. One resulting risk was that some long-standing American allies would start to hedge their bets and explore other foreign policy options on their own, such as aggressively unilateral military decisions on the one hand, or the preemptive accommodation of US adversaries on the other—either of which might be destabilizing regionally and harmful to American interests.[103]

Much attention is paid in public to the ways in which Obama has been strategically assertive—notably, in relation to intelligence surveillance, special operations, the 2009 Afghan surge, and escalating US drone strikes against suspected terrorists. The administration's declared pivot to Asia is also frequently cited as evidence of international strategic assertion. Yet with regard to America's defense expenditures and military posture abroad, the president's overall approach has clearly been one of retrenchment. In real terms there have been multiple waves of US military cuts since 2009, and defense spending has gone down significantly as a proportion of the federal budget while domestic spending has gone up.[104] Another way to measure US military retrenchment during the Obama era is in proportion to the nation's economic activity. As a percentage of gross domestic product (GDP), defense spending was about 4.9% of America's GDP in 2010. By 2016, that proportion is projected to be a little over 3%. In other words, there was a striking decline in the proportion of national effort devoted to military affairs, just as intended and called for by the president. Certainly, some of this reduction in defense spending was due to the US drawdown in Iraq and Afghanistan, but not all of it.

Under Obama's direction, Secretary of Defense Robert Gates initiated some important military spending cuts in 2009 and 2010, locating inefficiencies and canceling the further production of numerous weapons systems such as the F-22 fighter aircraft. Toward the end of his tenure in 2011, Gates warned that further defense cuts would endanger America's ability to reassure its allies, deter its adversaries, and preserve international stability.[105] The defense cuts only accelerated. In the summer of that year, under the Budget Control Act of 2011, Congress and the president agreed on a package of federal budget cuts amounting to over $2 trillion across a ten-year period in the absence of subsequent agreement, under a process known as sequestration. Half of these total cuts were to come from defense spending; no international or strategic rationale was offered. To be sure, responsibility for this outcome was shared between President Obama, the Senate, and a Republican-led House of Representatives. Since sequestration was never averted, the US armed forces are now in the middle of what is in effect a trillion-dollar budget cut stretched out over several years. These cuts have been accompanied by some significant adjustments in US force posture and security strategy. The Obama administration's 2010 Quadrennial Defense Review—although rather vague on priorities—emphasized challenges such as climate change, disease, and globalization, while downplaying any US "war on terror" in comparison with the Bush years.[106] The administration's more concise 2012 Defense Strategic Guidance (DSG) went further in clarifying key assumptions, notably by abandoning the pretense that America's armed forces would be able to fight two major regional conflicts at the same time.[107] This 2012 guidance document also clarified that the United States would henceforth de-prioritize any heavy-footed counterinsurgency or ground campaigns, saying: "we will develop innovative, low-cost and small-footprint approaches to achieve our security objectives" and "U.S. forces will no longer be sized to conduct large-scale, prolonged stability operations."[108] Another clear indicator of retrenchment: in terms of the sheer quantity of weapons and personnel maintained by the US armed forces, the overall trend under President Obama starting in 2010–2011 is that the numbers of soldiers, marines, ships, and aircraft have declined significantly over time. This was not compensated for by increased spending on military research and development, procurement, or modernization. On the contrary, expenditures in those categories went down sharply between 2010 and 2014.[109] So the notion of a deliberate shift from a larger, "heavier" military force toward a smaller, "innovative," high-tech one was rather misleading. In fact, the administration in agreement with Congress cut both troops and technology through deep cuts to US defense spending beginning in 2011. Of course, as with its alliance system overseas, the United States under Obama still maintains a very wide array of military capabilities, strategic engagements, and commitments abroad. Still, the president's overarching direction in relation to US military power is clearly one of retrenchment.

Objectively, the overarching drawdown of military capabilities at home and abroad poses a number of distinct and profound problems for US grand strategy, as suggested by leading bipartisan panels, numerous independent experts, America's Joint Chiefs of Staff, and all four of Obama's own secretaries of defense. These problems go well beyond common observations of increased wear and tear on US military forces, serious though such observations are.

First, while there is less immediate expense in maintaining a smaller armed force—sized to handle only one major regional contingency rather than two, and with no intention of engaging in large-scale ground campaigns—there is obviously a trade-off in terms of the level of international risk involved. Naturally, as the United States downsizes its strategic presence overseas, this tends to be unnerving to America's allies and encouraging to its adversaries. Allies depend upon believable, material indicators of American commitment, including a strong military presence together with a credible readiness to use it. Adversaries are deterred by the same. Some of the leading strategic statements issued by the Obama administration, such as the 2012 DSG, do not really concede or spell out the implication of any such trade-off between cost and risk; instead, they simply take for granted that the increased level of risk is manageable.[110] In effect, current plans assume or perhaps hope that international adversaries will not take advantage of America's scaled-back ability to handle a range of possible military challenges. US adversaries might not be so forgiving. They might also misperceive the true extent of America's strategic commitments and capabilities, and test it, under the impression that the United States will not respond. Indeed, this is how many of America's wars have begun in the past. So a smaller force and a seeming indication of limited US strategic interests and capabilities is hardly an inherent guarantee of peace, either for the United States or for anyone else. On the contrary, it has often preceded the outbreak of war.

Second, as pointed out repeatedly by a wide range of American military and civilian officials, by congressional leaders from both parties, and by defense experts in and out of the administration, even the current and relatively modest defense posture outlined under the 2012 strategic guidance is incompatible with actual levels of US military spending since sequestration entered into force. In this very tangible and disturbing sense, capabilities and commitments are not at all aligned in American grand strategy today.[111] The 2012 strategic guidance was written under the assumption of about $500 billion in military budget cuts over a ten-year period. It was not written under the assumption of $1 trillion in cuts, as specified under sequestration. Yet these are the cuts currently underway. In the words of one widely respected defense analyst, Michael O'Hanlon of the center-left Brookings Institution:

> Such draconian cuts would jeopardize what I consider irreducible requirements in American defense policy—winding down current wars responsibly, deterring Iran, hedging against a rising China, protecting global sea lanes vital for commerce, attacking terrorists and checking state sponsors of terror, and ensuring a strong all-volunteer military as well as a world-class defense scientific and industrial base.[112]

One practical implication among many, as stated explicitly by a majority of the Joint Chiefs of Staff in congressional testimony, is that the US armed forces under sequestration are not capable of handling with confidence even a single major armed conflict.[113] In effect the US military during the post–Cold War period has gone from the stated ability to execute two major regional missions, to one such mission, to none at all. How this could be constructive for the security and stability of an American-led democratic order internationally remains something of a mystery. One finds the same disconnect between US military capabilities and strategic commitments, as between words and actions, in specific cases like that of the celebrated pivot to Asia. Under the policy of America's Asian pivot, the Obama administration rightly implies an increased United States need to counterbalance rising Chinese military power and assertiveness. Former secretary of defense Leon Panetta, for example, indicated several years ago that the US Navy would henceforth shift toward the Asia-Pacific theater. Yet despite the assurance of a bolstered American naval presence in East Asia, the London-based International Institute for Strategic Studies—hardly unfriendly to the Obama administration—finds little hard evidence of it:

> Panetta said that "the navy will reposture its forces from today's roughly 50/50 split between the Pacific and the Atlantic to about a 60/40 split between those oceans." But when examined in detail, the only addition to capacity in East Asia will be the four Littoral Combat Ships to be deployed to Singapore, with three amphibious vessels rotated through the region and two Joint High-Speed Vessels (JHSVs) deployed there.[114]

In other words, because of deep overall cuts to the US Navy, a higher percentage of existing American vessels deployed to East

Asia amounts to no significant increase in actual numbers—only a dramatic decrease in the number of ships deployed to other regions, such as Europe and the Middle East. To think that the Chinese have not noticed this distinction would be absurd. In absolute terms militarily, the United States is really not much stronger in East Asia than it was five or ten years ago. Meanwhile, Chinese military expenditures—including naval expenditures—have grown dramatically over the same period of time.[115]

America's international retrenchment under Obama has led some thoughtful observers to suggest that the president's true grand strategy is one of offshore balancing, whereby the United States exits from any forward military commitments to the Eurasian mainland.[116] At the very least, he has moved the nation's security policies in that direction. Multiple elements of American grand strategy under Obama match what we would expect to see with a strategy of offshore balancing. These elements include, for example, a clearly declared unwillingness to engage in any further large-scale ground campaigns on the Asian continent; relatively deep cuts in defense spending; an emphasis on long-range strike capacity, militarily; a deep aversion to putting American "boots on the ground"; and a keen preference for US allies to take the lead themselves in facing international security challenges. The 2012 Defense Strategic Guidance, in particular, represents a remarkable shift in openly stated US strategic assumptions, in an offshore direction. It is for this very reason that one leading scholarly proponent of offshore balancing, Christopher Layne, identified the 2012 Guidance as a turning point in America's movement toward just such a strategy. In Layne's words:

Although cloaked in the reassuring boilerplate about American military preeminence and global leadership, in reality the Obama administration's new Defense Strategic Guidance

(DSG) is the first step in the United States' adjustment to the end of Pax Americana—the sixty-year period of dominance that began in 1945.[117]

The offshore trend under Obama is certainly striking. Still, the president has hardly adopted wholesale the recommendations of offshore-balancing advocates. The United States under Obama still maintains a wide array of military, international, and strategic commitments worldwide that go well beyond an offshore role. The Obama administration has not formally dismantled long-standing US alliance commitments in Europe and East Asia, as offshore balancers recommend. Nor has it cut defense spending as deeply as offshore balancers would like. Under a strategy of offshore balancing, the United States would not have surged into Afghanistan in 2009 or intervened in Libya during 2011. Nor would it have entertained any possibility of US armed intervention in Syria. American counterterrorism practices overseas, including drone strikes, surveillance, and intelligence operations, would presumably be scaled back under offshore balancing. By definition, US military bases on the Eurasian mainland would be abandoned. In all these respects, a true strategy of offshore balancing would go far beyond the retrenchments Obama has embraced, toward a very different paradigm more reminiscent of American grand strategy before World War II.[118] Obama has not embraced any such paradigm shift. He has, however, created his own distinct set of problems.

The Problem with the Obama Doctrine

American grand strategy under President Obama is a hybrid of various elements—including containment, bargaining, and even rollback in some cases—but in the end its most distinctive and consistent emphasis is on US retrenchment and international accommodation in order to focus on progressive policy legacies at home. Any fair-minded assessment of this strategy must note that the Obama administration has had certain international successes. The 2011 assault against bin Laden's secret compound is the most striking of these. There are also others. The administration—like its predecessor, and together with the US Treasury and Federal Reserve—did well in handling the international financial crisis of 2008–2009, which could have turned out much worse.[119] Obama maintains a relatively assertive campaign of drone strikes, special operations, and surveillance against al-Qaeda, which has had some good effect in continuing to wear down the traditional Pakistani-Afghan core of that terrorist organization. The administration's policy of strategic patience in relation to North Korea is essentially reasonable and welcome, though definitely incomplete. The same might be said of Obama's concept of a US pivot toward Asia. From the American public's point of view, the avoidance of new, large-scale ground combat entanglements beyond Afghanistan no doubt counts as a success in itself. Yet a number of caveats are in order. First, in cases where the administration has had some success—as, for example, in hitting bin Laden, containing North Korea, or pressing back against Chinese maritime assertion—it has been by embracing more hard-line strategies of deterrence, containment, or even (in the case of al-Qaeda) rollback. Second, while the Obama administration has had some genuine foreign policy successes, they are much more modest, uneven, and episodic than the president himself has suggested. When running for re-election in 2012, for example, Obama claimed to have ended two wars in Iraq and Afghanistan, placed al-Qaeda solidly on the path to defeat, maintained more than adequate national defenses, kick-started a brand-new democracy in Libya, engaged multiple US adversaries successfully through diplomacy, initiated worldwide processes of nuclear disarmament, and restored America's international standing with allies and foes alike. To put it mildly, this was overstating the case, and in multiple cases bears little relationship to stubborn facts on the ground. In reality, Obama's primary and overarching emphasis on strategic retrenchment, international accommodation, and domestic priorities has allowed multiple security threats to germinate overseas in ways that already hold very dangerous consequences for American interests.

On national defense, President Obama proposed and implemented deep military cuts beginning especially in 2011 that by the account of his own secretaries of defense have left the United States incapable of supporting its existing international commitments—not to mention any new ones, such as America's Asian pivot.

Al-Qaeda and like-minded jihadists have expanded operations in Syria, Iraq, Yemen, Somalia, Nigeria, Egypt, Libya, and across North Africa, especially in the wake of the Arab Spring. Al-Qaeda and the Taliban look to regroup and advance following America's troop withdrawal from Afghanistan. In Iraq, President Obama allowed allied status negotiations to break down, leading to the complete withdrawal of US forces from that country, with Iraq left as yet another arena for both Islamist terrorism and Iranian influence. Al-Qaeda splinter group the Islamic State of Iraq and Syria (ISIS) has established control over most of Iraq's Sunni Arab provinces, as well as large parts of Syria. ISIS is now rightly considered a direct terrorist threat to the homeland of the United States and its European allies.

The administration's stated commitment to nuclear abolition along with related gestures have left no single country more likely to abandon the bomb, and may actually render nuclear proliferation on the part of certain US allies more probable as they are unnerved by questions surrounding American foreign policy positions. Iran is on track to either acquire nuclear weapons or have international sanctions lifted while maintaining a virtual nuclear weapons capacity with American approval. The containment of North Korea, while certainly welcome, contains dangers of its own that the administration has not addressed and that will persist as long as the current regime in Pyongyang does.

Russia is asserting itself energetically to rebuild spheres of influence within the post-Soviet world and beyond, and to block American capacity in a variety of cases, despite Obama's attempted accommodation of Moscow over a broad range of issues including NATO expansion, missile defense, nuclear weapons, and human rights. China is asserting its newfound weight against the United States and its allies within the East and South China Seas, as elsewhere, both diplomatically and militarily—again, despite Obama's frequent attempts at engagement and reassurance. The risk of deterrence failure in East Asian skies and waters today is real, and serious questions exist regarding the constancy of America's regional commitments, especially given cuts in US armed forces together with the president's frequently declared desire to focus on domestic affairs.

In Egypt, President Obama helped push a long-standing American ally out the door, supporting that ally's replacement by Islamists openly hostile to US foreign policy goals, leaving the United States disdained by all Egyptian parties in the end. In Syria, eager to vindicate humanitarian principles while avoiding US military intervention, President Obama called for the overthrow of Assad, the support of relatively moderate rebels, and the prevention of growing Islamist extremism. Not one of these goals was actually implemented or achieved, as Syria's civil war became a regional catastrophe and a playground for violent jihadists. In Libya, President Obama embraced the overthrow of Mu'ammer

Gaddafi, only to provide little technical, political, or material support to the succeeding and nascent democratic government. Libya is now a failed state and in effect a safe haven for Islamist terrorists, warlords, and organized crime.

Traditionally, the most astute foreign policy realists have recognized that a strategy of retrenchment is not in itself a guarantee of international success. For one thing, it has to actually be implemented carefully and competently, and in world politics this is no small thing. When a great power retrenches, naturally this can be encouraging to its adversaries and disturbing to its allies. Within the particular arena of international relations, retrenchment is easily taken as a sign of growing weakness. An honest analysis would suggest that such a course involves certain inevitable trade-offs and must at the very least be conducted with keen skill, prudence, and rigorous self-awareness.[120]

Students of grand strategy have also long recognized that there are inevitable trade-offs between low-cost strategies and low-risk ones.[121] A grand strategy that is more light-footed and less expensive in immediate terms may have obvious appeal, but it can easily carry with it the risk of stimulating fresh international challenges. Put another way, an American strategic posture based upon military options, cuts, and flexibility that Secretary of Defense Hagel himself called "severely constrained" will in fact be severely constrained, and this naturally introduces certain dangers, as Hagel said, "especially if crisis occurred at the same time in different regions of the world."[122] Under President Obama, there has been a clear and unmistakable movement in the direction of a more low-cost grand strategy, with some necessarily increased risk for American interests overseas. Yet Obama's characteristic response to that development is to deny that any such trade-off exists. Nor does this appear to be simply the result of White House public relations efforts. Obama seems to actually believe that when it comes to his favored international policies, there is no trade-off between cost and risk. This attitude of denial is profoundly unrealistic and is itself the cause of much additional trouble for the United States overseas.

A similar problem exists in relation to Obama's deeply held assumption that international cooperation will necessarily follow from American accommodation. As a general rule, foreign governments or transnational actors do not feel obliged to alter their basic policy preferences or to make unwanted concessions of their own simply because an American president is accommodating, restrained, or articulate. This is not how international politics works. If the interests, goals, and priorities of other national governments align with those of the United States on specific issues, then those governments will cooperate with Washington on those issues. If not, they won't. Either way, whether we like it or not, the goals and priorities of foreign governments are defined by those governments, and not by the president of the United States. Any American president can alter the costs and benefits for other countries to cooperate with the United States on specific matters, by offering specific incentives or disincentives, but he cannot literally redefine how other governments view their own vital interests, and it is delusional to think that he can. If Washington offers a particular policy concession to another government in exchange for some concrete, reciprocal concession of real interest to the United States, then that is one thing. Such negotiations are at the heart of international diplomacy. But to make the concession beforehand—unilaterally, as it were—or to offer it up broadly to the entire planet as a whole in the hopes of unspecified reciprocity from particular countries, is to ignore the normal workings of international relations.

The usual complaint about Obama's foreign policy is that he never quite lived up to the transformational rhetoric or sweeping expectations of his 2008 campaign. That is hardly surprising, or even very interesting, since nobody could possibly live up to such gossamer expectations. Still, in a way that is exactly the point. The essential problem with the Obama doctrine is that it is based upon a sincere but fundamentally mistaken and unrealistic theory of international relations. When Obama ran for president in 2008, he suggested that most US foreign policy problems abroad were due to America's own policies under George W. Bush, and that if only the United States adopted a more accommodating approach, there could be dramatic progress toward international cooperation on a wide variety of issues. In truth this was a profoundly self-centered argument, both in relation to the United States and to Obama himself. Violent or intractable transnational and international conflicts and rivalries on a whole host of issues are not actually unusual in world politics. They existed long before Obama was president and will continue to do so. The international system possesses far less moral unity and collective police power then a single stable city, state, or country. The challenges of world politics are therefore not analogous to community organization at the local level. US presidents do not hover over the international arena as disinterested assemblers and observers, nor should they. The task of an American president is not to play the role of pope or UN secretary-general. The task of a US president is to promote US national interests overseas, guided to be sure by a sense of both prudence and justice. Obama is for many Americans a kind of inspirational personal bridge between races, as well as a bridge between his own country's past, present, and future. This is fine, but any desired projection onto the international realm is mistaken, not to mention pretentious. Obama may be a bridge for many Americans; he is not and cannot be a bridge between nations.

In a way, however, Obama has already achieved much of what he desired with his overall strategy of international retrenchment and accommodation, and that is to reorient American national resources and attention away from national security concerns and toward the expansion of domestic progressive reforms. He appears to sincerely believe that these liberal domestic initiatives in areas such as healthcare and finance will also bolster American economic power and competiveness. Actually there is good reason for skepticism here, since high debt and heavy-handed, constantly changing federal regulations may very well undermine long-term US economic growth. But either way, Obama's vision of a more expansive governmental role in American society is well on its way to being achieved, mostly without from his point of view debilitating debates over national security concerns. In that sense, especially since he was re-elected in 2012, several of his leading strategic priorities have already been accomplished.

3

The Domestic Politics of the Obama Doctrine

Under the Obama doctrine, the United States accommodates and retrenches internationally in large part so the president can focus on leaving behind liberal domestic policy legacies. This entails targeted counterterrorist strikes and assertive foreign policy adjustments when necessary, but for the most part represents a shift from guns to butter, a downscaling of military weight and presence, and an avoidance of any heavy US footprint overseas—a strategy pursued both on its own merits in Obama's view and in order to avert domestic political risk. President Obama keeps the final strategic decisions in his own hands, in consultation with a tight inner circle of White House advisers sensitive to his priorities. The resulting paradox is a highly centralized decision-making process in which clear and internally coherent foreign policy decisions in specific regional cases are often deliberately avoided or delayed, in order to minimize domestic political risk. During his first term in office, Obama found considerable domestic success with this approach. Democrats largely supported him, even when they had qualms about some of his decisions regarding the use of force overseas. Republicans criticized him but had difficulty agreeing on a superior international alternative. Most political independents appreciated both an assertive counterterrorist policy and an otherwise light US footprint abroad. For Obama, the successful May 2011 strike against bin Laden's secret compound removed counterterrorism as a politically vulnerable issue area, at least temporarily. Running on a re-election platform of "ending wars," "Bin Laden is dead," and "nation-building at home," Obama did something no Democrat had done since 1964: he turned foreign policy into a clear electoral advantage for his own party. In effect, he used national security as a wedge issue. Moreover he used this advantage to further implement an overarching grand strategy of international accommodation and retrenchment in his second term—again, with the evident goal of preserving and expanding domestic progressive policy legacies. Whether the Obama doctrine will continue to benefit Democrats so clearly heading toward 2016 is an entirely different question; there are already multiple signs it may not.

Public Opinion

Alexis de Tocqueville, generally an astute admirer of the US system of government, believed it to be ill-suited to the conduct of international relations. He was convinced that in a democracy like America's, an erratic and poorly informed public opinion would overpower and derail the possibility of a serious foreign policy. As Tocqueville put it, "a democracy finds it difficult to coordinate the details of a great undertaking and to fix on some plan and carry it through with determination in spite of obstacles."[1] Luckily, the great French writer was not entirely right about this. More recent research tends to discredit the notion that public opinion is simply erratic, unstable, or irrational when it comes to basic questions of foreign affairs.[2] To be sure, the general public in the United

States (as in other countries) does not play close attention to most international policy issues much of the time, and there are indeed sometimes changes or swings of opinion in the popular mood on such issues. In fact there seems to be a historical pattern of cyclical upswings and downswings in the public's support for American activism abroad. But these opinion swings are usually based upon real-world experience and are not necessarily irrational. In the wake of World War I, for example, the general public—defined here as the adult population of the United States—had no interest in repeating that particular wartime experience. In the wake of World War II, the general public was much more willing for the United States to remain engaged internationally on a regular basis, especially given the looming threat from the Soviet Union. During the mid-1970s, after the US exit from Vietnam, public opinion shied away from any similar interventions and indeed from foreign policy concerns altogether. By 1980, following the Soviet invasion of Afghanistan, the American public was once again ready to countenance a tougher national security stance. During the presidency of Bill Clinton, after the fall of the Soviet Union, the general public viewed foreign policy as a low priority. Following the terrorist attacks of September 11, 2001, much of the public was ready to pay attention and support military action overseas for several years. None of these shifts in popular feeling were unreasonable, per se. They did, however, create certain political incentives for politicians—including presidents—to either resist or support assertive US foreign policy strategies, depending on the swing of the cycle in public opinion.

Under Obama, the state of popular opinion on foreign policy issues has been fairly clear. Public opinion polls taken between 2010 and 2013 by organizations such as Gallup, the Pew Research Center, and the Chicago Council on Global Affairs all tell a similar story: the general public within the United States was tired of recent war efforts, focused on domestic economic concerns, and generally averse to new military interventions overseas.[3] In other words, the United States was in the midst of a significant downswing in another cycle of public opinion against strategic activism. This downswing actually began during the second term of President George W. Bush, in response to American frustrations in Iraq, and accelerated under President Obama. A 2011 Pew Research Center poll found that some 58% of Americans wanted the United States to "concentrate on problems at home," rather than "be active in world affairs."[4] Clear majorities within the United States opposed the prospect of armed intervention in both Libya 2011 and Syria 2013.[5] Support for US military efforts in Afghanistan underwent a steady but dramatic decline beginning in 2010–2011, with a remarkable 67% of Americans concluding by July 2013 that the Afghan war was "not worth fighting."[6] The popular desire within the United States to remove US troops from that conflict grew at a similar rate. Public awareness of budgetary constraints and mediocre economic growth only reinforced such feelings. Overall, the popular preference has been for a lighter international footprint than the United States exercised a decade ago.

Any inference, however, that the American public has suddenly embraced isolationism during the Obama era needs to be sharply qualified. On a range of specific issues, majorities of the general public remain willing to support key components of US grand strategy. For example, about two-thirds of Americans support the use of drone strikes against suspected terrorists; less than 20% oppose them.[7] An overwhelming majority also supported US airstrikes against the Islamic State of Iraq and Syria by September 2014.[8] On the issue of Iran, multiple polls have shown that well over 50% of Americans would support US airstrikes against that country, rather than allowing it to develop nuclear weapons.[9]

On defense spending, Gallup found in 2013 that only 36% felt the United States spent too much on national defense.[10] On the issue of Sino-American relations, the general public within the United States is if anything more worried about the rise of Chinese power—especially in its economic aspect—than are most US foreign policy elites.[11] According to polls conducted by the Chicago Council on Global Affairs, there is no majority support among the general public for dismantling most US bases or alliances inherited from the last seventy years.[12] Over 50% of Americans still believe that it is important for the United States to remain the world's most influential country as well as its leading military power.[13] So it is not as though the general public is demanding a systematic end to America's world role. Popular feeling regarding US international commitments is more mixed, ambivalent, and sometimes even hawkish, depending on the precise issue and how it is framed.

The general public tends to be more skeptical and pessimistic than liberal opinion elites regarding the possibilities for international cooperation through accommodation. Yet as one can see from the polling results above, in strictly political terms, certain components of President Obama's grand strategy have not been a bad fit with American public opinion. In particular, the combination of drone strikes and special operations against al-Qaeda terrorists, together with a clear desire to both exit from and avoid major military interventions on the ground, is not only part of the Obama doctrine—it is popular with the general public. On an important range of issues related to the interrogation, detention, and targeting of suspected terrorists, Obama's policy practices moved away from a civil libertarian position after he entered the White House. This disappointed the Left, but reassured the center of the country politically. On counterterrorism, specifically, Obama moved back to or even beyond many of the actual practices of the Bush administration. But this was hardly because Obama had no core political convictions. On the contrary, he very much wanted to safeguard a progressive domestic policy agenda and viewed debates over issues like Guantánamo Bay as something of a distraction. He therefore moved to the center on selected national security matters, precisely to save political capital in pursuit of his domestic agenda. It may also be that once in office, he realized the practical limitations of a strict civil libertarian position in relation to terrorists.

In any case, this combination of counterterrorism with modest international retrenchment and a light footprint overseas was a fair reflection of what the median American voter wanted, and during his first term at least, the general public gave Obama relatively high approval ratings on foreign policy issues as a result. In Gallup polls taken during 2012, for example, between 36% and 45% of the public approved of the president's handling of the economy. This was roughly similar to the low ratings he received on that issue for most of his tenure as president. On foreign policy, by comparison, he received approval ratings of between 47% and 49% in the very same polls.[14] This was hardly a ringing endorsement, but at least it put him out of the danger zone politically on international issues, and indeed this is exactly what Obama achieved during his first term in office: he stayed out of political danger on foreign policy and national security, and particularly for a Democratic president looking to leave a substantial domestic policy legacy, that was a truly significant achievement.

Interestingly, during the summer of 2013, Obama's foreign policy approval rating dropped below 40% in multiple polls and never really bounced back to his first-term levels. To some extent, this dovetailed with an overall decline in the president's popular approval across the board, but there was also enough of a distinctly steep and sudden drop in his foreign policy scores worth noting. The initial catalyst seems to have been his handling of the 2013 Syria crisis. While the general public was no more enthusiastic than Obama about the prospects of US airstrikes in Syria, voters also appear to have been disturbed by the president's foreign policy leadership style, which frankly came across as dithering and indecisive.[15] Ironically, his evident desire to consider every last possible objection to his own Syria policy may have been self-defeating politically, since in the end the overpowering impression was simply one of weak, confused leadership. As of mid-2014, his foreign policy approval ratings had not recovered.[16]

This goes to a more fundamental point: merely sticking close to the polled preferences of the median voter on a variety of specific policy issues is not the same thing as having a coherent or internationally effective grand strategy. Nor is it really necessary, even in domestic political terms, for presidents to follow polled majorities on every foreign policy issue. The voters elect a president to lead the country on foreign policy, among other things, with the understanding that he or she bears unique responsibilities not shared by every other citizen. Most voters neither have, nor claim to have, vast expertise on complicated international and military issues. The implied precision of public opinion polls on such issues can therefore be rather misleading. Large sections of the general public do not have strong preferences or even an attentive interest in relation to numerous detailed questions of foreign and national security policy. Nor is a lack of attention to international events the same thing as isolationism. Isolationists have fixed, detailed, and intensely held views on foreign policy issues. The general public on the other hand has views that are rather more ambivalent, fluid, and deferential both to national leaders and to pragmatic policy success. If and when a president decides to act in foreign affairs, a certain percentage of the American public will rally to his side, at least for a time, after which point he will be judged in terms of results.[17]

At the end of the day, US grand strategy is made by presidents, not by the general public. Public opinion sets broad constraints, and elected officials are obviously sensitive to such constraint or they would probably not be elected in the first place. But the very fact of popular uncertainty and ambivalence when it comes to foreign policy both permits and requires presidents to act, choose, and make decisions between a range of possible options in a serious and coherent way. Presidents can speak out on foreign policy matters, shape the popular debate, and try to nudge the trends of opinion. And even when unable to convince popular majorities of their chosen course on some specific question of foreign affairs, the fact is presidents can and often do pursue it anyway, when they believe it is the right thing to do. In other words, when it comes to foreign policy strategies, presidents can lead, and when they do, if they are successful, the public tends to follow. The real question is whether presidents are prepared to spend political capital on international issues that are truly vital. So it is reasonable to judge American grand strategy under Obama not only in terms of whether it fits with the apparent preferences of the median voter on a number of specific issues, but also in terms of whether it represents a model of presidential leadership abroad that is actually in the national interest.

Party Politics

While the American two-party system revolves primarily around domestic issues, it does influence the country's grand strategy, and this influence operates in several ways. First, as Democrats and Republicans compete for elected office, they try to appeal to swing voters, differentiate themselves, divide the opposition, and find winning issues, while simultaneously holding together broad coalitions of their own. This is no less true of presidents and their opponents: foreign policy debates are often caught up in the process of party competition. Second, the members of each political party as a whole—among the general public, Congress, interest groups, and opinion elites—have distinct views or preferences in relation to foreign policy. These preferences may be shaped by specific material interests, ideological convictions, or some combination of the two, but either way, the two major parties are not identical in terms of their broad foreign policy outlook. Moreover, there is some diversity within each party between different factions or tendencies when it comes to international affairs, and the strength of these multiple tendencies varies over time.

Public opinion on foreign policy issues differs according to party; it also differs according to the level of attention paid to the issues. Elite opinion-makers—defined as that small percentage within both parties which pays close attention to international affairs, articulate its views in public, and has some impact on the rest of popular opinion—hold different foreign policy views from the general public. Extensive research by political scientists such as Ole Holsti suggests that both public and elite opinion within the United States can be categorized along two distinct dimensions in relation to foreign policy. The first dimension, "cooperative" or dovish internationalism, corresponds with support for the United Nations, transnational governance, peaceful diplomacy, arms control treaties, foreign aid, humanitarian objectives, and the nonviolent resolution of international conflict. The second dimension, "militant" or hawkish internationalism, corresponds with support for defense spending, covert action, and the use of force overseas, including preemptive strikes. Dovish internationalists emphasize the possibilities for global peace and cooperation through multilateral coordination; hawkish internationalists see the world as a dangerous place and view US military power as central to staving off national security threats.[18] What is interesting in these results is that there is no apparent relationship between supporting military as opposed to nonmilitary tools of US leadership overseas. In other words, some Americans support the use of both military and nonmilitary instruments of US grand strategy; some support one or the other; and some support neither. Those who support both can be called internationalists. Those who support neither can be called isolationists or anti-interventionists. Those who support the military but not the rest can be called hawks. And those who support only nonmilitary instruments can be called doves.

One way to think about the relationship between party politics and American grand strategy over the years is to consider the changing strengths and affiliations of these four major tendencies within each party: internationalist, anti-interventionist, hawk, and dove. Quite simply, for the last forty years at least, conservatives have tended to be foreign policy hawks, while liberals have tended to be doves. These tendencies appear to be related to domestic policy convictions and deeply rooted philosophical beliefs that are unlikely to disappear soon.[19] At the same time, opinion elites in both parties have tended toward various forms of internationalism, whether hawkish or dovish, while the general public is more ambivalent and cycles through periods of disengagement.

Party political support for America's global role has shifted historically, with numerous twists and turns. During the 1930s, a bipartisan consensus inside the United States opposed direct intervention into major foreign wars. The Japanese attack on Pearl Harbor erased that isolationist consensus and allowed for the rise of an internationalist alternative, cemented by the Cold War's onset after 1945. Conservative anti-interventionists, like Senator

Robert Taft (R-OH), and liberal doves, like former secretary of commerce Henry Wallace, were either won over or politically defeated by other US party leaders, and by the mid-1950s the new foreign policy consensus was firmly in place. Every early Cold War president, from Harry Truman to Lyndon Johnson, pursued a strategy of robust internationalism centering on the containment of the Soviet Union and its allies. The GOP's presidential nominee in 1964, Senator Barry Goldwater (R-AZ), was uninterested in multilateral organizations but if anything more hawkish than his opponents in both parties, rejecting containment in favor of anti-Communist rollback. The truly lasting breakdown in America's internationalist consensus came in the wake of the Vietnam War. The US experience in that war triggered a genuine fracturing of bipartisan agreement over foreign policy issues. In particular, it saw the rise of a newly dovish form of liberal internationalism, committed to multilateral cooperation but opposed to US military interventions overseas. Initially, this new dovish inclination was not exclusively associated with either political party. Democrats especially were torn between hawkish and dovish factions. But the Democratic Party's nomination of Senator George McGovern (D-SD) in 1972 indicated that antiwar liberals had captured their party's high ground, and voters began to realign somewhat on foreign policy and military issues, with doves trending Democrat and hawks trending Republican. Ronald Reagan's pursuit of a hawkish American internationalism in the face of the Soviet Union only solidified these partisan trends, which well outlasted the end of the Cold War.[20]

For the Democrats, every presidential candidate since McGovern has had to wrestle with the dilemma of hawk versus dove on foreign policy issues. This is not so much because of historical memory; after all, McGovern's 1972 nomination was a long time ago. Rather, it is because the demographic and ideological makeup of the Democratic Party began to change dramatically during the Vietnam era, and these changes have persisted and continued right up to the present. Indeed the Obama coalition owes a great deal to George McGovern. The base of the Democratic Party is very different today from what it was under Harry Truman: considerably more dovish, domestically oriented, and liberal on cultural issues. Those components of the old New Deal coalition most inclined to hawkish foreign policies—southern and working-class white men—have shifted toward the GOP. Some of the leading voting blocs within the Democratic Party today are college-educated liberals, unmarried women, younger voters, and racial minorities, all of whom tend to be especially skeptical of US military intervention overseas.[21] At the same time, many Democratic leaders, including President Obama, understand that for both political and meritorious reasons they cannot simply replicate McGovern's plain antiwar stance, and the party's foreign policy establishment inside the Beltway is certainly less dovish and more internationalist than its liberal base. So each Democratic president since Jimmy Carter has walked a tightrope between policies and factions—dovish versus hawkish—with greater or lesser skill, luck, and success. Carter's tightrope walk was especially unbalanced. Obama's was more fortunate and dexterous, politically during his first term as president.

Republicans, for their part, have usually been less divided than Democrats over foreign policy and military issues, at least since the late 1960s. Hawks have dominated the GOP, and with its anti-interventionist strain subdued, the party has generally been united behind various types of muscular internationalism under every Republican president since Dwight Eisenhower. The 2003 invasion of Iraq, and its subsequent frustrations, certainly raised the question of what a conservative foreign policy should look like. Staunch Republicans in the Obama era still tend to be significantly more hawkish than the average American voter.[22] This is one reason that candidates like Ron Paul and Pat Buchanan were unable to come anywhere near securing the GOP's presidential nomination in previous election cycles. But another lengthy period in exile from the White House forced Republicans into a serious discussion of foreign policy issues, and during the Obama era conservative anti-interventionists made a comeback.

Overall, the pattern in US party politics for several decades after the Vietnam War was that national security hawks predominated within the GOP, while Democrats wrestled internally between internationalist and dovish impulses. In strictly political terms, up until very recently, this pattern tended to help Republicans more than Democrats. Indeed a standard complaint from liberals and progressives was that the GOP used national security as a wedge issue to divide Democrats from one another.[23] A more objective way of putting this would be to say that Republicans usually agreed on national security issues more than Democrats did. Yet we are now well into a different era—the Obama era—in which observers perceive that history has turned upside down, with Republicans in complete disarray and Democrats united behind prudent international policies. Are such perceptions accurate?

The short answer is: not exactly. Democrats nationwide continue to be internally divided over central US foreign policy questions regarding the use of force. In a May 2011 Pew poll, for example, a majority of Democrats wanted to "remove [US] troops as soon as possible" from Afghanistan; less than half favored keeping the troops there "until [the] situation has stabilized."[24] On military spending, a February 2013 Gallup poll found that 51% of Democrats felt the United States still spends too much on national defense; only 12% felt it spends too little, with the remaining 35% viewing existing levels as about right.[25] On the question of whether "the best way to ensure peace is through military strength," the Pew

Research Center found that Democrats are divided roughly in half, with 44% saying they agree with that statement.[26] The same division is found over the question of whether the United States should strike Iran to prevent its acquisition of nuclear weapons, with 46% of Democrats saying they would approve such an attack.[27] On the issue of drone strikes, some 64% of Democrats support their use against suspected terrorists, with a vocal minority in strong opposition.[28] A clear majority of Democrats opposed the prospect of US intervention in both Libya and Syria. Moreover the pattern is that on such questions, of all major political and ideological groupings, liberal Democrats are usually among the most opposed to the use of force. So it can hardly be said that the Democratic Party is unified today when it comes to a variety of international and military issues. If anything, there is significant and articulate opposition from the more liberal, dovish wing or base of the party to a range of Obama's foreign and national security policies.

Many Democrats would much prefer in principle to rein in drone strikes, stay out of Libya and Syria militarily, withdraw all troops from Afghanistan, shut down Guantánamo Bay, avoid armed conflict with Iran, cut US defense spending, avoid further trade agreements, and focus attention and resources on the promotion of a progressive domestic policy agenda. Yet the great majority of Democrats also say that on balance they approve of Obama's handling of US foreign policy.[29] This is partly because mainstream Democrats perceive—quite rightly—that the president shares their ultimate concerns on a broad range of domestic and international issues, and that he has been careful to factor in those concerns when making specific foreign policy and national security decisions. There is nothing like winning elections under a sympathetic figure to help paper over secondary factional differences within a political party, and Democrats have now won two presidential elections in a row under a leader they largely like and support. Obama has in fact straddled the dovish and hawkish elements inside the Democratic Party with considerable political success. Moreover on the great popular issues that truly animate and preoccupy America's two great parties in the current era, having to do with the federal government's proper role in the nation's economy, liberal Democrats are united in opposition to conservative Republicans and have no greater ally than the current president. So on those occasions where President Obama has taken the lead on some military or foreign policy issue overseas, even in contradiction to liberal or dovish preferences, a significant number of Democrats have rallied behind him in support.[30] This pattern is nothing new, historically; Republicans showed the same deference toward George W. Bush when he authorized the invasion of Iraq. Indeed the tendency since the Vietnam War is very clear: all things being equal, political partisans are more willing to trust and follow a president of their own party when it comes to foreign policy issues. Today, this tendency helps create the impression that Democrats agree on foreign policy fundamentals, when such agreement does not actually exist.

With regard to Republican foreign policy views in the Obama era, some of the most common journalistic perceptions or misperceptions have been the following: first, that under the influence of the Tea Party, GOP conservatives have abandoned their previous support for hawkish foreign policies and now support isolationism; second, that "neoconservatives" still dominate Republican foreign policy thinking; and third, that the GOP is in complete disarray, with no clear tendencies at all when it comes to international or military issues.[31] Of course, the above three claims are mutually contradictory—they cannot all be true at the same time. As it happens, all three claims are mistaken, or at least badly overstated. The mood at the base of the GOP, and among its congressional representatives, has moved away from distinctly neoconservative assumptions. During the Obama era, anti-interventionists have clearly risen in influence within the Republican Party. Taken as a whole however, strict anti-interventionists are still a minority and dissident GOP faction. Conservative Republicans—including Tea Party Republicans—remain relatively hawkish and hard-line on a wide range of national security issues, compared to Democrats and independents.

There is undoubtedly a rising and vocal anti-interventionist faction within the Republican Party today. Working from venues such as the libertarian Cato Institute, *Reason* magazine, and the *American Conservative*, anti-interventionists argue for a very deep retrenchment of US strategic commitments overseas. During the 1920s and 1930s, this strain of foreign policy thinking was dominant within the GOP under leaders such as President Herbert Hoover and then senator Robert Taft (R-OH). Only an intense anti-Communism convinced most conservatives to abandon this tradition after World War II. The GOP's anti-interventionist tradition resurfaced after the collapse of the Soviet Union, and was led by spokesmen such as Pat Buchanan and Representative Ron Paul (R-TX), but it remained a political liability for presidential candidates inside the Republican Party long after the fall of the Berlin Wall. Today, it is less of an obvious liability. Every year of the Obama presidency before 2014 saw the incremental rise of Republican anti-interventionism on one foreign policy issue or another. Ron Paul's son, Senator Rand Paul (R-KY), has been especially effective at articulating and popularizing anti-interventionist concerns within the GOP and beyond. In watered-down form, such concerns seem like a good fit for the times. Republicans have indeed shifted focus from international activism toward domestic fiscal and constitutional concerns, and the party's conservative base—like the general public—is in no mood for nation-building or humanitarian intervention overseas. Yet principled GOP anti-interventionists recommend much more than a tactical shift in mood or policy: they call upon the United States to scale back dramatically on a very broad range of military expenditures, bases, and international alliance commitments inherited from the last century.[32] Whether discussing American policy toward China, Russia, defense spending, jihadist terrorists, drone strikes, or Iran's nuclear weapons program, a common anti-interventionist theme is that the primary cause of US security challenges is the provocative and aggressive nature of American foreign policy itself. As we shall see in a moment, there is no evidence that most Republican conservatives agree with this broad contention, and plenty of evidence against it. GOP anti-interventionists may be better positioned right now, politically, than at any time since Robert Taft ran for the Republican presidential nomination in 1952. Nevertheless, strict anti-interventionists remain a minority GOP faction, even inside the Tea Party.

Regarding the supposed death of conservative foreign policy hawks: on a wide range of issues, Republicans continue to be more hawkish than the average American, with GOP conservatives most hawkish of all. Republicans are still much more likely than either Democrats or independents to say that the "best way to ensure peace is through military strength."[33] Only 17% of Republicans feel that the United States spends too much on national defense; a plurality of 45% feel it spends too little.[34] Between 70% and 80% of Republicans say they would support US airstrikes rather than allowing Iran to build nuclear weapons.[35] A similar percentage of GOP voters supports drone strikes against suspected terrorists.[36] When President Obama decided on a US military surge in Afghanistan in 2009, he received his strongest support from Republicans.[37] And an overwhelming majority of

Republicans supported airstrikes against the Islamic State of Iraq and Syria by September 2014.[38]

Tea Party Republican views on American foreign policy are especially misunderstood by outside observers. The Tea Party movement arose in 2009 primarily in opposition to the president's domestic agenda, over issues such as deficit spending. Foreign policy has never been the movement's primary concern. It is therefore often assumed that Tea Party supporters must be isolationist. Yet multiple polling results over the years demonstrate that Tea Party members are actually more inclined than the average American to support US military commitments abroad, not less so. For example, in 2011 the Pew Research Center found that of the following three political groupings—Democrats, Tea Party Republicans, and non–Tea Party Republicans—Tea Party supporters were the least likely of all to say the United States should "reduce military commitments overseas" in order to "reduce the national debt." The same poll found that Tea Party supporters were of all three groups the most opposed to cuts in US defense spending, and the most inclined to say that the best way to ensure peace is through military strength.[39] A majority of Tea Party Republicans are therefore neither dovish nor isolationist when it comes to foreign policy. They are, however, fiercely protective of US national sovereignty, and typically unenthusiastic about foreign aid, the United Nations, and humanitarian intervention overseas. We find the same, distinct combination of foreign policy views looking at the statements and votes of numerous nationally prominent Tea Party figures such as Senator Ted Cruz (R-TX). In other words, most Tea Party supporters are not attracted to "cooperative" internationalism. They are simply hard-line American national security hawks.[40]

To be sure, the specific mood among Republicans on foreign policy issues has shifted over the past decade. Under President

George W. Bush, the GOP rallied behind a war on terror, an invasion of Iraq, and a "freedom agenda" to democratize the Middle East, with the understanding that all three items were mutually related. This was the approach known as neoconservative. Under Obama, GOP support for the war on terror continued, but support for certain types of US military intervention within the Middle East dried up considerably. A large number of American conservatives, at both the elite and the popular level, worried that democracy promotion and large-scale ground interventions within the Arab world only empowered radical Islam. The events of the Arab Spring did nothing to ease this concern. After the experiences of the past decade in Iraq and Afghanistan, there was a feeling of war-weariness even among many GOP security hawks, and a much greater sense of skepticism that the United States could help successfully reshape Muslim societies in a democratic direction. Moreover this sense of skepticism dovetailed with an overpowering focus on domestic issues including fiscal and constitutional concerns. The Tea Party exemplified this focus. GOP conservatives were united and energized in opposition to President Obama's domestic agenda. They were neither united nor energized any longer by concepts of Middle Eastern democratization through US military intervention. Furthermore the conservative belief that the federal government simply spends too much money took a toll on GOP support for numerous international expenditures.[41] Whether the disturbing rise of the Islamic State of Iraq and Syria would encourage a full reversal of this anti-interventionist trend remained to be seen.

Another factor shaping Republican foreign policy debates today is of course generalized conservative GOP opposition to President Obama. Just as Democrats are more likely to rally behind the decisions of a president they like and support on other issues, so too are Republicans. In the case of President Obama, we have a president who many staunch conservatives view as quite literally threatening to traditional American forms of limited government. Republicans feel just as strongly and negatively about President Obama as Democrats came to feel about George W. Bush. It is hardly to be expected that a bipartisan foreign policy would be easy under such circumstances. Moreover many Republicans, even when they favor some specific foreign policy decision taken by President Obama, simply do not trust him to carry it out in a coherent fashion. This lack of trust flows partly out of prior and existing disagreement with him on a wide range of other issues. It also flows from having observed the president's management style as commander in chief over the course of his time in the White House.

Part of the confusion surrounding journalistic depictions of Republican "isolationists" is that conservatives and liberals support different versions of US activism overseas. Most GOP conservatives today do not oppose American international leadership, but they differ from liberal Democrats on the question of how America should lead. Conservatives—including Tea Party conservatives—are still more likely than liberals to favor a hawkish form of internationalism, including higher levels of defense spending, robust counterterrorism, and military support for US allies overseas. Liberals are more likely than conservatives to favor a cooperative form of internationalism, including support for the United Nations, humanitarian policy projects, and the pursuit of multilateral agreement on issues such as climate change and arms control.[42] These tendencies are quite consistent with broad patterns in US party politics for over forty years now. So if the question is whether Republican foreign policy thinking in the country at large is now predominantly isolationist, the answer is no. Republicans remain more hawkish than Democrats. But it does not follow that neoconservative ideas dominate as they did a decade ago. This simplistic dichotomy of neoconservative versus isolationist hardly captures the true range of foreign policy views inside the GOP.

Electoral Politics

American elections and American grand strategy influence one another. Elections influence grand strategy, in the sense that a new administration may decide to pursue foreign priorities different from those of its predecessor. Even congressional midterm elections, while generally fought over local and domestic matters, can influence American foreign affairs. International and security policies are not always leading issues in a US presidential election. Yet even when they are not, the general public expects a president—as well as any serious presidential candidate—to display a certain level of resolution, competence, and knowledge in relation to such issues. Moreover it is often the case that foreign policy and national security concerns really do play into presidential election results. Depending on the mood of the electorate, swing voters may reward incumbent presidents for displaying strong international leadership, or for keeping the country out of war.

A common myth regarding the electoral politics of US foreign relations is that presidents "wag the dog," or resort to war overseas, to divert attention from domestic problems and help win re-election. There is very little historical or empirical evidence to support such theories. If anything, presidents tend to shy away from the use of force internationally as they come up for re-election.[43] This is because they understand that the general public within the United States, while favoring strength on national security, prefers on balance for the country to be at peace. Incumbent presidents up for re-election when America is already at war usually try to campaign on a platform of strong and continuous wartime leadership, and if enough voters find this convincing, it can work. But US involvement in prolonged military stalemate overseas tends to eventually hurt whatever party is in power, even in congressional midterm elections, and has more than once led an incumbent president to step down rather than run for office again. There is not a single case over the past century where a US presidential candidate ran in peacetime on a platform calling for war, and won. This raises an interesting possibility, understudied by political scientists: under certain conditions at least, an incumbent president's re-election chances might actually be strengthened by downplaying rather than emphasizing international security challenges.

The politics of foreign policy during the 2008 presidential election, while unhelpful to Republicans by historical standards, did not favor either party decisively. To be sure, persistent and intense dissatisfaction with President Bush and the war in Iraq opened the door for the general public to hear relatively dovish arguments on foreign and national security policy from a plausible presidential candidate. Illinois's junior senator Barack Obama appeared to be just such a candidate: reasonable, articulate, intelligent, and self-disciplined. In the Democratic presidential primaries that year, Obama secured a majority of delegates very much on the appeal to liberals of his clear, longtime position against the war in Iraq. Still, there was no guarantee that a comprehensive antiwar stance would necessarily have the same appeal to swing voters. The Obama campaign understood this dilemma, crafting a foreign policy platform that included a promise to take the fight more aggressively to al-Qaeda and the Taliban in Afghanistan, while exiting from Iraq "responsibly."

In the end, those voters most concerned about Iraq voted for Obama. Yet the very success of the Bush administration's surge strategy in 2007–2008 meant the Iraq war was not the dominating issue it had been. Voters most concerned about terrorism—a roughly similar number to those most concerned about Iraq—voted for Republican presidential candidate Senator John McCain (R-AZ), by an overwhelming margin. Polls also indicated that voters had an easier time picturing McCain as commander in chief than Obama. So on the whole, international and security issues provided no decisive advantage to either candidate. The single biggest factor working in Obama's favor was simply the sheer unpopularity of President Bush by 2008. A strong majority of voters disapproved of the incumbent president and were ready turn the page on him and his party. The global financial crisis beginning that September only reinforced such feelings of dissatisfaction and benefited the Obama campaign. Under these circumstances, McCain did well to win twenty-one states. The final election result represented a chance for Obama and the Democrats to govern, in domestic as well as foreign affairs, with united control of the White House and Congress. There is little hard evidence that it represented any massive leftward shift in the average voter's ideological preferences, on either US foreign or domestic policies as a whole.[44]

The incoming president's foreign policy and political teams assumed office with great confidence that GOP approaches toward American national security had demonstrably failed. The new administration was especially determined to overhaul counterterrorist practices from the Bush era—a central campaign theme of Obama's. Yet numerous polls from 2009 and 2010 suggested that Republicans were still favored over Democrats on key components of national security and defense.[45] Issues of counterterrorism proved to be unexpectedly thorny for the new president. On a wide range of complicated policy challenges related to the surveillance, targeting, detention, and interrogation of suspected terrorists, the

Obama White House often found itself on the defensive, criticized by Republicans, backtracking on previous commitments, and disappointing Obama's liberal, antiwar supporters. A number of attempted terrorist attacks within the United States, including a successful one at Fort Hood, Texas, only highlighted the salience of the issue along with Obama's potential weakness on it. When the administration tried to shut down Guantánamo Bay and hold a civilian trial in New York for 9/11 mastermind Khalid Sheikh Mohammed, even many Democrats rebelled. In a word, the new president remained vulnerable to critique from Republicans and dissent from Democrats on matters of counterterrorism, even as he tried to press a very ambitious domestic policy agenda.

It was within this context that Obama framed his autumn 2009 Afghanistan strategy review, under powerful and conflicting political cross-pressures. On the one hand, he needed to demonstrate toughness, preempt GOP criticism, and keep his campaign promise to focus on Afghanistan. On the other hand, as his leading political advisers reminded him, the president needed to mollify antiwar Democrats, protect domestic priorities such as healthcare reform, and prevent the Afghan conflict from becoming his own version of Vietnam. To neglect either set of considerations might ultimately endanger his re-election chances. The final decision announced that December was to approve a surge of some 33,000 additional US troops into Afghanistan. At the same time, Obama announced that said troops would begin withdrawing from the conflict in July 2011. Strategically and militarily, the two halves of this announcement worked against one another: if the Taliban knew when US forces were leaving, they could simply wait out the American withdrawal. In domestic political terms, however, Obama found both halves of the stated policy to be helpful. The announcement of a US troop surge helped stave off Republican criticism in 2009–2010 that Obama was weak on national security, while the announcement of a timeline for American withdrawal helped reassure antiwar Democrats that military engagement in Afghanistan would not last indefinitely. As the president told Senator Lindsey Graham (R-SC) in explaining the mixed message, "I can't lose all the Democratic Party. And people at home don't want to hear we're going to be there for ten years." "You're right," Graham said. "But the enemy is listening too."[46]

The successful American raid against Osama bin Laden's secret compound in Abbottabad, Pakistan on May 2, 2011, had a dramatic effect on the politics of foreign policy inside the United States. President Obama deserved credit for signing off on this bold, well-considered action, and he received it. The jump in the president's approval ratings was only temporary, but the subsequent electoral impact was truly significant. While Republicans had a range of valid criticisms to make of Obama's counterterrorism policies, in political terms that issue was now off the table for the GOP heading into 2012.[47] The White House understood this dynamic and took full advantage of it. Not only did the Abbottabad raid become a centerpiece of the president's re-election campaign; the event also freed him to argue that with bin Laden finally gone, it was time to end America's wars and come home.

On June 22, 2011, Obama announced the beginning of US troop withdrawals from Afghanistan. Declaring that "the tide of war is receding," he specified that the United States would remove 10,000 troops by the end of the year, along with a further 23,000 by September 2012.[48] The speed and scope of the planned withdrawal was hard to justify militarily. If American forces in Afghanistan were vital to US counterterrorism efforts, as the president had said repeatedly, then there was a powerful argument against withdrawing those forces in such large numbers in the middle of the 2012 combat season. But domestic political considerations contradicted military ones. The White House was determined to have US troops from the initial surge visibly on their way home well before the president's re-election. Moreover, American public opinion was shifting against the Afghan war by 2011. This actually put Obama in a good position on the issue, politically. The overwhelming majority of Democrats and independents agreed that the president's planned troop withdrawals from Afghanistan were happening either at about the right pace or not quickly enough. Even traditionally hawkish Republicans were increasingly divided over this question and disaffected by the war.[49] The White House no longer felt vulnerable to GOP criticism on either counterterrorism or Afghanistan; if Republicans wanted to argue for a more extended US combat presence in that country, this would only benefit the president.

As Obama prepared for an intense re-election campaign, the GOP presidential primaries revealed both the extent and the limits of that party's foreign policy divisions. One early candidate, former Utah governor Jon Huntsman, argued for retrenchment from Afghanistan, cuts in defense spending, and US focus on East Asia.[50] Several candidates popular with the Tea Party, including Representative Michele Bachmann (R-MN) and Texas governor Rick Perry, called for an essentially hawkish foreign policy but with deep skepticism regarding US nation-building in Libya and Afghanistan. Longtime libertarian Representative Ron Paul (R-TX) received a more courteous hearing than in previous years, arguing for a grand strategy of strict nonintervention. But while outside observers spoke of resurgent Republican isolationism, in reality Paul's extreme foreign policy stance was a liability and not an asset in the GOP primaries.[51] While many grassroots conservatives had certainly lost enthusiasm for a Bush-like "freedom agenda" in the Middle East, they were not yet ready to embrace Paul's sweeping critique of America's global role. Paul held his core supporters—roughly 10% of Republicans nationwide—but did not win a single state primary. Almost 90% of GOP primary voters cast their ballots for three candidates—former Massachusetts governor Mitt Romney, former Speaker of the House Newt Gingrich, and former Pennsylvania senator Rick Santorum—who expressed relatively hawkish criticisms of Obama on issues including the Iranian nuclear program, counterterrorism, Sino-American relations, alliance management, military spending, and US international leadership. And for all the criticism of the 2012 Republican primary process as unserious, in the end, the most serious of the candidates won the nomination.

International relations were not the primary concern on most voters' minds in the 2012 presidential election, but insofar as such issues mattered, they worked in Obama's favor. Most polling throughout the fall campaign showed the president with a clear advantage over Governor Romney on foreign policy issues, and exit polls from election night showed the very same thing.[52] This was not due to any terrible weakness on the part of either Romney or his campaign. The former Massachusetts governor offered the voters a mainstream version of Republican internationalism, critical of and more hawkish than Obama to be sure, but hardly extreme. The underlying conditions of 2012 simply did not favor the GOP nominee on foreign policy. An incumbent president who had hunted down Osama bin Laden, and yet was also in tune with the popular mood regarding US military interventions overseas, was always going to be hard to beat on international issues, and Republican strategists knew it.

The one truly dramatic foreign policy event to occur during the 2012 campaign was a September 11 terrorist attack on a US diplomatic mission in Benghazi, Libya, killing several Americans including the US ambassador to that country. This attack and others like it overseas appeared to run against Obama's re-election claim that "Al Qaeda is on the run," and consequently was understood by both presidential campaigns to be potential political dynamite. But for whatever reason—popular indifference, media filtration, a mangled critique—the issue never really caught on among independent swing voters. Swing voters tend to give incumbent presidents the benefit of the doubt on US foreign policy, unless they are convinced it has been disastrously handled overall, and in 2012 they were not so convinced. The killing of Osama bin Laden gave President Obama an exceptionally compelling defense against charges of weakness on national security. At the same time, the American public was now disinclined toward further military interventions overseas, so any GOP arguments that the United States needed to be more assertive in such cases as Afghanistan, Syria, Libya, or Iraq—however plausible on their own merits— did not resonate powerfully with the general public. Indeed for those voters most concerned about foreign policy, the desire to avoid another war seemed paramount. The Romney campaign understood these electoral dynamics, and at key moments such as the third televised debate with Obama decided to emphasize Romney's careful demeanor rather than to go on the offensive.[53] Conservatives and GOP foreign policy hawks were frustrated by this decision, as by the apparent reluctance of many elite media outlets to take the Benghazi issue seriously. Yet even if Romney had somehow scored a nationally televised blow against the president over the handling of Benghazi, there is very little evidence that it would have altered the final electoral outcome. Independent swing voters gave Obama credit for keeping the United States out of yet more military engagements and for completing the hunt against bin Laden. The general public was simply not in the mood to hear more hawkish foreign policy arguments in 2012. Its attention was focused elsewhere, on domestic economic concerns. Republicans hoped that popular disapproval of the president's handling of economic issues would defeat him, but in the end

Obama did what incumbent presidents usually do when up for re-election during years of modest economic growth: he won.[54]

Obama's re-election put him in a rarified category of modern two-term presidents, and having campaigned on a platform of liberal economic populism, he could only be expected to claim vindication for his declared vision. Even in the face of fierce conservative opposition, the domestic policy legacies of his first term would be preserved and advanced. The president's foreign policy approach dovetailed with these domestic political priorities. An overarching emphasis on US retrenchment internationally—leavened by the aggressive pursuit of core Al-Qaeda leaders—had indeed played well with the general public, not only assisting the president's re-election campaign, but also allowing him for the most part to focus on liberal domestic policy objectives. Looking forward, Obama's second inaugural address in January 2013 indicated the essential priorities. Making a sweeping argument for a liberal interpretation of the American creed, the president called for "collective action," "care for the vulnerable," and "rules to ensure fair play" in a "modern economy," insisting that "when times change, so must we." International affairs received very little attention.[55] Meanwhile, Obama restructured his foreign policy team and installed loyalists that he knew would attend to his concerns: Senator John Kerry (D-MA) as secretary of state, former senator Chuck Hagel (R-NE) as secretary of defense, and former UN ambassador Susan Rice as national security advisor. The appointment of Hagel, in particular—a Republican with foreign policy views by this time very similar to Obama's—was understood to be of special significance, in that Hagel's role would be to oversee a shrinking US military. It had not been uncommon in the past for Democratic presidents to appoint a Republican secretary of defense, drawn from the more hawkish wing of the GOP, to help secure bipartisan support for internationalist US policies. This would be the first time that a Democratic president appointed a relatively dovish Republican to help secure bipartisan support for a continuing US military drawdown at home and abroad. The national shift from guns to butter would continue.[56]

Congressional Politics

No president has exclusive authority over the making of American grand strategy. The US Constitution specifies that certain powers related to foreign policy and national defense are reserved to Congress. The president is the nation's commander in chief, with explicit authority to make treaties and appoint ambassadors overseas. Congress retains the power to fund or defund US international and military expenditures, approve ambassadorial and cabinet appointments, declare war, and ratify treaties. This separation of powers between the executive and legislative branches is sometimes described as an "invitation to struggle" over US foreign policy. In reality, the informal powers of Congress and the president are not coequal when it comes to international affairs. Congress certainly has the ability to make its influence felt, and does so through pivotal mechanisms of funding, ratification, publicity, oversight, and procedure. Yet in practice, chief executives of both parties—including President Obama—have exercised and claimed a considerable degree of command authority over US foreign affairs and national security. By custom, international pressure, and historical evolution, the power to make foreign policy has tended to gravitate toward presidents. This has been especially true when Americans perceive some dire external threat, at moments of crisis, or initially during wartime. During the late 1950s, for example, Congress was relatively deferential toward the White House on national security issues; there was little political incentive to be otherwise. The same was true in the months immediately after the terrorist attacks of September 2001. When America's wars have ended or gone badly, and the political incentives shift, then Congress always reasserts itself, as it did after each world war and after Vietnam.[57]

We are now in the middle of a period of congressional reassertion that really began during the second term of President George W. Bush, in response to US frustrations in Iraq. The fact that today the Democrats control the White House, while Republicans control the House of Representatives, has not lessened the sense of congressional pushback. Republicans are no more inclined to defer to Obama than Democrats were to Bush. Congress is more polarized along party lines right now than it has been for generations. Inevitably this affects foreign policy debates. Still, the ideological and partisan polarization within Congress today is primarily over domestic issues, not international ones. As a result, we see interesting cross-cutting divisions and alliances over questions of grand strategy, within and between the two parties. Members of Congress are not motivated only by political factors when considering international or military matters; many also have strong internal convictions on such matters. It is precisely those differences in conviction, interacting with domestic political contexts, that have driven intraparty factionalism over US grand strategy in the Obama era.

During the 2010 congressional midterm elections, Republicans took control of the US House of Representatives, picking up sixty-three seats. These massive gains were powered by popular dissatisfaction with the state of the economy, and by a widespread feeling among independent voters that both President Obama and congressional Democrats had overreached on critical issues like healthcare reform.[58] The impact of the Tea Party on incoming conservative freshmen was strong. Still, the new House majority was hardly "isolationist." On the contrary, while highly critical of the president overall, House Republicans were on balance more supportive of internationalist policies in 2011 than were House Democrats on central issues such as Afghanistan and free trade. If anything, the new GOP majority pressured Obama from a hawkish direction over counterterrorism, arms control, Israel, missile defense, and economic sanctions against Iran. Yet there was also a palpable shift in priorities among congressional Republicans, in comparison to the Bush era. Rather than emphasizing rock-solid support for US military spending, many congressional Republicans now put fiscal priorities first and foremost, and prior GOP support for democracy promotion within the Middle East was replaced by much greater skepticism regarding the possible fruits of US intervention.

A dramatic struggle between Congress and the White House over raising the US debt limit in the summer of 2011 left long-term military spending trajectories caught in the axle of conflicting fiscal priorities. While all parties involved in the 2011 debt ceiling crisis claimed to want reductions in the annual budget deficit, their clashing preferences for how to get there were abundantly clear. Most congressional Democrats preferred to reduce the deficit by raising taxes, cutting military spending, and preserving domestic social programs. Most congressional Republicans preferred to reduce the deficit by cutting domestic spending rather than raising taxes or cutting defense too deeply. Congressional Democrats and the White House settled on a negotiating position by which roughly half of all spending cuts needed to come from the military. The majority of congressional Republicans were unhappy with such deep defense cuts, but even more committed to reducing overall government spending. The two sides therefore agreed, under the Budget Control Act of 2011, to $1.2 trillion in overall spending cuts over a ten-year period starting in 2013, along with an additional $1.2 trillion in cuts over the same period of time under a process of sequestration in the absence of subsequent agreement. US defense spending would be cut over ten years by approximately $500 billion under the Budget Control Act and by another $500 billion in the event of sequestration. Apparently neither side in these negotiations initially expected sequestration to ever occur. But as Congress and the president continued their political trench warfare over US budgetary priorities without resolution, sequestration went into effect, along with the additional long-term cuts in defense. One of the multiple ironies of this entire episode was that most congressional Republicans never wanted such deep military reductions in the first place. Still, they had revealed by their actions that preserving US defense spending was no longer the top priority it had once been, and of course for President Obama higher levels of defense spending were never a top priority at all.[59]

Growing bipartisan fatigue with US military interventions abroad reflected itself in Congress. Congressional Republicans, in particular, were skeptical of the Obama administration's arguments for US intervention in Libya and Syria. Since a significant percentage of congressional Democrats were inclined to support Obama, in spite of antiwar pressure from the party's liberal wing, this created some striking new patterns of division within Congress from 2011 onward regarding the use of force overseas.

Initially, with regard to Afghanistan, congressional resistance to an expanded US war effort came primarily from Democrats, not Republicans. The 2009 military surge decision was never popular with the base of the Democratic Party. By the time of Osama bin Laden's death, two years later, the overwhelming majority of congressional Democrats were prepared to vote in favor of accelerated US troop withdrawal from Afghanistan. Equally interesting was the nascent Republican Party splintering over this issue. In May 2011, twenty-six GOP House members joined most

Democrats in calling for clear exit deadlines—a sign of mounting fatigue with America's Afghan war, across party lines. The antiwar measure failed by a margin of only 215 to 204.[60] Phased withdrawal of US troops beginning a few weeks later appeased some antiwar feeling, but congressional dissatisfaction with costs and outcomes in Afghanistan only continued to build.

American military intervention in Libya triggered even greater resistance from Congress than did Afghanistan, and in a much shorter period of time. Most congressional Republicans never supported war over Libya in the first place, and many of them feared that such intervention would only encourage the rise of radical Islam in that country. The fact that President Obama received explicit approval to intervene in Libya from the Arab League, but not from the US Congress, was widely viewed among Republicans as both an insult and a disturbing precedent. This, they felt, was "Obama's war," and a very badly managed one at that. In June 2011, the House of Representatives issued a stinging rebuke of the administration's Libya policy, in a nonbinding resolution that passed with the support of 223 Republicans and 45 Democrats. A more aggressive resolution proposed by antiwar representative Dennis Kucinich (D-OH) to terminate America's Libyan intervention gained 87 Republican votes and 61 Democrats.[61] For dozens of GOP members to vote in this way regarding an ongoing US war effort overseas was truly something new. House Republicans seriously considered defunding military involvement in Libya. In the end, the Gaddafi regime collapsed before congressional opposition mounted any further.

In the case of Syria, most House Republicans were again disinclined to support US military intervention, for similar reasons as in Libya: first, the risk of unintentionally empowering Islamist forces; second, a deep distrust over President Obama's handling of the matter; and third, strong opposition from their own constituents, including many grassroots conservatives at the base of the GOP. When Syria's dictator, Bashar al-Assad, launched an especially blatant chemical weapons attack on civilians in the summer of 2013, Obama felt bound to respond—both to preserve what he called an international norm against the use of chemical weapons and to enforce his own declared "red line" against their use in this case. The United States prepared to launch limited airstrikes against the Assad regime. Public opinion polls inside the United States showed strong opposition across party lines to such airstrikes, with opponents outnumbering supporters by a ratio of roughly two to one.[62] Deciding to ask Congress for approval this time, Obama discovered deep resistance. The best estimates were that any use of force resolution during September 2013 was headed toward defeat in the US House of Representatives and possibly even defeat in the Senate. The great majority of House Republicans, in particular, were opposed to military intervention in Syria, as were a large number of liberal House Democrats.[63] In the end, a diplomatic agreement with Russia, negotiated in Geneva, forestalled the immediate possibility of US airstrikes against Assad. There remained profound doubts as to whether this agreement would be fully enforced. But from the point of view of the White House, the United States avoided a military intervention that President Obama clearly did not want in the first place, along with the high likelihood of a formal rebuff from Congress. Obama's handling of the Syrian crisis had been visibly incoherent even in the eyes of many of his core supporters, but the general public was relieved to have avoided yet another US military engagement within the Middle East.[64] The issue disappeared from the front pages of American newspapers, at least temporarily, leaving Assad in power and free to crack down on rebel forces. Congressional debates over Ukraine and Iraq in 2014 continued to reveal a pattern of cross-cutting divisions and partisan confusion over major foreign policy issues. Significantly however, congressional Republicans were largely united by the end of that summer over the specific need for a more coherent and assertive US approach against the Islamic State of Iraq and Syria.[65]

Presidential Leadership

It is customary when examining US foreign policy and grand strategy to catalog all the ways in which presidential decisions are shaped and constrained by domestic political pressures. Still, disembodied pressures do not make foreign policy decisions: presidents do. As national heads of state, presidents are uniquely positioned at the apex of the American political system, where international pressures meet domestic ones. In practice, presidents have a striking ability to set the agenda and lead on foreign policy, if and when they choose to exercise such leadership. They are granted considerable status and resources to that end, along with a certain amount of leeway, by Congress, public opinion, the bureaucracy, and their own political parties. To be sure, there are always myriad pressures directed at the president during this process, from all directions, international as well as domestic. But it is precisely for this very reason that the president's role is so central. Any conceivable foreign policy decision usually involves a range of apparent domestic and international trade-offs, costs, and risks. It is the president, in the end, who decides which particular risks will be taken, and which will not; what exact trade-offs will be made; and what precise options will be chosen. Under specific circumstances, strategic alternatives exist, and presidents choose between them. It therefore makes a great deal of difference who occupies the White House, and what his individual foreign policy beliefs, personality, experiences, managerial style, and overarching priorities are.[66]

Like all previous presidents, Barack Obama has his own specific foreign policy decision-making style, personality, and procedural preferences, a mixture of strengths and weaknesses. These features are related to, but distinct from the substantive content of a president's foreign policy beliefs. In Obama's case, three features in particular stand out: first, a highly centralized decision-making process, converging on the White House; second, a president tolerant of policy ambiguity, sometimes to the point of excess; and third, a keen sensitivity to domestic political considerations. All three features have been very evident since 2009, reflect Obama's core inclinations, and appear unlikely to change.

First: American foreign policy under Obama is highly centralized in the Oval Office. In the words of Obama's first secretary of defense, Robert Gates: "His White House was by far the most centralized and controlling in national security of any I had seen since Richard Nixon and Henry Kissinger ruled the roost ... The controlling nature of the Obama White House and the NSS staff took micromanagement and operational meddling to a new level."[67] President Obama surrounds himself with a tight inner circle of de facto foreign policy advisers based within the White House. This inner circle includes and has included speechwriters like Benjamin Rhodes, key National Security Council staff like former deputy Denis McDonough, longtime supporters and associates from the 2008 campaign and Chicago before that, political advisers like David Axelrod and Valerie Jarrett, and national security advisors such as Thomas Donilon and Susan Rice who have the president's confidence. Key members of this inner circle, with notable exceptions including Donilon and Rice, possessed no executive branch foreign policy experience prior to 2009. Many are relatively young, and like Obama they view themselves as having overcome old partisan debates regarding the Cold War and Vietnam. They have in common the president's trust, based on demonstrated fealty; a broadly similar foreign policy outlook shared by him; a willingness to stay on message; and for the most part little executive experience before entering office. Vice President Biden, while of a different generation, and certain members of his staff are part of this inner circle, depending upon the issue. Leading cabinet officials are not.[68] Obama's first national security advisor, James Jones, was either unable or not permitted to emerge into an inner-circle role.[69] Secretary of Defense Robert Gates was one of the most effective such secretaries in the history of that office, but he was not a member of Obama's inner cadre.[70] Secretary of State Hillary Clinton carved out her own distinct policy niche over time, rebuilt her political capital, showed loyalty toward Obama, and enjoyed favorable press coverage, but she was never really inside the president's inner ring.[71] Secretary of State John Kerry and Secretary of Defense Chuck Hagel were not within the White House cadre either, but were understood to be loyalists toward the president who would implement his overarching priorities on international policy and defense while taking the lead on selected issues from time to time.

Obama, while critical in the abstract of centralized presidential power over national security, has in practice conceded very little in the way of executive authority. He understands that when it comes to foreign policy, the president's role is absolutely critical. He is therefore determined to keep the central foreign policy decision capacities in his own hands, so that the final outcomes reflect his own core priorities. To say that he prides himself on his analytical and decision-making capabilities would be an understatement. He has tremendous confidence in his ability to personally dissect, articulate, and manage various stages of the foreign policy process. He does not really believe that he needs one or more big-picture foreign policy strategists in the room when he is making the crucial decisions. He is determined to play that role on his own.[72]

When faced with a major policy dilemma, Obama likes to gather a wide range of information and recommendations, listen to assembled experts, and ask them probing questions. He takes his time making decisions, keeps his own counsel, and has a strong aversion to being pinned down. He is frequently willing to compromise on policy specifics and accept imperfect solutions in order to achieve incremental progress toward his long-term objectives. Temperamentally, Obama is self-contained and even-keeled. His typical demeanor in decision-making settings is sober, businesslike, calm, and clinical. While capable of friendly good humor in public, and of inspiring great affection from his admirers, up close he remains emotionally detached from all but a very few. He has great confidence in the power of carefully chosen words, including his own, to move people and achieve common ground. He believes that careful, informed deliberation and analysis can help build consensus and reach better decisions. One of his characteristic methods, rhetorically and analytically, is to detach himself from two opposing camps, sympathize with each, and then attempt to "transcend the debate" by insisting that the differences between the two camps are less than commonly believed.[73] No doubt many of the above qualities and inclinations were influenced by Obama's legal training, and by his experience as a community organizer in Chicago. The overarching style is one that tends to be especially appreciated and valued within academic circles. But while Obama brings certain undoubted strengths into the policy process, his decision-making style has its downsides as well.

The qualities that make for an effective community organizer, legal instructor, or academic—and even the qualities that make for an effective politician—are not necessarily the same qualities required for an effective chief executive or foreign policy president. The task of a president is not simply to explore and articulate policy contradictions, but to resolve them and then act on that resolution. Indefinite pliancy, profound ambivalence, and a disinclination to commit are hardly unmixed virtues in the field of grand strategy. There comes a time when a president's role is to make a decision, even a potentially unpopular or risky one, and then enforce that decision so that it sticks. Occasionally Obama has done exactly that, for example with the 2011 strike against bin Laden. Unfortunately, the more common decision-making pattern on key foreign policy issues has been to veer toward drift, indecision, and endless ambiguity. This pattern has been so common since 2009 that it appears a reflection of the president's basic decision-making style. Major international issues wait on the backburner, for want of executive attention. Clear decisions on vital foreign policy matters tend to be made very late, if they are made at all. Repeated instances of delay and ambiguity unnerve US allies, leaving little time to consult with them—an ironic commentary upon a president who prides himself on the restoration of America's diplomatic standing. Once Obama's attention is focused, he typically drafts and delivers an eloquent, nuanced public address, laying out all sides of an issue. These speeches often sound as if they were made by a thoughtful outside critic, rather than by the existing chief executive. Still, however thoughtful, speeches are not self-executing. Having announced a chosen international course, a president needs to be tenacious in ensuring its practical enforcement and implementation, not only in relation to bureaucratic actors but also overseas.[74]

One last distinctive feature of the foreign policymaking process under President Obama is his exceptionally high sensitivity to domestic political considerations. Certainly, many previous chief executives have incorporated a shrewd awareness of domestic politics into their foreign policy decision-making; the current president is hardly the first to do so. Still, the proportion of time and energy spent by the Obama White House on considerations of public presentation, media framing, domestic electoral impact, and preemptive political defense of foreign policy decisions is truly striking even by modern standards. Leading political advisers participate directly in major foreign policy decisions to monitor the relationship of foreign and domestic politics.[75] The president's chosen inner ring of formal and informal White House foreign policy advisers are also known for their keen political antennae and ability to stay on message, even when prior foreign policy experience is lacking.[76] One sympathetic chronicler, James Mann, calls this White House inner circle "the Obamians." In Mann's words, "the Obamians tended to know less about the nuances and subtleties of an issue, and they were less concerned with practical details of governance. They were, however, more adept at providing a determined opposition to the Republicans, and much better at figuring out what to say in public about foreign policy."[77] Mann is an author who, on balance, likes and appreciates the president's foreign policy. Some former Obama administration officials have been less flattering about the central place of domestic political considerations. Robert Gates, who of course also served as defense secretary under George W. Bush, observed that "political considerations were far more a part of national security debates under Obama."[78] In the words of Vali Nasr, now dean of Johns Hopkins School of Advanced International Studies, and a leading State Department official between 2009 and 2011:

The President's habit of funneling major foreign policy decisions through a small cabal of relatively inexperienced White House advisers whose turf was strictly politics was truly disturbing. The primary concern of these advisers was how any action in Afghanistan or the Middle East would play on the nightly news, or which talking point it would give the Republicans.[79]

In a way, Obama's sensitivity to domestic considerations in the foreign policymaking process dovetails with his determination to avoid being pinned down. By engaging in a light-footed and detached approach to foreign policymaking, even in cases where he intervenes overseas, the president limits his own liability along with America's. This may encourage substantial strategic incoherence in specific cases, but it preserves Obama's political capital, which is never invested too deeply, and it allows him to focus primarily on domestic policy goals. The president reserves the right to make the final foreign policy decisions, and to make them in a fashion involving considerable drift and ambiguity, precisely in order to limit domestic political risks. Moreover he sincerely believes that the United States should tread lightly abroad and retrench even as it intervenes. The resulting pattern is a highly centralized foreign policy process, in which—paradoxically—unambiguous strategic decisions are deliberately averted and delayed. During Obama's first term, this process served his aims fairly well, insofar as the avoidance of US liability overseas matched the inclinations of the general public. But the impression of ambivalent presidential leadership on international matters could not be entirely prevented, and beginning with the case of the 2013 Syria crisis the impression of indecision was so strong as to be damaging politically.[80]

One key factor in the decision-making process that has obviously changed since 2009 is that Obama and his advisers possess far more executive experience than they did when he first became president. There have been some important tactical adjustments in Obama's foreign policy approach over time. Early in 2009 for example, we saw an especially strong emphasis on international accommodation, with diplomatic outreach to Iran, Obama's Cairo speech, the Copenhagen climate summit, a "G-2" with China, the Russia reset, and a Middle East peace push. Then the president seemed to become rather more hawkish, with escalated drone strikes, the Afghan surge, the bin Laden operation, a Libyan intervention, and the pivot to Asia. What is interesting, however, is that after 2012—as international security challenges in relation to US defense spending, al-Qaeda, Afghanistan, Syria, Russia, Iran, China, North Korea, and Iraq began to pile up—Obama took this as all the more reason to maintain a broad course of American retrenchment. In other words, there was really no sign of any fundamental revision in his basic foreign policy assumptions, priorities, or decision-making style after coming into office. We know from both political psychology and historical example that most presidents tend to keep operating on inbuilt policy assumptions, even when contrary evidence piles up. It usually takes either a truly dramatic shock, or a new administration altogether, to bring about a major revaluation of existing ideas. Curiously, this resistance to contrary evidence in foreign affairs appears to be even truer of highly educated, self-confident, and intelligent people with certain core ideological convictions—a description that certainly fits the current president. Obama is very flexible on tactics and takes great care to project an aura of sensible calm, but his characteristic response when his core beliefs or ambitions are tested is to bristle, not to bend. He is therefore particularly unlikely to admit or even perceive that a foreign policy based upon faulty international assumptions is failing or has failed, and of course from his point of view it has not. He has already achieved much of what he desired with an implicit strategy of US accommodation and retrenchment, namely to reorient American resources and attention away from national security concerns and toward the expansion of progressive domestic reforms over a full two terms as president. From his particular perspective, the Obama doctrine has been a striking success.

Looking Ahead to 2016

For much of the Obama era, particularly in his 2012 re-election campaign, the domestic politics of the Obama doctrine worked in the president's favor. The general public was unfocused on international issues and skeptical of military interventions. Republicans remained relatively hawkish on national security but faced a risen anti-interventionist faction internally. Democrats were inclined to support Obama. An electoral political dynamic of initial (2009–2010) presidential vulnerability on the issue of terrorism was dramatically eased by the 2011 strike against bin Laden, and then capped by a 2012 incumbent advantage on foreign policy issues based upon claims of strong counterterrorism, "ending the wars," and "nation-building at home." But it would be a mistake to assume that these trends will continue in linear fashion or that they will work equally well for the Democratic Party's next presidential candidate in 2016. Early in his second term, the president's foreign policy approval ratings dropped dramatically. Obviously much will depend on events and on how the two major parties respond.

Will the Obama doctrine have domestic political success moving ahead? Will the Democratic Party's next presidential candidate be advantaged on foreign policy issues, as Obama was in 2012? Here the possibilities are wide open. In 2012, the Democrats were led by a charismatic incumbent president who had just overseen a successful strike against Osama bin Laden the previous year. Conditions will be quite different in 2016.

Whoever the Democratic Party runs for president, he or she will not possess the advantages of an incumbent commander in chief on foreign policy and national security issues. Even if the popular mood remains ambivalent regarding US international leadership, it is entirely possible that a compelling Republican candidate with a clear and convincing message could regain the GOP's traditional advantage on international issues. To be sure, any persuasive GOP candidate will have to reassure the public that he or she will be careful on questions of military intervention, but this problem is not as overpowering as commentators sometimes suggest. In fact on the specific question of which political party "will do a better job of protecting the country from international terrorism and military threats," Gallup found in September 2013 that the general public has favored Republicans over Democrats during most years since 2008, with 2012 as the outlier.[81] If the GOP had really lost its traditional edge on national security issues for all time due to George W. Bush and Iraq, then these polling results would have been impossible. In any case, the only way to win the argument for an internationally serious and robust security strategy is to make it. The current mood of the general public is rather disengaged and downbeat regarding America's global role. Still, the pattern in US history is that these downswings in mood never last forever. Events are already occurring abroad to trigger renewed concern inside the United States over international security challenges. Ironically, President Obama's own grand strategy has left some such events more likely, insofar as it invites aggressive behavior from hostile actors overseas. In the end, the United States always bounces back from these periods of disengagement and counterpunches. The only question is when.

4

Republican Alternatives to the Obama Doctrine

Political scientists used to argue that the United States would be better served by a responsible two-party system with some significant ideological and programmatic difference between the country's two major parties. They got their wish. Over the past half-century, Democrats and Republicans have diverged not only over economic but also cultural and social issues such as crime, abortion, and civil rights. Social and economic liberals have gradually moved out of the GOP and into the Democratic Party, while conservatives have done the reverse. Both the voting base and to an even greater extent the congressional representatives of the two major parties are now polarized along ideological lines.[1] In practical and comparative terms, this means that national Democratic Party leaders lean toward liberal policy assumptions, while GOP leaders lean toward conservative ones. Inside the Republican Party, conservatives of various types play a preponderant role among party activists, elected officials, donors, supportive foundations, sympathetic media outlets, and above all, GOP voters. Some two-thirds of self-identified Republicans within the United

States call themselves conservative. There will continue to be vital debates over what exactly this conservatism implies for specific domestic policy recommendations. Certainly, Republicans must develop constructive domestic policy proposals that appeal to at least some moderate and independent swing voters; current battles between the Tea Party and establishment forces will have to be overcome.[2] But the GOP will no doubt remain America's more conservative party, just as the Democrats will remain America's more liberal party into the foreseeable future. The overwhelming majority of Republicans agree that President Obama's domestic economic approach has led to federal government excess in terms of domestic expenditures, deficits, regulations, and legislative overkill. Within the GOP, a broad inclination toward domestic economic conservatism is actually a unifying force.[3] On foreign policy however, Republicans and conservatives are clearly less united than they were a decade ago.

What exactly is the current state of play inside the GOP on foreign policy issues? The conventional wisdom varies between several mutually contradictory assertions: first, that neoconservatives are still dominant; second, that Tea Party isolationists are now preponderant; third, that Republicans have learned nothing from Iraq; and fourth, that the GOP possesses no clear foreign policy leanings whatsoever. As it happens, all four claims are mistaken. In reality, Republicans are engaged in a healthy internal debate over some alternative foreign policy approaches, which is exactly what you would expect of a party out of power. New ideas are percolating, and serious reflection on international challenges is well underway. But the GOP's foreign policy alternatives do not boil down to simply neoconservative on the one hand and isolationist on the other. Nor are most Tea Party supporters truly isolationist. The truth is actually a little more complex, and a lot more interesting.

In the following pages, I suggest that when it comes to US foreign policy there are three main factions or schools of thought within the Republican Party today, each of roughly equal importance: anti-interventionists, internationalists, and nationalists. All three groups are largely conservative, but they disagree about the implications for American grand strategy. Conservative anti-interventionists favor a strategy of deep retrenchment, including strict avoidance of foreign wars, cuts in defense spending, cuts in foreign aid, and cuts in America's military presence, bases, and alliance commitments overseas. Conservative internationalists hold the opposite view, supporting US foreign policy activism and global leadership in both its military and nonmilitary aspects. Conservative nationalists are skeptical regarding foreign aid, nation-building, and multilateral humanitarian interventions—especially as handled by President Obama—but continue to favor strong national defenses and an unyielding stance toward US adversaries overseas.

Republicans are more evenly divided over foreign policy issues today than at any time since the early 1950s. For a variety of reasons, including the contingencies of the primary process, it is entirely possible that a conservative anti-interventionist such as Senator Rand Paul (R-KY) could win the Republican presidential primaries in 2016 or beyond. Yet this might be in spite of his foreign policy stance, rather than because of it. Clearly, an anti-interventionist stance is not the severe disqualifier that it used to be in conservative circles. Whether it is actually an electoral asset in a Republican primary is another question. One crucial factor will be the direction conservative nationalists take. The GOP's conservative nationalists have grown deeply skeptical of foreign interventions under Obama, but they are still quite hawkish on a range of national security issues, and as it turns out Tea Party supporters tend to be conservative nationalists rather than strict anti-interventionists. This is just one illustration of the way in which a simplistic dichotomy of Republicans as either neoconservative or isolationist is positively unhelpful and misleading.

The important thing for outside observers to understand is that support inside the Republican Party for a relatively hawkish foreign policy still extends, as it long has, well beyond the precincts of neoconservative intellectuals. The GOP's most dedicated anti-interventionists have gained considerable impact during the Obama era, but they remain a minority within their own party under some serious disadvantages in a presidential primary. Even now, the majority of conservatives and Republicans do not actually support any comprehensive disengagement or profound retrenchment of US military power overseas. In fact, two of the three leading GOP factions examined—conservative nationalists and conservative internationalists—concur on aggressive counterterrorism, robust military spending, a firm line toward adversaries such as Iran, support for core US alliances, and a more muscular foreign policy approach than the one pursued by President Obama. Republican conservatives remain, of all American political constituencies, rather hawkish on national security issues. This means that while an anti-interventionist could conceivably win the GOP nomination, so too could a conservative nationalist or internationalist. Nor is it obvious that a carefully developed stance of conservative internationalism would necessarily perform worse in a general election than a neoisolationist one—more likely, the opposite. The stakes of the current debate are therefore very high. For the first time since General Eisenhower narrowly defeated Senator Robert Taft for the 1952 Republican nomination, the basic foreign policy direction of the Republican Party is truly up for grabs between some dramatically different visions regarding America's role in the world.

Conservative Anti-interventionists

Conservative anti-interventionists look to avoid foreign wars, cut military expenditures, scale back on US alliance commitments, and keep the costs of American grand strategy to a bare minimum. This has been a rising sentiment on the right during the Obama era, dovetailing with a popular loss of interest in foreign entanglements. To a greater extent than at any moment since the early 1950s, anti-interventionists today are an important faction within the GOP, representing at the very least a significant minority of opinion on a wide range of foreign policy and security matters. Indeed on a few select issues such as the September 2013 prospect of US airstrikes on Syria, the anti-interventionists have been in the majority. They possess a growing network of think tanks, opinion journals, and elected officials to represent their views, in which libertarians play a special and prominent role. One such official, Senator Rand Paul (R-KY), is a serious contender for the Republican presidential nomination in 2016. Conservative anti-interventionists believe that under President Obama, the United States has not scaled back far enough overseas, whether in terms of military interventions, defense spending, strategic commitments, drone strikes, the "war on terror," or international expenditures in general. The GOP's anti-interventionists therefore favor a new grand strategy of deep retrenchment. At its most pristine—for example, as advocated by the Cato Institute, the nation's preeminent libertarian think tank—such a policy would disentangle the United States from existing US alliance commitments in Europe, Japan, the Philippines, and South Korea. Conservative anti-interventionists remain under some serious disadvantage politically, but for the first time since Senator Robert Taft (R-OH) ran for the GOP's presidential nomination against Dwight Eisenhower, they have a genuine prospect of seeing their favored champion head the Republican Party in a general election.

Public opinion polls from the Obama era reveal a striking rise in anti-interventionist sentiment within the GOP, compared to only a few years ago. According to Pew Research Center studies from 2013, a slight majority of Republicans said the United States does "too much" to solve world problems and should "mind its own business" overseas.[4] Other polls showed similar results. A plurality of Republicans indicated in March 2011 that they did not believe America's Libyan intervention to be of vital interest to US national security.[5] The Gallup organization found that well over 50% of Republicans were opposed to prospective US airstrikes on Syria in September 2013.[6] Over 80% believe the United States should reduce foreign aid expenditures.[7] Significant minorities of Republicans oppose drone attacks on suspected terrorists; disapprove of US airstrikes against Iran; and support cuts in military spending. Among the GOP's Tea Party supporters, some 43% said that Edward Snowden's leaks regarding NSA surveillance served the public interest.[8] Several of these numbers are not radically different from recent polling results of Democrats and independents. But that is exactly the point. During the George W. Bush years, conservative Republicans tended to be very staunch supporters of US military engagements overseas. These days, conservatives are much more divided between competing factions and tendencies over foreign policy issues. The GOP's anti-interventionists have been on the rise under Obama—and that is a major story in itself.

There is clearly historical precedent for today's conservative anti-interventionists. In the years just prior to World War II, anti-interventionism was the dominant foreign policy perspective among conservatives, as among Americans generally. The United States at that time maintained certain overseas holdings such as the Philippines, but otherwise avoided strategic alliances or commitments on the European and Asian mainland. The spectacle of Nazi German military conquests in 1939–1940 forced a great debate over US foreign policy that was especially divisive within the Republican Party. Conservative anti-interventionists like three-time presidential candidate Senator Robert Taft (R-OH) argued that US intervention against Hitler's Germany was strategically unnecessary and would fatally corrupt American traditions of limited government. Such arguments carried considerable weight among congressional Republicans, especially those from Midwestern states. The Japanese attack on Pearl Harbor dealt a blow to the political beliefs, unity, and influence of conservative anti-interventionists from which they never fully recovered. But a rump faction of Midwestern Republicans led by Taft—while rallying to the war effort against the Axis powers—remained unhappy with America's new international role. A staunch anti-Communist, Taft nevertheless argued against early US Cold War policies including the Marshall Plan and the formation of NATO as costly and provocative. After the outbreak of the Korean War in 1950, he seized the moment to lay out an alternative foreign policy vision based upon the avoidance of costly international commitments such as a US military ground presence in Europe.[9] In 1952 he ran one last time for the Republican Party's presidential nomination, losing in a close race to General Dwight Eisenhower. Ike's nomination and election, together with his successful encouragement of a new foreign policy consensus, represented the final defeat of the GOP's Taft wing. Anti-interventionists were marginalized within the Republican Party for the rest of the Cold War.

The collapse of the USSR created a new opportunity starting in the early 1990s for conservative anti-interventionists to make their case. Libertarian and paleoconservative intellectuals called on the United States to disinherit its global strategic role. Very few Republicans were won over to that argument at the time. The memory of Ronald Reagan's bold, effective facedown of the Soviet threat remained the model for mainstream conservatives in thinking through new foreign policy challenges. Conservative commentator Pat Buchanan ran for the GOP presidential nomination on an anti-interventionist foreign policy platform twice during the 1990s, and then finally as an independent in 2000, but with very little success. In truth, even after the end of the Cold War the anti-interventionist position was a liability rather than an asset within a Republican Party presidential primary, where most voters remained relatively hawkish on issues of national security. This underlying political dynamic also continued to bedevil presidential runs by Representative Ron Paul (R-TX), the leading voice for libertarian and conservative anti-interventionists over a period of many years. Eventually, though, the ground would begin to shift.

The reasons for the rise of conservative anti-interventionism within the GOP over the past decade are not hard to discern. When President George W. Bush decided on the invasion of Iraq, only a small minority of conservatives and Republicans voiced outspoken opposition. A new magazine, for example, the *American Conservative*, was cofounded by Pat Buchanan in 2002 specifically against war in Iraq, and more generally against US internationalist policies dating back to World War II. At first, this point of view had few friends inside the Republican Party. Over time, however, as the Iraq war turned sour, the anti-interventionist position began to gain some purchase among a portion of otherwise staunch Republicans. Barack Obama's inauguration as president encouraged fresh numbers of GOP conservatives to turn against US military engagements in general. New interventions in Libya (2011) and possibly Syria (2013) were now viewed by many conservatives as ill-managed, likely to help Islamist radicals, overly expensive, and quite possibly unconstitutional. Even America's war in Afghanistan—strongly backed by most Republicans, as late as 2009–2010—lost support on the right over time, as grassroots conservatives and their congressional representatives came to view Hamid Karzai's Afghan government as wasteful, corrupt, and ungrateful for US support. To some extent, this shift in GOP feeling against overseas military intervention was simply a reflection of broader trends in American public opinion, but it also reflected some concerns distinct to conservatives. Having turned toward a primary focus on the excessive scope and expense of yet more federal government programs, many conservative Republicans tended to be increasingly concerned in the Obama era by the financial cost of US military intervention abroad. They tended to be concerned by legal issues surrounding the use of force by a liberal president whose constitutional fidelities they very much doubted. And they tended to be concerned by what they viewed as President Obama's extremely poor and indecisive handling of the military interventions themselves.

Today, conservative anti-interventionists are a significant political force and faction in relation to foreign policy issues within the Republican Party. They benefit from a number of factors and trends distinct to this moment. Americans right now are overwhelmingly concerned by domestic economic issues and problems rather than by foreign affairs. The continuing weak recovery from the recession of 2008–2009 only reinforces this domestic concentration, along with a keen awareness of fiscal constraints. The general public is skeptical of new military interventions or nation-building projects overseas. This popular fatigue with foreign wars and international expenditures extends well into the Republican Party. Conservatives in particular are focused mainly on resisting and if possible rolling back President Obama's domestic agenda. The GOP has been reshaped by this resistance in a populist libertarian direction, with its epitome in the Tea Party and its primary attention on domestic economic and constitutional concerns. This obviously has spillover effects into foreign and security issue approaches, even when sometimes unintentional. As Kim Holmes of the conservative Heritage Foundation notes, for many on the right, the maintenance of US military spending is not the top priority it once was. [10] Instead, the more powerful priority is in cutting government spending of all types. International and foreign aid expenditures, especially, have fewer Republican defenders these days. Many conservatives now complain that Obama's handling of current US military engagements and counterterrorism practices such as NSA surveillance are not only incompetent but unconstitutional and contemptuous of congressional authority. Most Republicans simply do not trust Obama to carry out a coherent foreign policy. All of these factors add up to a dramatic change in conservative foreign policy mood from a decade ago, and work in favor of anti-interventionists inside the GOP.[11]

The leading champion of conservative anti-interventionists right now—and a possible Republican presidential nominee in 2016 or beyond—is Ron Paul's son, Senator Rand Paul (R-KY). Rand Paul was elected a US senator from Kentucky in 2010, as part of a wave of new GOP leaders closely affiliated with the Tea Party. The common consensus on Paul among those who know him best seems to be that he shares much of his father's core conviction on foreign and domestic policy but is more interested in building coalitions and winning elections in order to put those ideas into practice.[12] He is a talented politician and has a proven ability to use the Senate floor in order to publicize the causes in which he believes. This, along with his evident sincerity and a devoted following among libertarians, makes him a formidable political figure, especially since the center of gravity within the

Republican Party has moved several degrees in his direction during the Obama era.

On foreign policy, Rand Paul has laid out a variety of positions that set him apart from many of his Republican colleagues in the Senate.[13] He argued for accelerated US disengagement from both Iraq and Afghanistan over a period of several years. In June 2011, he called on Congress to end ongoing US military operations in Libya. He is a leading critic of American foreign aid overseas and has called for deep cuts in such aid. He also argues for significant cuts in military spending. He is a vocal critic of US drone strikes against suspected terrorists and made national headlines in March 2013 by engaging in a lengthy filibuster over the issue of drones. He suggests that the threat from al-Qaeda has been overplayed by both the Bush and the Obama administrations. He criticizes current policies related to the targeting, detention, and surveillance of suspected terrorists as destructive of civil liberties. He opposes NATO expansion. He describes the Obama administration's 2013 chemical weapons agreement with Russia and Syria as a possible model for nonproliferation efforts in North Korea and Iran, and suggests that America needs to be more willing to embrace diplomatic engagement in such cases. He has repeatedly said no president may take the country into hostilities overseas, even on a small scale, without explicit authorization from Congress. He opposed further sanctions against Iran early in 2014, in the belief that existing US diplomatic efforts would work better without them. He is highly critical of American involvement in international economic institutions such as the IMF, the World Bank, and the WTO. He recommends the United States shrink or shut down many of its military bases overseas.

Evidently, Senator Paul understands that his father's exact foreign policy presentation is a problem in a presidential election.

The younger Paul disdains the term "isolationist." In fact, he calls himself a foreign policy realist. So far, the senator has been a little vague about which precise international commitments he would cut and which he would retain. This is not at all unusual for a first-time presidential candidate looking to build support and master the issues. For example, Paul has stated that in the case of Israel, he seeks no immediate end to US foreign aid but would instead reduce financial support to Tel Aviv gradually. Similarly, regarding America's military presence abroad, Paul indicates that he "doesn't want to close all overseas military bases just yet."[14] Still, his overall policy preferences are unusually clear. As president, Paul would pursue conservative and libertarian goals on domestic economic and constitutional issues, alongside an anti-interventionist foreign policy. With regard to the latter, he would look to cut costs significantly, reduce international expenditures, avoid US interventions overseas, keep a very tight lid on military spending, and dismantle a number of existing commitments abroad. In terms of the basic strategic options laid out in chapter 1, this would represent a strategy of deep retrenchment, well beyond what Obama has done. What makes this so interesting politically, heading into 2016, is that such a foreign policy strategy would be considerably more dovish for all practical purposes than the one likely to be advocated by leading Democratic presidential candidates such as Hillary Clinton. There have been a number of elections since World War II where the Republican and Democratic presidential nominees were about equally hawkish—but there have been none thus far where the Republican was clearly the more dovish of the two.

Some of Paul's most vocal supporters in the libertarian and conservative anti-interventionist firmament take the argument for US international retrenchment much further than he has. Foreign policy analysts at the Cato Institute, for example, call quite consistently for the termination of a wide range of specific US alliance commitments dating back to the 1940s and 1950s. The most recent *Cato Handbook for Policymakers*, published just after Obama's election to the presidency, specifically outlines the following recommendations for American foreign policy:

- "Eliminating most U.S. defense alliances"[15]
- "Redeploy troops in South Korea, Europe, and Japan to the United States"[16]
- "Cut the size of the Army to 25–30 brigades"[17]
- "Reduce the Navy to 200 ships"[18]
- "Fully withdraw U.S. forces from outdated cold war deployments in Asia and Europe"[19]
- "Terminate, within three years, all defense treaties with South Korea and the Philippines, and withdraw all American military units from those countries by that deadline"[20]
- "Rescind, within three years, the informal commitment to defend Taiwan"[21]
- "Withdraw all ground forces from Japan within two years"[22]
- "Withdraw from the World Bank"[23]

Cato's current director of foreign policy studies, Justin Logan, added in 2012 that on the question of whether the NATO alliance should continue, "it is time to declare the alliance a relic of the past and put NATO out to pasture."[24]

The policy merits or demerits of the above stands, and of their overarching logic, will be discussed in the final chapter. Obviously it would be useful to know if Senator Paul, as a possible presidential nominee, agrees with them or not. For now, the only thing to note is that a large number of Republicans, including a large number of grassroots conservatives around the United States, do not share the Cato Institute's stated position on the termination of most US alliance commitments overseas.

Conservative Internationalists

At the other end of the Republican Party foreign policy spectrum are the GOP's internationalists. Conservative internationalists have taken the leading role in Republican foreign policy approaches since World War II, although not without fierce competition from time to time. During the great debates of 1940–1941 over escalating US intervention in World War II, GOP internationalists played a critical part in arguing for American aid to Great Britain on moral, economic, and strategic grounds against Nazi Germany. The Japanese attack on Pearl Harbor settled that debate and left the internationalists predominant within the GOP on foreign policy issues. Republican internationalists were able to win the party's presidential nomination every four years beginning in 1940 and culminating with Dwight Eisenhower in 1952. The Eisenhower years cemented a working consensus within the GOP and within the United States around an internationalist policy of vigorous Cold War anti-Communism, entailing a wide range of costly and significant institutional, economic, diplomatic, and military American commitments spread all around the world. Every subsequent Cold War Republican president—including Richard Nixon, Gerald Ford, Ronald Reagan, and George H. W. Bush—pursued some version of this same policy, albeit with considerable variation from one administration to the next. The collapse of the Soviet Union left conservative internationalists dominant on foreign policy issues among Republican Party leaders, partly because of the widespread feeling that Reagan's approach in particular had been vindicated. Still, this left more than one version of conservative internationalism available.

When George W. Bush ran for president in 2000, for example, he argued for a version skeptical of nation-building. After the shock of September 11, 2001, Bush became convinced of the need for a different approach, energetically embracing interlocked concepts of Middle Eastern democracy promotion, aggressive counter-terrorism, rogue state rollback, and preventive warfare against Saddam Hussein's Iraq. GOP foreign policy was thus reworked in a strikingly idealistic and assertive direction. For several years, this approach had strong or at least sufficient domestic backing. Frustrations in Iraq lost Bush the support of political independents by 2006, and Obama's years as president eventually led an increasing segment of GOP conservatives to question internationalist policies of any kind. Altogether, there have been some broad continuities in the history of conservative GOP internationalism since World War II—but also important variations in the particular form and degree of success under specific Republican presidents.

Conservative internationalists, past and present, support military along with diplomatic and economic instruments of US foreign policy activism.[25] They favor clear American leadership internationally, support a forward US strategic presence overseas, and are comfortable with the current and historical institutions behind American national security policy. Conservative internationalists believe US interests abroad to be extensive, and perceive multiple threats to those interests from numerous autocratic powers as well as violent nonstate actors. They see Russia and China as competitive toward the United States in important respects; support robust counterterror policies against violent jihadists; and are skeptical of diplomatic accommodations toward Iran and North Korea. Conservative internationalists favor strong presidential leadership when it comes to foreign and national security policy. They are basically optimistic about America's latent capabilities relative to its adversaries. They favor robust levels of defense spending, to support US military advantages, and in the belief that American military power undergirds a stable international order. In terms of basic strategic options for the United States, conservative internationalists oppose any deep retrenchment, and prefer strategies of engagement, containment, and sometimes regime change. They generally argue for staunch support of traditional US allies overseas. Conservative internationalists support a sufficient level of US foreign aid as indispensable to America's influence and role as a world power. They support participation in international economic institutions as essential to the promotion of an open economic order overseas. Conservative internationalists favor free trade enthusiastically, as beneficial to the American economy. No less important, they believe the promotion of trade will lead to an international system freer, more prosperous, and friendlier to US strategic interests. They frequently favor democracy promotion abroad, for similar reasons. Conservative internationalists often support the use of shrewd, assertive diplomacy with US adversaries overseas, so long as it is backed by hard power and is not pursued as an end in itself. They favor a selective multilateralism that works through international institutions where possible, without viewing such institutions as having veto power over US national interests.

The GOP's conservative internationalists are distinct from liberal internationalists in important ways, for example in emphasizing cooperation among sovereign democracies rather than institutions of global governance.[26] The form of internationalism favored by American conservatives is rather different from the version favored by contemporary liberals. Conservative internationalists tend to place greater emphasis on defense expenditures, military support for overseas allies, and robust counterterrorism, while liberal internationalists tend to emphasize the desirability of arms control agreements, diplomacy with rogue states, supporting the United Nations, and multilateral action on climate change.[27] These practical differences in policy emphases have deep roots historically and ideologically. To a much greater extent than conservatives, liberal internationalists place primary weight on the central role of multilateral institutions in solving international coordination problems and resolving disputes between nations without force. Conservative internationalists tend to be more skeptical that multilateral institutions hold such great capacity, but are willing to work through them where possible. Conservative internationalists also tend to be more full-throated than liberals in arguing that diplomacy must be armed with force in order to be effective. Simply put, when it comes to the use of sticks and carrots as US foreign policy instruments overseas, liberals tend to have greater faith in carrots, while conservatives tend to have greater faith in sticks. Certainly, liberals can sometimes be quite energetic in arguing for sticks including military intervention abroad, especially for humanitarian reasons. But ever since the Vietnam War, liberal internationalists as a whole tend to be more ambivalent about America's use of force overseas than are GOP internationalists.[28]

Conservative internationalists are not monolithic. After all, this is a group that by definition includes Henry Kissinger as well as John McCain. They frequently debate among themselves a significant range of philosophical inclinations and fine-tuned policy positions, including the exact possibilities for diplomacy with US adversaries, the relative importance of democracy promotion and human rights as foreign policy priorities, the precise use of force overseas, the desirability of multilateral agreement on specific matters, and the need for military preemption versus deterrence. Some are more hawkish and hard-line than others, some more idealistic, some more pragmatic, and this is true not only at the level of punditry but also of voter preferences and practical politics. There are conservative internationalists among Midwestern Republicans, in the South, the Northeast, and within the Chamber of Commerce. There are also articulate exponents among public intellectuals, including neoconservatives.

Neoconservatives can be defined as one subset of conservative internationalists, favoring an especially muscular idealism in foreign affairs. Even here though, there are shades of opinion. First-generation neoconservatives like Jeane Kirkpatrick warned that pushing human rights issues in relation to US partners could destabilize allied governments and allow for the rise of even worse regimes.[29] Some current authors commonly described as neoconservative, such as columnist Charles Krauthammer, have been similarly skeptical that the Arab Spring's revolutions would produce democratic governments friendly to the United States, while others like Robert Kagan have been much more optimistic.[30] During the Bush years, popular commentary placed tremendous weight on the policy influence of neoconservative intellectuals. Without dismissing that influence entirely, it must be said that the crucial foreign policy decisions under President Bush were made by President Bush, for his own reasons and in his own way.[31] For several years after 9/11, these reasons appeared to align significantly with neoconservative thinking, notably in Bush's embrace of democracy promotion and rogue state rollback by way of Iraq. Yet already during Bush's second term, neoconservatives lost as many foreign policy arguments as they won. The broader point is that an obsession with neoconservatives actually obscures many of the true reasons for the underlying strength of a distinctly Republican internationalism over repeated generations since World War II. In fact, GOP support for a relatively hawkish American internationalism long predates the rise of neoconservative thinkers, and extends well beyond their precincts, even now.

When it comes to GOP foreign policy, conservative internationalists possess a number of enduring political, intellectual, and organizational strengths that should not be minimized. Every Republican presidential nominee since the end of the Cold War has argued for some form of conservative internationalism. This would certainly include the party's 2012 nominee, former Massachusetts governor Mitt Romney. A clear majority of potential GOP presidential candidates for 2016 also lean toward or espouse a conservative internationalist approach. This would include, for example, former Florida governor Jeb Bush, New Jersey governor Chris Christie, Louisiana governor Bobby Jindal, Senator Marco Rubio (R-FL), Representative Paul Ryan (R-MN), and former senator Rick Santorum (R-PN). Most former executive branch officials within the Republican Party lean toward some version of conservative internationalism at the end of the day. So does much of the GOP's congressional leadership. The US Senate's Republican caucus is still a bastion for conservative internationalists, of whom John McCain (R-AZ) and Lindsey Graham (R-SC) are only the most assertive and outspoken. Conservative internationalists influence and maintain an impressive network of journals, foundations, think tanks, and multimedia sounding boards for their arguments. A number of important interest groups on the political right and center-right share internationalist positions. During the Bush years, for example, one striking new development in Republican foreign policy was the linkage of evangelical political commitment to foreign aid and human rights concerns in Africa and beyond. For many of the GOP's conservative evangelicals, that foreign policy connection is not about to disappear. Moreover a great number of Main Street Republicans in every region of the country understand that America's current economic well-being is increasingly bound up with conditions overseas, and that this militates against any strict isolation from world affairs. Overall, internationalist sentiment is still fundamentally stronger among American conservatives and Republicans nationwide than often perceived. This is especially true regarding questions surrounding the use of force abroad by the United States. So the continuing strength of conservative internationalism is not simply based upon a small number of influential and well-placed advocates. It is also based upon the fact that a large segment of Republican voters, to this day, lean toward conservative internationalist policy positions. Polling from the Obama era bears this out.

Depending upon the particular foreign policy issue under discussion, conservative internationalists typically make up at least a third and sometimes a solid majority of voters inside the GOP. Indeed, Republican conservatives are of all American political groupings in the Obama era the most supportive of an assertive foreign policy against international security threats. Some 79% of Republicans say it is "very important" for the United States to remain the world's leading military power, and a similar proportion of 73% say it is very important for the United States to remain the world's most influential country.[32] Between 60% and 70% of Republicans say they support the use of force by the United States to end state support for terrorism, stop genocide, and prevent the spread of weapons of mass destruction.[33] In August 2014, over 70% of Republicans said that they supported US airstrikes against the Islamic State of Iraq and Syria.[34] Even the prospect of US military interventions under President Obama into Libya and possibly Syria gathered a large minority of support among conservative Republicans in 2011 and 2013, respectively. Almost half of Republicans indicated in March 2011 their belief that US intervention in Libya was the right decision.[35] Over two-thirds of Republicans regularly say they would support US airstrikes against Iran rather than allow that country to acquire nuclear weapons.[36] On military spending, the most common response from Republican voters when polled is to favor spending more—not less—on national defense. Less than 20% favor further military cuts.[37] On counterterrorism, an overwhelming majority of Republicans support American airstrikes and military attacks on terrorist encampments overseas. Over two-thirds of GOP voters support US drone strikes against suspected terrorists. Some 41% of Republicans say that current counterterrorism policies under Obama do not go far enough in protecting Americans from attack.[38]

Foreign aid is not popular with the general public, partly because the level of aid is overestimated, but a majority of Republicans actually favor current or increased levels of US aid to Africa as well as Israel. Indeed a solid majority of Republicans tend to feel very warmly toward Israel, viewing it as a key US ally, and supporting its defense if attacked.[39] On the basic question of whether the United States should dismantle its traditional alliance commitments overseas, a majority of Republican voters say no. Indeed GOP voters are more supportive of maintaining these commitments than are Democrats. Majorities of Republicans support the use of American troops to defend traditional US allies such as South Korea, Israel, and Taiwan if attacked. With regard to South Korea, for example, over two-thirds of Republicans say they would favor US military aid to South Korea if attacked. GOP majorities also favor a broad continued American strategic presence in Europe, East Asia, and the Middle East. According to a 2012 YouGov poll, over three-quarters of Republicans agree the "U.S. must maintain its current naval forces in Asia and the Pacific to protect the cargo ships that carry most of the trade between the United States and Asia." A majority of Republicans agree, and only 18% disagree, that "the U.S. should maintain the NATO alliance because we share common values and political systems with other NATO countries." And over two-thirds of Republicans say the "U.S. must keep a strong military presence in the Middle East to prevent terrorist attacks against the U.S. homeland."[40]

Conservative internationalists today are obviously not the dominant influence they were a decade ago, but they are still a major force quite capable of contending for leadership of the Republican Party. Despite the trends of recent years, the GOP's more hawkish instincts on a range of US foreign policy and military issues have deep roots historically, politically, ideologically, and institutionally—and those instincts are not about to disappear any time soon.

Conservative Nationalists

The third and final foreign policy group within the Republican Party today is conservative nationalists—a group that can go in different directions on issues of American grand strategy, depending upon the circumstances. The GOP's conservative nationalists carry special support from the South, the interior West, white working-class voters, Tea Party supporters, and those Republicans calling themselves "very conservative." While more inchoate than other GOP foreign policy factions, conservative nationalists form a recognizably distinct tendency quite common these days in the US House of Representatives and at the base of the Republican Party. Conservative nationalists support a powerful US military, have no trouble believing in concrete threats to American security, and no objection to the use of force against such threats when convinced it is appropriate. At the same time, conservative nationalists view multiple aspects of the liberal internationalist tradition—including foreign economic aid, nation-building, diplomatic accommodation, humanitarian intervention, and greater multilateral organization—as naive, wasteful, unlikely to earn foreign gratitude, and threatening to US national sovereignty. This set of concerns has been especially highlighted during the Obama years. The GOP's conservative nationalists view President Obama as basically weak and indecisive on matters of national security. Yet their primary focus today is on opposing his domestic agenda, not his international one. This sometimes creates the impression that they are isolationists at heart. They are not. Conservative nationalists remain rather hawkish and hard-line on a range of foreign policy and security issues—but they prefer international engagement on their own terms, rather than on liberal ones.

What follows is a fuller definition. Conservative nationalists are comfortable with the military aspects of US foreign policy activism: defense expenditures, covert action, strategic alliances, and preemptive strikes abroad if necessary. At the same time, they are profoundly uncomfortable with many of the nonmilitary aspects of US internationalism, including foreign aid, multilateral organization, nation-building, humanitarian intervention, and diplomatic concessions toward other powers. Historically, this leaves conservative nationalists open to a variety of strategic options ranging from nonintervention to regime change, but with little interest in classically liberal strategies of integration or accommodation. Conservative nationalists have little interest in legalistic or cosmopolitan projects for world order and global governance. In fact they cherish the preservation of America's national sovereignty as a primary goal in itself. They do, however, believe in the necessity of US military superiority over any conceivable adversary, and have no problem believing that such adversaries exist and must be faced down relentlessly. In a word, they favor the use of foreign policy sticks, but not carrots. This particular mixture of qualities leaves them easily misunderstood by common categorization, since they are neither internationalist nor isolationist, but simply hard-line national security hawks.[41]

Today's conservative nationalists are very much a part of what Professor Walter Russell Mead of Bard College calls America's "Jacksonian" foreign policy tradition.[42] This tradition—going back to President Andrew Jackson, according to Mead—has its geographic and demographic base in the nation's heartland, especially in the South and interior West but also among rural white voters and working-class conservatives nationwide. Jacksonians are antiestablishment cultural and political populists, generally skeptical of elite-sponsored humanitarian, multilateral, or idealistic projects overseas. They are intensely patriotic and take for granted the exceptional nature of the American experiment. Jacksonians tend to view the international political arena as a dangerous place, characterized by genuine threats, and resistant to progressive improvement. Their first instinct is not to intervene abroad. At the same time, they believe that honor, reputation, and commitments really do matter in international affairs, as in any other aspect of social life, and that weakness invites aggression. Jacksonians therefore favor strong foreign policy leadership, along with a robust American military, to match and overpower any real-world adversary. They have no objection to the use of hard power overseas, and when they see the United States as threatened or under attack Jacksonians are typically assertive and unyielding. They are keen to avoid any erosion of US national sovereignty and take a special pride in the nation's armed forces. Indeed both the officer corps and enlisted ranks of the American military tend to be disproportionately Jacksonian in background and temperament. This distinct combination of traits leaves Jacksonians a poor fit for the usual academic foreign policy dichotomy of realist versus idealist, or internationalist versus isolationist. The best way to describe them is as hawkish American nationalists—and it is exactly these conservative nationalists who form a critical plurality, pivot point, and median on foreign policy issues within the GOP today.

Jacksonians tend to be persuaded into foreign policy activism by the existence of concrete US adversaries overseas, not by what they view as internationalist abstractions. The history of the Republican Party since World War II shows the truth of this, and of the centrality of conservative nationalists in the formulation of GOP foreign policy approaches. In the days of FDR's New Deal coalition, Jacksonian America—including southern conservatives, western farmers, Appalachia, and working-class whites nationwide—voted Democrat. During the second half of the twentieth century, all of these subgroups eventually migrated toward the Republican Party, mainly over domestic issues dividing left from right, but also over foreign policy. Southern conservatives, for example, were alienated not only by national Democratic Party trends on domestic issues but also by the party's seeming abandonment of a hawkish anti-Communism after Vietnam. The migration of Jacksonian voters out of the Democratic Party and into the GOP had major consequences for the foreign policy positions of America's two major parties. It reinforced the hawkish tendencies of the GOP, leaving Democrats significantly more dovish on issues of foreign policy.[43]

Longtime GOP conservatives, for their part, moved from an anti-interventionist foreign policy position toward a more hawkish and nationalistic one, first after the Japanese attack on Pearl Harbor in 1941, and then again after the onset of the Cold War in the late 1940s. The threat of Communism was sufficient in convincing most rock-ribbed conservatives to abandon peacetime foreign policy traditions of nonintervention. Even Senator Robert Taft sounded rather Jacksonian by the early 1950s, calling as he did for the rollback of international

Communism.[44] Antipathy toward Communism glued the GOP's conservative nationalists to overarching US Cold War strategies, while bringing new converts into the fold. In fact a leading complaint of conservative nationalists such as Senator Barry Goldwater (R-AZ) was that anti-Soviet containment did not go far enough to meet and turn back the challenge from the USSR and its allies. Goldwater—a pure foreign policy Jacksonian—won the GOP's presidential nomination in 1964, indicating the rising influence of hard-line southern and western conservatives inside the Republican Party. These Sunbelt conservatives were unable to capture the White House that year, but they indicated the long-term direction Republicans would take. When Ronald Reagan finally captured the presidency in 1980, it was clear the GOP's Jacksonians had arrived in power at the highest level, with a president who very much shared their point of view.[45]

Reagan wedded conservative internationalist policies to Jacksonian instincts, and in the end produced striking success on both the domestic political and international fronts. His example left a lasting impact—enough to prevent conservative nationalists veering too far from it. During the 1990s, after the collapse of the Soviet Union, many of the GOP's Jacksonians were tempted to abandon internationalist policies, especially as managed by President Clinton. Senate Foreign Relations Committee chairman Senator Jesse Helms (R-SC), for example, critiqued Clinton's policies on foreign aid, nation-building, arms control, the United Nations, and humanitarian intervention. However, Helms was equally adamant that the United States maintain robust armed forces, together with a hard-line stance against US adversaries overseas—a combination of concerns typical for conservative nationalists. The GOP's foreign policy Jacksonians were happy to rally around the party's 2000 presidential nominee, George W. Bush, on this basis.

After the al-Qaeda attacks of September 2001, both Bush and conservative nationalists were convinced of the need for a much more assertive strategy in relation to terrorist threats. For Bush, this came to include high hopes for the democratization of the Arab world, a cause in which he became sincerely convinced. For the GOP's Jacksonians, it had more to do with a prosaic determination to hunt down and punish anyone remotely threatening to the United States. Since conservative nationalists could see that Bush shared this determination, they rallied to him and his approach, including a "war on terror" along with the invasion of Iraq. Even when the postinvasion occupation of Iraq turned sour, GOP Jacksonians formed a phalanx opposed to US surrender in that war. Only some time after Bush left the White House did conservative nationalists truly begin to rethink their support for new and existing interventions overseas.

During 2009–2010, Republican nationalists backed US military efforts in Afghanistan, providing crucial bipartisan support for Obama's surge of troops into that country. The major story starting around 2011—in terms of internal GOP politics on foreign policy matters—was the peeling away of Jacksonian support for numerous internationalist policies centered on American military intervention, foreign aid, and democracy promotion overseas. This happened for several reasons. GOP nationalists began to experience distinctly Jacksonian sensations of disgust over seemingly uncooperative and ungrateful US allies at the head of Afghanistan's government. This made it increasingly difficult to argue for American economic support of such allies, especially when Republican nationalists never really liked most foreign aid programs in the first place. For Jacksonians, the feeling with regard to well-intentioned US interventions in the Muslim world as a whole turned sour. Conservative nationalists came to suspect that American military intervention was doing more to assist

Islamist radicalism than to combat it—and they carried this suspicion into new debates over Libya and Syria. Appalled by Obama's 2011 handling of US intervention in Libya, most GOP nationalists came out against it. The same pattern repeated itself in August and September 2013 in relation to Syria. Republican nationalists remained rather hawkish at heart, but their open disdain for Obama's leadership style and policy agenda across a wide range of issues no doubt influenced their stance in cases like Syria and Libya. Indeed the single biggest focus for the GOP's Jacksonians during much of the Obama era was to oppose President Obama, convinced as they were that his domestic policy agenda represented a grave threat to American traditions of limited government. Inevitably, the intensity of this conviction had spillover effects into US foreign and national security policies. It did not, however, indicate any necessary permanent turn toward either dovish or isolationist foreign policy preferences on the part of conservative nationalists.[46]

Nationalists currently share some foreign policy preferences with GOP internationalists, and some with anti-interventionists. Yet conservative nationalists do not simply fall "in between" the other two factions. The nationalists are a distinctive third group, with specific attitudes and preferences on a range of issues, and on certain questions they are not in the middle at all. For example, GOP nationalists tend to be of all Republicans the most staunchly conservative and the most fiercely opposed to Obama. They are especially skeptical of US diplomatic concessions, open immigration, and democracy promotion in the Muslim world. Like anti-interventionists, today's conservative nationalists are tired of US international expenditures, nation-building projects, and foreign wars. They share a deep suspicion of new military interventions right now—especially as handled by Obama. At the same time, the GOP's nationalists differ from its anti-interventionists in several important respects. Conservative nationalists continue to support: robust techniques of counterterrorism, including US drone strikes; close American alliance with Israel; a hard-line stance against Iran's nuclear program, including the threat of US airstrikes; increased levels of American military spending; and firm support for traditional allies overseas. Indeed a major complaint of conservative nationalists is that President Obama is insufficiently decisive when it comes to the promotion of American interests overseas. GOP nationalists believe in hard power, perceive multiple threats abroad, and are willing to use force and military aid to defend vital interests. They want the United States to remain the world's leading power and favor strong presidential leadership to that end—but foreign policy is not their current primary focus. In this sense, conservative nationalists represent the average Republican voter today.

While conservative nationalists are not as separately well organized as other GOP foreign policy factions, they are at least as numerous, aligning with a range of venues, voters, and party leaders associated with the Republican Party's base. Conservative nationalist arguments can be frequently found, for example, in the pages of *National Review*; at the Heritage Foundation; and on conservative talk radio. Grassroots conservative lobbies, activists, and interest groups, including those affiliated with the Tea Party, regularly support nationalist foreign policy positions. The Republican House freshman class of 2010—a group that delivered GOP control over the US House of Representatives—is more nationalist than anything else. Indeed, nationalist foreign policy positions today represent the most common positions as well as the center of gravity inside the GOP's House majority. Several presidential candidates from 2012, including both Representative Michele Bachmann (R-MN) and Texas governor Rick Perry espoused conservative nationalism in foreign affairs. So does

Texas senator Ted Cruz, a possible presidential candidate in 2016.[47] Former Alaska governor Sarah Palin is another leading example of an instinctive conservative nationalist.[48] Not coincidentally, all of the politicians just mentioned tend to draw special ire from the nation's center-left bicoastal elites. In part, this is because figures like Cruz and Palin are so clearly "very conservative." Yet within Republican Party politics, that is precisely their strength. In a way, the GOP's nationalists need no separate foreign policy network to distinguish them from internationalists on the one hand, or anti-interventionists on the other. The nationalists' true network is simply among American conservatives, writ large—and this is a wider and broader network than those possessed by any other single Republican faction.

The Tea Party connection to conservative nationalism is especially noteworthy. Outside observers often assume that the Tea Party must be isolationist or anti-interventionist on foreign policy issues, in the mold of stalwart libertarian and former US representative Ron Paul (R-TX). It is certainly true that a vocal minority of Tea Party supporters favor Ron Paul's exact foreign policy philosophy. The majority, however, do not. According to a range of public opinion polls, the more common set of foreign policy views expressed by Tea Party supporters since 2009–2010 has been a hawkish American nationalism, skeptical of new interventions in Syria and Libya to be sure, but supportive of robust counterterror campaigns, strong national defenses, and a hard-line stance toward multiple US adversaries overseas. Much of the confusion on this topic is due to the fact that for Tea Party supporters, foreign policy is not their primary concern. The Tea Party developed as a reaction to President Obama's domestic policies in 2009; its core concerns are limited government, excessive federal spending, and constitutional conservatism at home. This domestic focus has obviously had some spillover effects on American foreign policy. Still, a primary focus on domestic issues is not the same thing as a strong or clear commitment to isolationism. In fact, most Tea Party supporters are not isolationist at all. They simply focus on domestic matters and put special emphasis on the preservation of American national sovereignty.[49]

Tea Party supporters are much more likely than Democrats or non–Tea Party Republicans to say that the "best way to ensure peace is through military strength." They are particularly likely to favor "getting tough with China" over international economic disputes.[50] Professor Brian Rathbun of the University of Southern California finds that most Tea Party supporters have no objection to the military component of America's international presence. What they object to is the idealistic aspects of liberal internationalism. In a word, the Tea Party is largely and classically Jacksonian in its approach to foreign affairs.[51] Indeed some of the GOP's leading figures elected into office with Tea Party support, such as Florida US senator Marco Rubio, are staunch conservative internationalists and inveterate foes of isolationism. What all of this means is that the current intra-Republican debate over basic US foreign policy options will continue inside the Tea Party and inside the conservative movement, since GOP nationalists can move in multiple directions depending upon the circumstances. The Tea Party's most dramatic symbol—the historic Gadsden flag, with its coiled snake on a yellow background declaring "Don't tread on me"—illustrates these different directions quite vividly. The snake's declaration can be seen as a preference for nonintervention, if possible. It can also be taken as a refusal to retreat and a warning of combat if remotely challenged. This is exactly the combination of foreign policy instincts embraced by conservative American nationalists, to this very day.

Foreign Policy in the 2016 Elections

How will divisions between conservative foreign policy factions play out in the coming years? Specifically, how might foreign policy and national security issues interact with the 2016 Republican presidential primaries and general election?

One striking new feature of today's intra-Republican factionalism over foreign policy is how evenly balanced the three main groupings are. GOP anti-interventionists, nationalists, and internationalists each have their own distinct political strengths and weaknesses, but at least for the moment, the three groups are roughly equal in political potential. This has not always been true. During the mid-1950s under President Eisenhower, strict anti-interventionists were thoroughly marginalized within the Republican Party, and they remained marginal well after the fall of the Soviet Union. While a few figures like Ron Paul and Pat Buchanan held a torch for them over a long period of time, the GOP's anti-interventionists have only recently reemerged as a genuinely important faction politically. Conservative "Jacksonian" nationalists, for their part, have long been a powerful force at the base of the Republican Party, but in practice conservative internationalists have dominated GOP foreign policy approaches since World War II, usually in alliance with these same nationalists. Today, the possibilities for implicit alliance between various factions go in multiple directions. One possibility is that the traditional coalition between conservative internationalists and Jacksonian nationalists will be rebuilt in some form. This would be consistent with every Republican presidency since the 1950s. Another possibility is that a new, enduring alliance will form between Jacksonian nationalists and conservative anti-interventionists. This would most closely resemble the Republican presidencies of the 1920s, from Warren Harding to Herbert Hoover. Under either scenario, the GOP's nationalists hold the trump card; they can determine which way the Republican Party pivots on foreign policy, if they choose to do so.

In presidential primaries, most voters normally cast their ballots on issues other than foreign affairs, and this will probably also be true in 2016. For that very reason, the international policy stance of the winning candidate is far from predetermined. Successful coalitions in US party politics are built across multiple issue dimensions, of which foreign policy is only one and hardly the most important from the perspective of most voters. Yet the very fact of widespread voter indifference to foreign affairs allows successful candidates considerable room to lead on these issues, and to advocate international policies in line with their own beliefs. The American political system does not provide for a leader of the opposition, until the nomination of a presidential candidate. It is the party's presidential nominee that brings or tries to bring unity, coherence, and a clear party platform on international issues. In the end, most Republicans will support the party's nominee in the November 2016 general election, whatever their particular foreign policy preferences. This gives the party's nominee a remarkable degree of leeway in defining GOP foreign policy.

A successful Republican candidate in 2016 will have to address conservative nationalist concerns, at the very least, in order to secure the party's nomination. Conservative nationalists will play a pivotal role in determining whether an anti-interventionist or an internationalist emerges triumphant from the primary process. Anti-interventionists will have to reassure that they can stand up for American interests abroad. Internationalists will have to reassure that they are not overeager to embark on new military interventions. It is entirely possible that a leading Republican presidential candidate might argue for conservative internationalism in foreign affairs, and link this approach to an attractive stance on domestic issues, a well-organized campaign, or a winning personal appeal. The fine balance between anti-interventionists, nationalists, and internationalists right now within the Republican Party allows for this range of possibilities. In a sense, it frees up candidates to argue their core convictions, since any one of several foreign policy stands might accompany victory in the GOP primaries.

The champion of conservative anti-interventionists in 2016 will in all likelihood be Senator Rand Paul. Paul's task would therefore seem to be among other things winning over conservative nationalists into a new anti-interventionist foreign policy coalition. The challenge Senator Paul has in building this coalition is that conservative nationalists and anti-interventionists differ very significantly in substance. They agree on certain questions such as humanitarian intervention and foreign aid. But on a wide range of other issues including defense spending, drone strikes, counterterrorism practices, Russian and Chinese foreign policy behavior, Iran's nuclear weapons program, and support for core US allies, conservative nationalists are relatively hawkish and distant from the anti-interventionist philosophy. Senator Paul for his part feels that President Obama should scale back on US drone strikes overseas, cut military spending further, and make more of an effort to conciliate Iran diplomatically. He believes that on the whole Obama has been too aggressive in pursuing a war on terrorism continued from the Bush era, and at the same time insufficiently willing to pursue diplomatic engagement with rival powers.[52] The problem for Paul is that this is not how most Republicans feel about Obama's foreign policy. The most common GOP complaint outside the Beltway is hardly President Obama is "too tough" when it comes to counterterrorism, or that he has not given diplomatic engagement with Iran and other countries enough of a chance. This is not how most grassroots conservatives feel. It is not how most Tea Party supporters feel. To be sure, it is how many liberal Democrats feel. But Paul will not be running as a Democrat.

Paul's foreign policy difficulties are multiplied by the challenges typically faced by movement candidates on the right. GOP presidential primaries have followed a fairly predictable pattern for over a quarter century now: insurgent candidates initially favored by conservative or libertarian movement activists tend to fail. Partly, they fail for lack of organizational and financial strength, which wears them down during the arduous primary process. Partly, they fail for lack of broad voter support. Most Republican primary voters are not actually on the far right. Even fewer Republicans are specifically libertarian—about 12%, according to the Brookings Institution.[53] Roughly two-thirds of GOP voters describe themselves as conservative, but of those, about one-half say they are only "somewhat" (as opposed to "very") conservative. The candidate favored by those who self-identify as somewhat conservative always wins in the end. This type of candidate is generally a known figure with considerable political experience, a reassuring character, and a center-right approach to politics, acceptable to GOP conservatives.[54] Such winning candidates always have one further crucial quality: they typically favor some version of Republican internationalism in foreign affairs. Fringe candidates, ultraconservative candidates, insurgent movement candidates, and foreign policy anti-interventionists such as Pat Buchanan and Ron Paul tend to lose. The question of course is whether 2016 will be any different—and in particular, whether a conservative anti-interventionist could win the nomination this time around.

Senator Paul must be considered an insurgent candidate, with special and intense initial support from libertarians. This would seem to predict that he loses the GOP nomination, if recent patterns are any indicator. Yet the precedent from the previous quarter-century may not hold. In fact Paul should be considered a serious contender for the 2016 Republican nomination, for multiple reasons. His populist libertarianism on domestic issues is a reasonably good fit for the mood of many GOP voters right now. The opening primary state of New Hampshire is relatively friendly territory for him. He is a talented politician well-liked by grassroots conservatives, and his distinct libertarian worldview gives him a core network of staunch supporters inherited from his father who will regard his candidacy as a genuine cause. This same quality also gives him a significant base of financial donors, both large and small, unavailable to previous insurgent candidates. Paul clearly understands that he must reach out beyond his father's core supporters to build a broader coalition and is already trying to do so. The demeanor he typically strikes is earnest rather than threatening, and this together with his unorthodox policy positions may have some crossover appeal outside of the GOP's conservative base—at least this is what Paul's supporters hope. A dovish foreign policy stance is hardly a traditional path to the Republican nomination, but electorally it appears less of a flat disqualifier than it used to be.

One interesting scenario is that Senator Paul wins the nomination not because of, but in spite of his anti-interventionist foreign policy views. This, too, is a real possibility. Party primaries tend to be more unpredictable than general election results, and with multiple candidates running, the various contenders might slice up the vote and run through the states in surprising ways. For example, even if Paul's foreign policy views still represent only a minority of GOP primary voters, multiple other candidates running as national security hawks might divide up the remaining vote, leaving Paul at no disadvantage numerically. And of course the majority of voters these days do not cast their ballot over foreign policy at all, but over issues of domestic politics and personality quite separate from international affairs. All of which is to say: while more of a foreign policy anti-interventionist than any GOP nominee since the 1930s, and in this sense unconventional within the modern Republican Party, Rand Paul really does have a chance to win the 2016 presidential nomination. Recognition of this new political reality should help focus the minds of the GOP's internationalists and security hawks.

I have suggested that given the current formation of the Republican Party, it might go in one of two very different directions on foreign policy issues: either Jacksonian-isolationist or Jacksonian-internationalist. Which of these fundamental directions would most likely benefit the GOP in a presidential election? And how might foreign policy issues help shape the electoral outcome in 2016?

Republicans should face a more favorable environment in the 2016 presidential election compared to 2012.[55] Swing voters are historically more inclined to turn against the party controlling the White House after eight years than after four. International affairs may not be the single leading issue these days, but in a general election foreign policy is always an important threshold issue in the sense that voters expect a potential president to demonstrate the degree of knowledge, temperament, plausibility, and competence expected of a commander-in-chief. Any winning presidential candidate in the near future from either party will certainly need to reassure swing voters that he or she would be careful and prudent rather than reckless or bellicose on questions of military intervention. But in American politics, this much has always been true.[56] It was true during the Cold War and is still true today.

On many leading foreign policy issues, the median US voter right now is ambivalent—not isolationist. The general public is indeed war-weary but remains willing to support key elements of America's forward international role. Most voters do not cast their ballots on strongly felt preferences over most foreign policy issues most of the time. This means that US political leaders—and especially presidents—play a crucial part in translating popular preferences into practice and in determining exactly what American foreign policy will be. Presidential candidates in fact have a certain amount of room to lead their party and their country by indicating what international direction they think best for the United States. Because of deep partisan differences over domestic issues, most Republicans will vote for the Republican candidate in 2016, and most Democrats will vote for the Democratic candidate, regardless of foreign policy. The election will likely be fought above all as a referendum on Obama, a reflection on the state of the economy, and a choice between liberal versus conservative domestic policies. This actually gives presidential nominees a certain amount of freedom in defining their party's foreign policy stance heading into the general election, so long as they do not outrage large numbers of fellow partisans on issues of central importance.

For most (not all) presidential elections between 1952 and 2004, the GOP held an advantage on foreign policy issues as the perceived party of strength on national security. Today, the Republican Party's critics—both internal and external—sometimes suggest that the memory of Iraq has wrecked the GOP's national security advantage for all time. It is of course true that the growing unpopularity of the Iraq war hurt the Republican Party badly during George W. Bush's second term. Obama also erased any GOP issue advantage on foreign policy in 2011–2012, temporarily at least, with the strike on bin Laden. Yet Republicans continued to be viewed as the stronger party on key issues such as terrorism between 2008 and 2010. By late 2013, President Obama's approval ratings on foreign policy had dropped considerably, and the GOP was once again viewed as preferable on issues of national security.[57] Apparently, the general public is increasingly disturbed by the president's foreign policy leadership style. In any case, there is no reason to simply assume that Obama's foreign policy advantage from his re-election campaign will automatically replicate for the Democrats in 2016. The circumstances of 2011–2012 were rather unusual. In strictly political terms, Republicans were never likely to gain a foreign policy issue edge over an incumbent president running for re-election who had just authorized a successful strike on the leader of al-Qaeda. There will be no such incumbent in 2016.

Presidential elections are among other things a referendum on the previous four years.[58] If the existing president is unpopular, then a nominee from the same party cannot altogether escape the association with an unpopular incumbent. John McCain was a very different person from George W. Bush in 2008, just as Hubert Humphrey was a very different person from Lyndon Johnson in 1968, but when an incumbent is unpopular it envelops and drags down his would-be successor. President Obama's overall approval ratings have hovered around 40% since the summer of 2013—not as low as Bush's by the end of his second term, but still not at all good. If a majority of Americans continue to disapprove of Obama by 2016, and to feel the country is on the wrong track, then voters will hold the Democratic Party's 2016 presidential nominee responsible for Obama's performance, regardless of candidate messaging. This includes voter evaluation of incumbent performance on foreign policy issues. A party's presidential nominee can try to distance him or herself from a weak incumbent, but if voters disapprove of a president's foreign policy, inevitably this hurts any would-be successor from the very same party. To be sure, presidential nominees from the party out of power must develop credible, appealing, and constructive policy alternatives. But asking voters to reflect on the failure or success of an existing president's foreign policy record is quite rightly a major part of what opposing nominees can and should do.

Obama's approval ratings on foreign policy, specifically, dropped down to about 40% during the summer of 2013 and stayed at that level (sometimes lower) well into 2014.[59] To some extent this was probably a reflection of a broad drop in the president's overall popularity. But the president's foreign policy ratings also showed distinct downward movement apart from his general approval and for the first time in his presidency were consistently lower than his overall ratings. It is therefore reasonable to surmise that by 2013–2014, an increasing number of swing voters were beginning to disapprove of Obama's management over US foreign policy as revealed in specific cases like Syria and Ukraine. The growing impression of international policy weakness and indecision was too striking to fully ignore, even for a general public still unfocused on foreign affairs and disinclined to intervene abroad. Witness the results of a December 2013 Pew Center poll asking voters whether President Obama was "too tough," "about right," or "not tough enough" on foreign policy matters. Among the general public, 5% of Americans said Obama was "too tough," 51% said "not tough enough," and 37% said "about right."[60] Again, this was a poll taken from the general public—not just Republicans. In effect, neoisolationist critics align with the 5%, rather than with the 51% on this issue. The suggestion that Obama is best criticized as "too tough" or "too aggressive" on foreign policy is therefore probably not a winning strategy for the GOP.

As of now, the leading presidential candidate on the Democratic side is former secretary of state Hillary Clinton. Clinton's claim will be that she is a strong, experienced foreign policy leader with the instincts and background to take on international challenges. There is much to critique in Clinton's record at State, but Republicans will need to take seriously the task of how to match or defeat her on foreign policy issues. The argument of GOP anti-interventionists is that the best way to critique a candidate like Clinton is to attack her as too hawkish on foreign affairs. To be sure, there has been little popular enthusiasm within the United States for humanitarian intervention in locations such as Libya—a cause supported by Secretary Clinton in 2011. But the general implication that Clinton is too assertive on national security issues would probably backfire on Republicans, as swing voters actually appreciate a sense of toughness on such issues. Clinton is better critiqued as too liberal, too continuous with Obama, and too ineffectual at State, than as too assertive on national security.

Conservative anti-interventionists make the interesting argument that a dramatically new Republican foreign policy posture of strategic disengagement will win fresh recruits to the GOP.[61] This fails to consider the kind of countervailing effects common in electoral politics. A strict anti-interventionist position on foreign policy issues could easily lose the GOP more voters than it gains. Certainly, a Republican neoisolationist turn might win over some low-information independent voters who resent all American engagement overseas. But left-liberal doves would probably still vote Democrat in any case, on domestic issues. And in the meantime, the GOP would have alienated a broad range of voters in the middle and on the right who at the end of the day reject strict nonintervention and instead value strength on national security. This is the ultimate irony of the neoisolationist argument: in their eagerness to respond to the Democrats' temporary 2011–2012 advantage on foreign policy issues, the GOP's anti-interventionists might unintentionally hand that advantage over to Democrats like Clinton well into the future.

In sum, a neoisolationist stance is neither optimal nor necessary for Republicans politically. In fact it would be a great gamble for the GOP to adopt such a stance in a general election. Many attentive voters in both parties would rightly view a neoisolationist policy position as basically impractical and unserious—as an indication that Republicans are not yet ready to govern. It could even split and demoralize many Republicans heading into a general election. American voters may be domestically focused right now, but they will still reward a sense of strong, capable, and successful leadership in foreign affairs. Lately, this is not the sense they have received from President Obama. On the contrary, there is a growing impression of drift and enervation with regard to the president's foreign policy. This gives Republicans an opening to make their case. It is entirely possible that with the right candidate, a certain kind of Jacksonian internationalism could work well for Republicans in the 2016 general election. Such a foreign policy stance would include among other things bedrock support for American allies overseas, firm deterrence of US adversaries, assertive counterterrorism, reinforced national defenses, and an overarching mentality of peace through strength. I call this conservative American realism. In the next chapter, I offer some thoughts on what such a stance might look like.

5

Conservative American Realism

In the early 1980s, President Ronald Reagan pursued a national security strategy aimed at pressuring the Soviet Union comprehensively. He authorized a US military buildup, supported anti-Communist insurgents, downplayed the need for any immediate arms control agreement, and publicly described the Soviet system of government as dysfunctional and illegitimate. At the same time, he refused to entangle great numbers of American troops in protracted, inconclusive combat on the ground. This combination of features had the effect of preserving domestic political support for an assertive grand strategy. It also had the effect of eventually forcing the USSR into major concessions. Reagan is often described as an idealist, and in many ways he was. But his national security strategy also contained powerful elements of what might be called conservative American realism.[1]

Conservative American realism is one alternative to the Obama doctrine. A conservative American foreign policy realism would emphasize supporting American allies and resisting American adversaries internationally. It would emphasize strategic planning, bolstered deterrence, and presidential leadership on behalf of a genuinely prudent US forward presence. This includes identifying concrete US interests along with real, current challenges to those interests. The precise recommendation is for what I call strategies of pressure against US adversaries and competitors overseas. Targets fall into three main categories: great power competitors, rogue state adversaries, and jihadist terrorists. In all cases, I make specific policy proposals based upon a certain reorientation away from common US errors of the post–Cold War era. I suggest that a foreign policy stance something like this could win domestic political support in upcoming GOP presidential primaries, in a general election, and beyond that as a component of governance under the next Republican president.

First Things First

Foreign Policy Realism

One common theory regarding President Obama is that he is a realist on foreign policy. According to this theory, Obama has appropriated the international approach of Republican presidents such as Dwight Eisenhower and George H. W. Bush, along with their political success over foreign policy issues, by pursuing a grand strategy based upon realist assumptions.[2] If the evidence presented so far in this book is correct, then it should be clear that President Obama—whatever his other qualities or strengths—is not a foreign policy realist. Obama's starting point on foreign policy seems to be a desire to avoid international controversies and entanglements, in order to focus on liberal domestic reforms. He generally refuses to impose strategic coherence on specific regional or functional American policies abroad that might risk his overarching domestic goals. He is willing to give inspirational speeches regarding international matters, but not necessarily to enforce them. For a US commander in chief, he puts unusual emphasis on the possibility of triggering international cooperation through detached reason, discussion, concession, and his own unique personality. The whole approach has been highly self-referential, with a special emphasis on public relations. To be sure, Obama is generally calm and even-keeled in how he presents decisions. He is also tactically very flexible. But this in itself is not realism. In the words of one of President Obama's leading first-term advisers on China policy, Jeffrey Bader: "the president and his spokespersons were not focused on the balance of power or Realpolitik."[3]

Foreign policy realists see the international system as a competitive arena. The lack of any genuinely effective overarching power to enforce law and order at the international level means that nation-states count mainly on their own devices—and on those of their allies—to protect vital national interests. Realists are by no means unaware of moral obligation in world politics, but they view a leader's primary moral obligation as the safety and security of his own country, which in turn requires seeing things as they are, rather than as we wish they were. Realists are skeptical of transformational or progressive visions of world politics. They believe that the underlying features of international relations have never really changed that much over time. This is one reason they view the study of history as instructive. Realists emphasize the centrality of geographic location and distributions of power in shaping and constraining the menu of options available to any country's leader—a study known as geopolitics. They caution against strategic overextension and moralistic crusades disconnected from geopolitical conditions. They welcome the intelligent use of diplomacy. But realists also warn that diplomacy must be backed by force; that strategic competition between major powers is historically normal and will continue; and that military instruments are by no means outmoded as a central tool of world politics in our own time. Realist foreign policy recommendations therefore tend to look different from classically liberal ones. Rather than relying too heavily on the promotion of global governance, international law, multilateral institutions, economic interdependence, democracy, and human rights, realists focus on what Hans Morgenthau called the "workmanlike manipulation of perennial forces" to promote achievable national interests including a peaceful and favorable balance of power overseas.[4] These perennial forces and techniques of influence include concrete military and economic rewards as well as punishments—or stick and carrots, in more prosaic terms—to give diplomatic injunctions real bite. Leading realist scholars since World War II include the aforementioned Morgenthau, E. H. Carr, Reinhold Niebuhr, Nicholas Spykman, George Kennan, Henry Kissinger, Kenneth Waltz, Robert Gilpin, Stephen Walt, John Mearsheimer, and Robert Art.[5]

For Americans, foreign policy realism is a corrective, rather than a starting point. Americans of all parties have long believed that the spread of classically liberal norms, free exchange, and popular forms of self-government abroad will ultimately lead to a more peaceful and friendly international system. That belief is not about to change, but it can and should be tempered by a realist understanding of international security dilemmas as they actually exist. Realism has no necessary connection to any particular domestic political program. In practical terms, neither liberals nor conservatives will be satisfied with a foreign policy that ignores their domestic priorities. Recent iterations of academic realism, in particular, are often too abstract and detached from day-to-day challenges to be of much use to policymakers. Commentators inside the Beltway, for their part, sometimes use the word "realism" to describe a preferred foreign policy decision even where there is little or no connection to realist insights. The Center for the National Interest, a foreign policy think tank, is a rare example of a Washington institute devoted to realism in international relations. Even among serious foreign policy realists, however, there are important disagreements.

Realism is a mindset from which to approach international challenges, not a particular policy or strategy. Naturally the specifics of any such strategy must be worked out in detail. Indeed, foreign policy realists often disagree over day-to-day policy issues. They even differ over basic questions such as whether to retain America's forward presence abroad, or move "offshore" strategically. These differences must be clarified, in order to be useful. Nobody should pretend that presidents spend much time mulling over academic formulations of international relations. Nevertheless, in the case of several Republican administrations since Eisenhower's—including Ronald Reagan's—each president instinctively incorporated certain aspects of foreign policy realism into an overarching strategy in order to achieve practical international success.[6] There really has been a worthwhile tradition of Republican foreign policy realism over the years, even if it is quite distinct from the path recommended by most academics as well as by President Obama. The pressing need for both Republicans and the United States today is to recover that worthwhile instinct for what might be called conservative American realism.

A conservative American realism would be distinct from many academic versions, as well as from President Obama's existing approach, in several key respects. Certainly, it would draw on the powerful realist insights mentioned above. But it would be *conservative*, literally, in working to preserve America's international status, security, and influence; in drawing on specifically conservative insights regarding statecraft; and in being tied to a conservative domestic political approach. It would furthermore be distinctly *American* in aiming to energetically promote concrete US interests against some very real adversaries overseas; in taking seriously the sovereignty of the United States as an independent constitutional and federal republic; and in accepting that Americans by nature neither will nor should completely abandon long-term hopes for the betterment of the international system. A foreign policy realism of this particular kind would be much closer to the historical practice of several successful Republican presidents than to the Obama doctrine. What international strategy for the United States would follow from such a conceptual readjustment?

US Interests and American Primacy

Any strategy should begin with a specification of national interests. America's vital interests include the defense of US territory from attack, terrorist or otherwise; the protection of US national sovereignty; the preservation of America's system of limited government at home; guarding the lives and property of US citizens overseas; the promotion and defense of American trade and investment internationally; the security of oil supplies from the Persian Gulf; and the maintenance of regional balances of power within Europe, the Middle East, and East Asia. Beyond that, Americans have a vital interest in the preservation of what can only be called US primacy. Indeed the protection of America's other national interests will be more likely if US primacy is maintained.

American primacy refers to a set of interlocking conditions in which the US retains more broad-based economic and military capabilities than any other major power, along with a greater ability than any rival to shape the international environment.[7] Primacy is a circumstance and an interest, not a strategy. In the case of the United States, however, primacy is also an historical reality, dating back to the end of World War II. During that war, Americans determined they would not return to a posture of strategic disentanglement; instead, they would play a new and more forward role in the world. The decisions of that period, culminating with the early Cold War, led to the creation of an American-led international system qualitatively different from any that had preceded it. Outside of the Soviet bloc, the United States helped nurture the development and maintenance of an open international order in which market-oriented democracies could flourish. After the collapse of the Soviet Union, this system was expanded to include several former Communist states. By historical standards, this US-led order has been an astonishing success. Much of the world is now far more free, democratic, prosperous, peaceful, and friendly to US interests than in previous generations. Yet we often take the benefits of this order for granted.

During the 1990s, commentators began to refer to America's "unipolar moment."[8] The word unipolar might be taken to mean that the US is all-powerful in world affairs—an obvious untruth. In fact, unipolarity simply refers to an international system in which one great power far outpaces all of the others in terms of its combined economic, military, and political capabilities. By that standard, it is not unreasonable to describe the current international system as unipolar.[9] Clearly, the United States is not the only major power in the world. China, Russia, Japan, India, Germany, France, and Great Britain all have claim to the title. This is why observers sometimes say that we live in a multipolar world—one in which multiple great powers exist. Yet such a description does not quite capture the outsized role the United States plays worldwide, along with its unique range of capabilities. Political scientist Samuel Huntington tried to address this tension by calling the post–Cold War order "uni-multipolar."[10] A less awkward framework is proposed by British international relations scholar Barry Buzan. Buzan suggests we live in an international system in which there are multiple great powers but only one superpower. According to Buzan, superpowers possess "broad-spectrum capabilities exercised across the whole of the international system," "first-class military capabilities ... and the economies to support such capabilities," "global military and political reach," and a claim to promote "'universal' values."[11] Great powers may be very impressive in one form of power or another and in one region as opposed to another, but only superpowers are influential worldwide in a wide variety of ways. By this standard, argues Buzan, the United States has been the world's only superpower since the collapse of the Soviet Union.

It ought to be self-evident, but seems to need repeating, that the preservation of American primacy is in the American interest. By definition, whatever other international and domestic interests, values, and goods Americans seek to conserve or pursue are more easily done if the United States is more powerful rather than less so. Under the conditions of US primacy, this advantageous power position has gone hand in hand with a specifically American international order outside the spheres of major authoritarian powers, and the continued existence of that US-led order has been of tremendous benefit to the United States. Economically, for example, Americans as a whole have benefited materially and dramatically from the operation of a global trading system in which the United States is the largest economy and final guarantor, and from the existence of an international financial system in which the US dollar remains—to this day—the leading reserve currency. This is not to mention the political, economic, and security benefits American primacy has brought for dozens of US allies. What Samuel Huntington said twenty years ago is no less true today:

> A world without U.S. primacy will be a world with more violence and disorder and less democracy and economic growth than a world where the United States continues to have more

influence than any other country in shaping global affairs. The sustained international primacy of the United States is central to the welfare and security of Americans and to the future of freedom, democracy, open economies, and international order in the world.[12]

America's Forward Strategic Presence

For almost seventy years, US primacy including a relatively benign international order has been buttressed and maintained through America's forward military presence overseas. This forward presence includes a great network of US defensive alliances, peacetime strategic commitments, force deployments, and military bases around the perimeter of the Eurasian continent. It also necessarily entails the maintenance of superior US military capabilities, along with a credible readiness to use them. America's forward strategic presence in Europe and Asia has undergone many important adjustments over the years, but the underlying continuities are striking. Basically, during the 1940s Americans rejected their traditional stance of strategic disengagement from the Eurasian continent, and they have never returned to that stance. The question today is whether such a return or at least partial return to disengagement might be tempting.

The most interesting arguments for strategic disengagement, deep retrenchment, and offshore balancing do not disparage the value of a favorable power position for the United States. Rather, they suggest that America's forward military presence on the Eurasian continent actually undermines the US power position by leading it into unnecessary costs and unnecessary wars.[13] This is a serious argument, and it deserves an answer. There is no doubt that numerous US military interventions under conditions of American primacy have been ill-managed, and in a few cases ill-advised. The key is to avoid confusing either the poor management or the unpopularity of specific interventions with the underlying argument for a forward strategic presence. If you don't like the costs of America's current world role, consider the alternative.

America's forward presence of alliances, bases, and strategic commitments serves several worthwhile purposes, when properly managed. It deters and contains US adversaries and competitors. It reassures US allies, which in turn prevents those allies from pursuing dangerous levels of armament including nuclear weapons programs. It helps buffer and dampen destabilizing military competition between allies and adversaries, by clarifying that the United States will act as a security provider of last resort. It upholds regional balances of power, making it more difficult for authoritarian competitors to gather strength uncontested. It protects global sea lanes and maritime choke points, easing the free flow of commerce and shipping worldwide. A forward strategic presence further allows the United States to more easily protect its economic interests overseas, including American trade, investment, and the steady flow of oil supplies issuing from the Persian Gulf. It buttresses the international strength of the American dollar as a global reserve currency, providing huge economic advantages for the United States. A forward strategic presence permits the United States to perform humanitarian and disaster relief efforts abroad when it chooses to do so. It allows the United States when necessary to intervene against its enemies, including terrorists, from an advanced posture rather than an impossibly distant one. It leaves the United States better able to protect the lives of its citizens overseas. These all are distinctly US interests. America's forward presence also serves numerous allied interests, whether fully appreciated or not. One need not be a hyperinterventionist to grasp that on the whole, the basic US strategic posture since World War II has done far more good than harm for Americans as well as for the rest of the world. It is in fact a crucial buttress not only of US capabilities but of a relatively democratic, prosperous, and peaceful international order. If America's forward strategic posture did not exist, we would have to invent it. Why throw it away?

Advocates of offshore balancing, deep retrenchment, and strategic disengagement often point out the costs of America's current world role. Because these human and financial costs are known, current, and visible, they are easily understood. For example, we know how much the United States spends on foreign aid or on national defense. What is less obvious, known, or visible, but potentially massive, are the possible costs and risks of dismantling America's current world role—and here, despite their stated realism, the advocates of disengagement often work from surprisingly rosy assumptions. If America's forward strategic presence abroad were abandoned, it would likely invite a range of very significant costs and risks, both for Americans and internationally. There is actually no guarantee that other democratic countries would step up and fill the gap in ways welcome to US interests. Without the United States as a stabilizing and pacifying force in regions such as Northeast Asia, great power warfare would be more difficult to prevent. So too would the proliferation of nuclear weapons on the part of US allies currently reassured by Washington's security guarantees. Major authoritarian powers would have greater leeway to advance. Jihadist terrorists in al-Qaeda would no doubt take any comprehensive American retreat as a victory, rather than as a reason to lay aside arms. In all likelihood, a world without a clear US forward presence would be less stable, less democratic, and more violent than the one we now live in. In the absence of an overarching American deterrent, heated interstate conflicts might be more common rather than less so. In the end, the United States would probably be pulled back into several of these conflicts, since vital American interests would in fact be at stake. Something like a new US forward presence would then have to be reconstituted, but at immense cost in blood and treasure—including from Americans. Indeed this is exactly what happened in the first half of the twentieth century, when the US intervened in World War I, then disengaged, only to find itself pulled back in by the 1940s at great cost to itself. A much less expensive solution would be to avoid strategic disengagement in the first place.[14]

In practical terms, proposals for deep US strategic retrenchment and disengagement are literally radical, as opposed to conservative. They uproot the current order, exaggerate the problems with it, and fail to appreciate its benefits. The unintended consequences of dismantling America's long-standing forward presence would probably be far greater and far worse than admitted or specified by its proponents. Any serious consideration of such radical proposals should weigh their possible downsides and closely scrutinize any promised gains.

US Capabilities and Resources

After specifying vital national interests, any serious strategy should offer a kind of net assessment of a country's available resources and capabilities, particularly as compared to those of its international competitors. There has been a great deal of talk in recent years about rising multipolarity, relative decline in US power, and the coming of a "post-American" era. Certainly when it comes to the possibility of constructive US influence overseas, the mood in America is far more pessimistic than it was, for example, in 2002–2003, and to some extent this pessimism has been hard earned. The combination of wartime sacrifices and frustrations in Iraq and Afghanistan, together with a severe recession followed by mediocre economic recovery, have encouraged a widespread feeling of strict US limitation and possibly national decline. This is a subjective mood, with real political consequences, and it has some factual basis. But the mood of pessimism and decline has now overshot its basis in reality. Those familiar with US history will understand this is hardly the first time such a pattern has repeated itself. As they did after Sputnik, Vietnam, and the 1980s economic challenge from Japan, Americans cyclically and periodically enter into earnest internal debate over their country's relative decline. Excessive optimism alternates with and is replaced by excessive and unrealistic gloom. If anything, Americans today tend to underestimate how powerful the United States really is. Objectively, the range of economic, military, and diplomatic capabilities available to the United States remains unmatched by any other country. True multipolarity has yet to arrive.

America's multidimensional advantages on the world stage can be measured in several ways. No other country enjoys the range of capabilities and resources possessed by the United States. These advantages and capabilities include, but are not limited to, the following:

- The single largest national economy in the world
- Financial markets of unmatched depth
- An extremely favorable geographical location, surrounded by friendly countries and separated by two oceans from any other major power
- Abundant natural resources including food, vital minerals, oil, and gas on a continental scale
- Dramatic improvements in the domestic production of shale gas
- Favorable demographics compared to any other major power

- An ability to receive and integrate large numbers of immigrants with relative success
- One of the three largest populations on the planet
- A high per capita income by international standards
- Most of the leading universities and research institutions in the world
- A persistent edge in technological and scientific innovation
- An exceptionally robust civil society
- An ideological framework in liberal democracy of sometimes broad and subversive appeal overseas
- A global alliance system, including most of the world's leading democracies, centered on the United States rather than any other country
- Armed forces far stronger than those of any potential challenger
- One of the two largest nuclear weapons arsenals in the world
- Unmatched military capabilities at sea and in the air
- A continued lead in the ongoing revolution in military affairs, combining the use of precision strikes with the latest information technology, and
- An underlying domestic political and constitutional order that is stable, peaceful, solid, and almost universally revered by US citizens of either party

No other major power holds this full-spectrum combination of resources and capabilities. The European Union is a vast conglomeration of wealthy democracies, peacefully integrated in many ways, but it does not perform as a single actor on key issues of international strategy, war, and peace. China is America's most plausible peer competitor, and of course Chinese economic weight has risen dramatically over the past quarter-century. Over the past decade, furthermore, the balance of military capabilities along the

East Asian littoral has shifted in favor of the Chinese and against the United States. Still, China does not possess a full range of capabilities like those listed above—and Chinese leaders know it. Other powers like Russia and India are either rising or resurgent, but again, they are not world powers akin to the United States. Nor is the US share of world GDP (gross domestic product)— one obvious measure of material power and potential—actually in dramatic decline. On the contrary, in spite of all the ups and downs in America's foreign policy, its share of world economic production has remained quite stable over the past twenty years, at a little over 20% of global GDP—significantly more than that of any other single country. The point of all these comparisons is not to beat American chests. Rather, the point is to locate some objective measure of comparative great power resources and to show that current talk of a post-American era under a new multipolarity is typically overstated.[15]

The United States does face a considerable range of very serious challenges, both domestic and international, to its continued primacy. Yet it also remains, in fact, the world's only superpower, with a broad range of capabilities to support that role. In strictly material terms, the United States has the resources and the capabilities to pursue a wide variety of international strategies, including some that preserve a forward US presence overseas. In truth, this is as much a question of American political will and choice as of resources. If America's underlying share of material capabilities internationally were terribly unfavorable, or in genuinely steep and inevitable decline, then of course a grand strategy of continued overarching retrenchment might be the most responsible option. But the United States still holds unmatched capabilities, and their imminent demise is hardly inevitable. If anything, under current circumstances there is a risk that excessive and ill-managed US retrenchment and accommodation feed into perceptions of American decline unnecessarily. And this is precisely what has happened under President Obama.

Challenges and Threats

A coherent strategy should specify threats to the national interest and distinguish between them. What are the chief international threats to American interests today? The tendency under President Obama has been to define national security challenges in terms that are fashionably vague and to downplay specific threats from specific international actors along with their underlying motivations. For example, the administration's 2010 Quadrennial Defense Review (QDR) spends considerable wordage on the term "clean energy," while refusing to mention "Islamism" or "jihadism" with reference to al-Qaeda. Similarly, the 2014 QDR never clearly identifies China as a strategic competitor.[16] There may be concerns of public diplomacy behind these omissions, but a president should at least be clear in his own mind regarding genuine threats to American interests, and it is not entirely obvious that such clarity currently exists. An identification of threat best refers to specific groups of human beings—whether state or nonstate actors—pursuing policies hostile or at least dangerously competitive toward the United States. There are three such categories of actor today. The first category contains great power competitors, namely Russia and China. The second category contains rogue state adversaries, primarily Iran and North Korea, although Syria and Venezuela could certainly be included. The third category contains Islamist jihadist terrorists—starting with but not limited to al-Qaeda—that wage a transnational war against the United States and its allies. More will be said about each of these categories in a moment, along with how to address them. The point for now is that important phenomena such as globalization, disease, failed states, ethnic conflict, climate change, humanitarian disaster, and even nuclear weapons are not necessarily threats to US national security, unless they interact with and are taken up by specific groups of human beings in ways hostile to the United States.

Allies and Adversaries

Obama's special emphasis on international accommodation and retrenchment is certainly different from the approach of his predecessor George W. Bush, but all post–Cold War US presidents have been influenced by certain common and classically liberal US foreign policy assumptions. The classical liberal tradition in American foreign policy thinking suggests that multilateral organization, democracy promotion, and economic interdependence will render ancient ("nineteenth century") patterns of realist power politics irrelevant as the world progresses toward a more liberal international order. Francis Fukuyama famously described this sense of post–Cold War liberal progress as the "end of history."[17] All of the last three US presidents, whether intentionally or not, shared and acted upon some key aspect of this classical liberal assumption. For Bill Clinton, "democratic enlargement" meant that the US could expand a zone of friendly market democracies—at minimal expense—to promote international liberal ends. For George W. Bush, at least after 9/11, a Middle Eastern "freedom agenda" joined to a doctrine of preemptive military action would help undermine support for anti-American terrorism by expanding democratic governance within the Arab world. For Barack Obama, multilateral cooperation over liberal priorities would be promoted through international accommodation. Each of these presidential assumptions was powerfully influenced by some aspect of classical liberal US foreign policy thinking, and each turned out to have a vital blind spot. The classical liberal international tradition is not entirely wrong—in fact it perceives certain things that realism does not—but it also contains conceptual weaknesses that in practical terms can lead to dramatic foreign policy errors. All post–Cold War presidents, whether Democratic or Republican, have in one way or another been overly optimistic regarding prospects for what can only be called the classical liberal "end of history." Meanwhile, history has not ended. To be more specific: historically recognizable patterns of geopolitics, strategic competition, and international violence have not entirely disappeared. Nor have most of America's authoritarian adversaries and competitors disappeared over the past twenty years. Indeed, for some time now, numerous autocratic governments have proven able to adapt, survive, and defy US wishes internationally.[18] The answer is neither to give up and come home, nor to think that all such challenges can be suddenly blasted away—much less, lectured into reasonable accommodation—but to prepare for some steady, robust, long-term competition with a number of serious international adversaries. In other words, a clear understanding that history has not ended and is not about to end should inform a realistic grand strategy.[19]

This leads to a certain shift in emphasis. The bipartisan US tendency since the end of the Cold War has been to prioritize classically liberal goals of either democracy promotion or international accommodation, on the assumption of inevitable progress. Conservative American realism would recommend a rather different mindset, precisely to better defend existing democracies against serious current threats. The expansion of human rights and multilateral cooperation are each worthwhile foreign policy ends and will not be abandoned, but neither one can be the single starting point for American grand strategy in a competitive international environment. Instead—and particularly given the predilections of the Obama administration—there must be considerably greater weight placed on simply supporting America's allies and resisting its adversaries overseas in a coherent, robust way. If the United States cannot distinguish clearly between its friends and its enemies internationally—and then act meaningfully on that distinction—protestations of liberal ideals will not be especially useful, and the United States will suffer for it.

Allies

Many Americans in the Obama era, including possibly the president himself, seem to view the US alliance system overseas as a tiresome burden. Particular and understandable ire is directed by Congress and the public toward extremely difficult allies such as Pakistan. But to generalize from such frustrations is to miss the forest for the trees. Considered as a whole, America's global alliance portfolio is a remarkable asset. In fact, it is historically unprecedented. The United States stands at the hub of a worldwide integrated network of formal and informal alliances and partnerships, centered on the United States rather than on any other nation, that help lock in stable, peaceful, and prosperous relationships between dozens of countries. This network includes a majority of the world's leading economies, as well as most of its great democracies. No other major power, current or historical, has held an asset anything like this. To say that it serves American interests would be an understatement; to toss it away or ignore it would be imprudent in the extreme. President Obama has certainly not dismantled this American alliance system, but for all his emphasis on the value of diplomacy, international standing, and reputation, he has frequently neglected US alliance relationships and allowed them to erode.

It is the nature of alliance relationships to oscillate between fears of entrapment and abandonment. Abandonment refers to the fear of being left alone by one's ally. Entrapment refers to the fear of being pulled by an ally into an unwanted violent conflict.[20] Under President Obama, the United States regularly acts as if it fears entrapment above all else, whether in Eastern Europe, the Middle East, or the China Seas. American allies in those regions consequently fear abandonment. In the abstract, both fears can be useful if a proper balance is struck between them, but there also comes a time when the pendulum swings too far one way or the other, and this is the state of Washington's alliance relations today. US allies currently fear that America may abandon them, and the extent of that fear is neither healthy nor productive. The United States under Obama is overly preoccupied with avoiding entrapment on the part of its allies, to an extent that may actually encourage rather than discourage violent conflict. In relation to core allies such as NATO, Israel, and Japan, the United States will have to act to defend those allies in any case, should it come to that. But if Washington gives the impression of endless ambiva-lence or disengagement, this could lead to some very dangerous misunderstandings whereby authoritarian adversaries believe America will never act forcefully, when it fact it eventually will. Nor is this danger purely hypothetical; it has occurred repeatedly in American history. Allies fearful of US abandonment may also act in other unproductive ways. They may lash out assertively in a manner unwelcome to American interests. They may even try to accommodate US adversaries in some cases, for lack of other options.[21] Certainly, there is a need to strike a balance between the twin dangers of entrapment and abandonment, but that is not the balance being struck today. Multiple US allies have been deeply unnerved by the president's efforts to accommodate inter-national rivals and retrench American power, as by the striking disconnections between presidential statements and material follow-through. There is a compelling case for recalibration here.

Existing US allies need to be supported concretely; a president's promises have to be kept; and words need to be backed with action. In short, being an ally of the United States has to mean something. Otherwise, we can be sure that America will ultimately find itself with fewer and fewer allies in a much less friendly world.

Adversaries

National governments and nonstate actors that pursue adversarial behavior toward the United States can be pictured along a continuum. Some, like the government of China, pursue highly competitive and assertive policies within the strategic realm, but at the same time hold multiple common interests with America—economically, for example. In such cases, there is considerable room for negotiation and mutual gain, alongside serious competition. At the other end of the continuum, there are bitter and intractable enemies like al-Qaeda, actively at war with the United States, with whom negotiation is impossible. American strategies must be calibrated toward the nature of the adversary, not to mistake a competitor for an enemy or vice versa. At the same time, none of these should be mistaken for simple partners, allies, or friends.

Western liberal opinion tends to regularly ask whether international adversaries are defensive, realistic, and essentially reasonable, or ideological, aggressive, and irrational. Evidence of operational pragmatism is then chalked up to an essentially reasonable and therefore malleable nature. This is a false dichotomy and a profound misunderstanding of international politics. The United States faces plenty of authoritarian adversaries abroad that are entirely capable of tactical practicality, instrumental rationality, and even negotiated compromises in the long-term pursuit of unfriendly purposes. These tactical flexibilities and basic purposes are often informed by overarching ideological frameworks so alien to current Western opinion that the true danger is in our failing to grasp them altogether. For example, numerous leaders and supporters of Egypt's Muslim Brotherhood adhere to a vile anti-Semitism so intense and widespread that Western opinion hardly takes it seriously.[22] We should take it seriously. Governments and forces deeply hostile to the liberal Western world frequently tell us with remarkable candor the exact content of their ideologies, purposes, and resentments, if only we care to listen. And since such adversaries invariably and quite sincerely view themselves as being threatened by insidious American influence, it is not especially helpful to ask whether their own self-perception is defensive. Most of the great dictators of the twentieth century would have said the same thing. It is simply narcissistic to assume that a conciliatory gesture or a well-intentioned reassurance will necessarily alter the basic intentions and perceptions of international actors pursuing long-term goals. US adversaries have their own reasons for action, apart from anything Americans say or do. In short, the United States today faces a number of international adversaries that are very real. It should pay them the compliment of taking them seriously.

Strategies of Pressure

In relation to its adversaries and competitors, the United States should conceive, develop, and implement strategies of pressure. This will entail, among other things, reviving the art of deterrence and coercive diplomacy. During the Obama years, the United States has repeatedly faced situations in relation to the East and South China Seas, Iran, Iraq, Syria, and Ukraine, just to name a few such locations, where both allies and adversaries have come to doubt the credibility of US deterrent or compellent warnings. Part of the problem appears to lie in a basic misunderstanding as to what deterrence and compellence actually require. Deterrence involves the threat of force to prevent some adversary from taking an unwanted action or aggression. Coercive diplomacy—or compellence, as it is sometimes called—involves the threat of force to press some adversary into undoing an action it has already taken. Most serious studies of deterrence and compellence agree that both require, at a minimum, the believable threat of punishment in a way that means something to the target.[23] Specifically, the target of a compellent or deterrent warning must fear that the state issuing the warning—the United States, for example—truly intends to back up its threat with superior force at the relevant point. This is especially difficult when issues are at stake of much more apparent interest to the target government than to the United States, which is precisely why the United States should either demonstrate a serious interest or make no ill-considered threat in the first place. Threats cannot be issued and then forgotten, or only one-quarter implemented. This undermines the reputation of a country and its leader for seriousness in foreign affairs. A sense of clarity, specificity, and urgency also helps. Punishment and threatened costs gradually ramped up bit by bit in an uncertain or incoherent fashion tend to be much less impressive than clear, credible, decisive action. Given the inevitable fog of interstate communication, and against a common intuition, excessive subtlety or complexity in such matters can actually encourage confusion and misperception—and even lead to war. Certainly, coercive diplomacy can be successfully combined with positive incentives for desired international behavior. Put another way, carrots can be combined with sticks. But in the absence of genuine sticks—or more to the point, in the absence of a credible readiness to use them—the United States is unlikely to shape the foreign policy conduct of its real-world competitors and adversaries in a manner conducive to US interests. This is no less true in the twenty-first century than it was in previous ones.

More generally, the United States should build upon rather than erode its existing forward presence, and apply a wider variety of policy tools than it currently does to pressure, contain, and frustrate its leading challengers overseas through robust hybrid strategies. Presidents need to be able to draw upon and sensibly integrate a broad range of instruments including alliance relationships, foreign aid, trade agreements, economic sanctions, covert action, well-maintained intelligence capabilities, diplomatic assets, forward bases and deployments, and a thoroughly prepared armed forces to gain meaningful leverage against US adversaries. The aim should be to impose costs, intensify pressure, and gain leverage against these adversaries in regionally differentiated ways. Depending on the case, such intensified pressure need not necessarily involve the abandonment of economic and diplomatic engagement, or the embrace of regime change as a stated US policy goal. In the case of China, for example, the United States is going to continue to pursue extensive economic engagement and diplomatic bargaining under any likely approach, as well it should. In all cases, however, there should be a conceptual and material shift in American strategy away from Obama's overarching emphasis on retrenchment and accommodation, toward an intensification of pressure against US adversaries and competitors.

Great Power Competitors

We can count on rising and resurgent authoritarian great powers to be a continuing challenge to American statecraft. The impact of multilateral institutions and economic interdependence has not led great power competition to altogether disappear. Russia and China are both autocracies possessed of considerable material capabilities, keen national pride, and a determination to assert their influence regionally and geopolitically. The United States can work with each of these powers in certain issue areas. But strategic competition between Washington, Beijing, and Moscow will persist, requiring steady American diplomacy, strong regional alliances, and a forward military presence on the part of the United States.

With regard to *Russia*, that country's 2014 seizure of Crimea and intervention in Ukraine represents nothing less than an attack and dismemberment on the territory and integrity of a major European nation. This is part of a long-term pattern whereby Putin attempts to rebuild a Russian sphere of influence within nearby countries, by any means necessary. Thus far, the West's response has been inadequate. If Putin and Russia are not forced to pay a heavy price for such aggressions, then naturally they will continue, raising the risk of not only further Russian assertion but even dangerous misunderstanding and possible deterrence failure in relation to America's existing NATO allies in Central and Eastern Europe. The United States can do a great deal against these dangers, without placing major combat units directly inside Ukraine. Specifically, the United States should institute broader economic sanctions against key sectors of the Russian economy, including finance, mining, defense industries, oil, and gas; provide fresh military aid to the government of Ukraine, including antitank and antiaircraft weapons, joint exercises, intelligence and surveillance capabilities, training, and advice; support economic reforms and political stability inside Ukraine with increased material, financial, and technical support; release American oil and gas for export to Europe, to ease Europe's import needs; deploy significant new and permanent US air and ground forces to existing NATO allies in Poland and the Baltic states; institute regular additional military exercises with NATO allies in Central and

Eastern Europe; enhance allied air, ground, and cyber defenses in the same region; relocate significant NATO facilities eastward, while indicating the centrality of territorial defense as a NATO priority; halt the long-term drawdown of American forces from Europe; and reinvigorate the pursuit of US and allied missile defenses in the region. Ideally of course this should all be done in coordination with the European Union, but if America's European allies cannot act in concert, the United States must lead. This would at least impose genuinely heavy costs on Putin's regime and make him think twice before his next move. In fact, it would make dangerous misunderstandings with Moscow less likely, because it would clarify that America will not tolerate incremental aggression against existing NATO allies in Central and Eastern Europe—allies it is bound to defend in any event.[24]

Beyond the issue of Crimea-Ukraine, the United States should institute hybrid strategies of pressure against Moscow to deter further aggression, impose costs on Putin's regime, support US allies, and protect American interests around Russia's perimeter. Clearly, Obama's attempted accommodation of Russia under the "reset" did not work; it contained too many carrots and not enough sticks. Even Obama may now realize this, although he would never admit it, but his subsequent temptation may be to walk away rather than institute vigorous competitive policies in relation to the Putin regime.[25] The United States should not simply disengage from Russia and its neighbors. A more realistic American strategy with regard to Putin's Russia would combine straightforward, hard bargaining in limited areas with significantly bolstered containment, balancing, and deterrence on a range of locations and dimensions. This more hard-nosed approach can still exist alongside long-term hopes for a more liberal Russia, but such hopes do not constitute a strategy, and they do not help us move toward that future goal. Insofar as

Russian politics contains liberal forces, however weak, they are not strengthened by either accommodating or ignoring the Putin regime. Putin's Russia is in fact engaged in a competition for influence with the United States and its allies in key regions including Eastern Europe, with implications for the success of democracy as well as multiple American interests throughout such regions. Much greater emphasis must therefore be placed on deterring, containing, and balancing Russian power assertions in a meaningful, credible manner within the former Soviet Union and beyond. The US aim should be the nurturance and protection of friendly and if possible market-oriented democracies, rather than dysfunctional autocracies integrated into a Moscow-centered "Eurasian Union" around Russia's vast circumference. Historical experience suggests that strategic vacuums in Central and Eastern Europe, in particular, are preferably filled by Western rather than Russian influence—and better filled than allowed to destabilize. The United States should and will continue to work with Moscow in a businesslike fashion on a number of issues including Afghanistan, counterterrorism, and nuclear nonproliferation, but the United States should stop operating under the assumption that generous accommodation toward Russia in any of these or other areas will lead to broader cooperation from the Putin government, because the record shows it will not. However lacking in global capacities, Putin's Russia is a serious competitor and must be treated as such. As James Sherr, the former head of the Russia and Eurasia Program at London's Chatham House, says of Moscow's foreign policy: "Partners, competitors and opponents who are ill-prepared for hyper-competition are at risk of being outmaneuvered, irrespective of the wealth, power or technology at their disposal. Those who believe that the West faces a choice between 'partnership' and 'confrontation' with Russia will be outmaneuvered systematically."[26]

In relation to *China*, the United States faces the likely prospect of a long-term peaceful strategic competition with a well-financed and sophisticated rival—less openly aggressive than Russia, but on balance more challenging. The first task is for Americans to realize that such a competition is already underway. Despite a fascinating variety of internal debates and pragmatic tactical adjustments, China's government has been perfectly capable for many years now of promoting the expansion of Chinese economic, political, and military power relative to the United States. Only when China's maritime assertions overreached strategically, during the early years of the Obama presidency, did Beijing unintentionally push a number of regional powers back toward the United States. With the American "pivot" to Asia, President Obama rightly declared a bolstered US presence in the region. Yet today there are profound doubts about the substance, constancy, and reliability of this presence. Under Obama, even with the pivot, the United States has clearly retrenched, placing considerable emphasis on reassuring and accommodating China. On a wide range of issues of great concern to Washington however, China has not been especially helpful. The US desire for cooperation and accommodation with Beijing has reaped surprisingly few concrete policy rewards. Obama has generally had his greatest success in the region when he has embraced policies of strategic balancing and deterrence. America's China policy should therefore be recalibrated. The United States should place greater emphasis on deterring China and reassuring US allies, rather than the reverse. While Beijing may not like it, this will actually lead to a reduced chance of deterrence failure arising from Chinese misperceptions of American weakness or disengagement. Rather than emphasizing legalistically that it takes no partial stance on maritime disputes between China and its neighbors, the United States should make it quite clear that it supports its own allies and will not tolerate regional aggression. Washington will continue to engage Beijing diplomatically and economically in any case, but the current need is for an adjustment in the direction of strengthened, believable, and convincing US balancing and deterrence, as opposed to mixed messages or sporadic detachment.

It is time to disabuse ourselves of the notion that simply trading with, investing in, and cooperating with China will necessarily liberalize that country's political system. This has been a central premise of US policy for a quarter-century, and the promised political liberalization has not occurred. Meanwhile, China has only grown stronger, with its one-party dictatorship intact. The United States cannot and will not try to isolate China from the global economy, as it once did with the Soviet Union; levels of economic interdependence with China are much too high for that. Still, the United States can and should pursue a more energetic and focused strategy of pressure, power balancing, and deterrence in relation to Beijing, in order both to support US allies and to bolster America's relative position within the Asia-Pacific. Specifically, the United States should strengthen US military capabilities in the region, invest significant political capital in completing the Trans-Pacific Partnership trade agreement, back regional allies and security partners more consistently, support Japan's growing regional security role, and encourage greater security cooperation between South Korea and Japan. The United States should further coordinate arms sales and defense industrial cooperation among allies to develop complementary capabilities, assist those allies to better protect their own air and sea spaces, implement export controls on American technologies useful to China's military, and explore options for additional basing or access arrangements in the Asia-Pacific. Finally, the United States should allocate additional military resources and investments to meet the increased security challenges of the region, field credible ballistic missile defenses against the full range of threats, and work with Asia-Pacific partners to create regional institutions that promote the above goals. Given that President Obama himself has already declared his verbal commitment to several of these proposals, the challenge is not so much in listing as in following through on them. The United States has announced a fresh interest in the Asia-Pacific. Now it actually needs to back that up more persuasively. For several years, popular and elite discussion of China's rise versus America's relative decline has been characterized by a kind of smothering defeatism. China is an impressive power, but it has its vulnerabilities, and the United States possesses a wide range of counterbalancing policy instruments if it chooses to use them. Nobody, including the Chinese, wants a Sino-American competition to turn violent. But the best way to prevent that, and at the same time secure a peaceful and free order within the Asia-Pacific, is to make it clear to Beijing that Washington is in earnest about maintaining its commitments in the region.[27]

Rogue State Adversaries

American strategy toward *Iran* needs to start from a clear recognition of the country's current regime and its foreign policy implications. Specific Iranian leaders like President Rouhani may be skillful tactical negotiators, but they are part of an Islamist dictatorship that is basically a determined and bitter adversary toward the United States and its allies within the Middle East and beyond. In recent years Tehran has supported terrorism in multiple countries around the globe, consistently lied about the nature of its nuclear weapon ambitions, plotted assassination attempts on American soil, and helped kill US troops in Iraq and Afghanistan. In fact the current regime holds a violent anti-Americanism as one of its founding tenets. To be sure, some of Iran's leaders such as Rouhani have proven capable of pursuing all of these ends in operationally flexible ways. Still, this regime is not about to become a cooperative partner in US designs for a benign regional security architecture, and American strategy should not be based on that false hope.

Economic sanctions and limited covert action have had some real impact on Iran's nuclear program in recent years, but because President Obama underestimates the depth of Tehran's hostility toward the United States—and because he has very limited appetite for any further measures—this existing pressure is at risk of being thrown away for token and inadequate concessions on the part of Iran. The United States need hardly abstain from diplomacy with Tehran altogether, but such diplomacy must be aimed at securing worthwhile agreements in the American interest rather than agreements for their own sake. As of 2014, there was a very real danger the Obama administration would accept an agreement with Tehran that essentially lifted economic sanctions and locked in Iran's nascent nuclear weapons capacity with official American approval. However well intentioned, there is no need for the United States to sign any such agreement; it would only strengthen the current regime and preserve its core nuclear weapon ambitions intact.

Historically, the mullahs of Tehran have been willing to concede on central diplomatic issues only when they operated under genuine fear of external force. American airstrikes against Iran would certainly constitute a fateful step, the full consequences of which include risks and costs both seen and unforeseen. There are intelligent arguments both for and against such strikes.[28] But in order for current efforts at coercive diplomacy to work, by definition, Iran's leaders must believe that devastating US airstrikes are a real possibility. In truth, today these leaders live in relatively little fear of the United States and its president. For this very reason, any American strategy aimed at divesting Tehran of its nuclear weapons program must carry far greater coercive pressure. Any serious US strategy must also comprehend the full range of Tehran's international aggression and push back against it, rather than self-limiting to the nuclear issue alone.

Tehran works actively to promote violence and instability, further Iranian interests, and counter American ones in Syria, Lebanon, Iraq, the Persian Gulf, and Palestinian territories. The United States could do considerably more to counteract this, with sophisticated, multidimensional, and competitive efforts of its own. It could adopt a much more comprehensive and well-coordinated strategy aimed at pressuring and frustrating the government in Tehran on multiple fronts. This could, for example, include a bolstered US deterrent in the region; fresh naval exercises, military coordination, and enhanced intelligence sharing with American allies; effective, strengthened theater missile defenses in Europe; and a more regular US carrier task force presence in and around the eastern Mediterranean and Persian Gulf. It could also involve foreign aid redirected to strategic ends; intensified economic sanctions, fully enforced; and increased covert action along with better intelligence gathering inside Iran itself.[29] American diplomacy in the region should work outward from US alliances, rather than frightening allies by going over their heads in an effort to accommodate Tehran. The focus should be on reassuring American allies, rather than reassuring Tehran. Both Iran and US allies need to understand and believe that the United States is not abandoning the Middle East. The region is certainly a frustrating one for Americans. It will be even more frustrating and dangerous if the belief continues to spread that US allies are not supported and US adversaries not resisted.

The United States can and should develop a more competitive, integrated strategy to pressure, deter, and impose costs upon the government of Iran, not only to secure genuine concessions on the nuclear issue, but also to take back the initiative regionally from a serious hostile power. Since the current Iranian regime is by its own design a US adversary, there is minimal tension between America's democracy agenda and its security agenda in this case. The United States has little to lose by highlighting human rights abuses inside Iran and by supporting the aspirations of Tehran's pro-democracy domestic opposition, such as it is. Drawing attention to Iran's human rights abuses is another way of pressuring the regime and of keeping faith with dissidents inside that country.

With regard to *North Korea*, the Obama administration offered diplomatic outreach, only to be energetically rebuffed. The administration then settled on a default policy of "strategic patience"—essentially, containing North Korea, and refusing to offer further concessions until Pyongyang first lives up to prior obligations. This policy at least has the advantage of avoiding further extracted concessions followed by predictably broken promises on North Korea's part. Yet strategic patience in this case has its own dangers as well. The hope after 2011 within the Obama administration was that Pyongyang's new ruler, Kim Jong-un, would steer North Korea away from weapons of mass destruction and toward domestic economic reforms. As it turns out, Kim has done the opposite, while imposing his domestic political supremacy ruthlessly. North Korea continues to work on the development of nuclear-tipped ICBMs (intercontinental ballistic missiles) capable of reaching the mainland United States.[30] Thus far, the North has been deterred from another major attack southward since the ceasefire of 1953, but it is not clear that it will be deterred forever. Kim and his surrounding circle may not understand that they do not have a reliable second-strike nuclear capability against the

United States. They may believe or come to believe that they possess massive coercive leverage against the United States and its allies—and they may choose to use it. Deterrence may fail. Indeed on a certain level it already has, if we consider Pyongyang's repeated violent aggressions and nuclear and missile tests against multiple American warnings.[31]

According to Georgetown University professor Victor Cha, director for Asian Affairs at the National Security Council from 2004 to 2007, what North Korea really wants is not a grand bargain whereby it denuclearizes in exchange for a range of economic and security benefits, but potentially a grand bargain whereby Pyongyang receives the following: continued possession of nuclear weapons; a wide range of economic and security benefits, including strategic assurances from the United States; equal recognition by Washington as a legitimate nuclear weapons state; and active American support in the continuation of the current regime.[32] In other words, Pyongyang wants an astonishingly one-sided and from an American perspective unappealing deal that no US president including Obama can or will accept. Yet the North may press for such a deal with continual threats, triggering repeat crises that carry with them deliberately escalated risk. For this reason, strategic patience by itself is inadequate; it simply allows Kim to become ever more bold and demanding.

Strategic patience as currently implemented also downplays the sheer barbarity and inhumanity of the North Korean regime internally, which even by hardened norms of international realpolitik ought to shock the world's conscience. Pyongyang maintains a massive system of work camps in which hundreds of thousands of prisoners are tortured and killed with arbitrary depravity. The United Nations has rightly singled out North Korea as uniquely awful even by authoritarian standards.[33] The government of

North Korea is essentially a gigantic money-laundering operation and international protection racket, run in the narrow interests of the Kim family and its elite supporters, at the expense of the elementary freedom, prosperity, or basic dignity of its ordinary citizens. The contrast with South Korea—a flourishing and democratic US ally—is very striking, especially since the two Koreas possess a common culture. Nor is the totalitarian nature of the North Korean government completely unrelated to its foreign policy. As long as this highly artificial Stalinist dictatorship exists, it will continue to be a vexing challenge to the United States and its allies—arming, extorting, and threatening when it can. In simple human terms, North Korea is an appalling disaster. The United States need not be reticent in powerfully condemning Pyongyang's constant outrages against the most basic conceptions of human dignity.[34]

The Obama administration has really developed no satisfactory answer to the challenge of North Korea. Indeed there is no easy answer. There is, however, the possibility of a more carefully calibrated and tightly focused strategy designed to pressure and deter Pyongyang while avoiding the very worst dangers. Managing the North Korean security challenge is for Washington a constant tightrope walk. The United States should of course be very careful not to take actions that might trigger another Korean war. Such a war could easily result in the death of hundreds of thousands of innocent civilians, both north and south of the demilitarized zone. A preventive strike against North Korea's nuclear weapons program obviously carries that precise danger. Even an openly stated US policy of regime change could conceivably encourage Pyongyang to lash out in desperate fashion. Yet the equal, parallel danger is that North Korea's rulers may think they can proceed unimpeded with continually greater aggressions, because of a perceived weakness in America's deterrent posture—and that seems to be the current risk.

The primary imperative is for any US president to realize that getting America's North Korea strategy exactly right is quite literally a matter of life and death, deserving close and careful attention. If Washington gives more teeth to its declared Asia pivot, this will help deter North Korea as well as China. The United States could improve security cooperation with South Korea and Japan; bolster America's naval presence in the region; strengthen US national and theater missile defenses; and enhance the defense capabilities of proximate US allies. Pyongyang is best deterred by robust US preparations, alliances, capabilities, and commitments that are crystal clear rather than the least bit uncertain. Beyond that, an American strategy of pressure should aim to weaken, frustrate, and erode North Korea's aggressive capabilities—not just contain them. An intensification and fuller enforcement of international financial sanctions, to which the North's shadow economy is vulnerable, is definitely in order. The US government also needs to pay greater attention to how the United States, South Korea, and China would each respond were the government of North Korea to collapse. China prefers to maintain North Korea as a buffer state. But this dysfunctional regime cannot last forever, and it is imperative that Beijing and Washington avoid open conflict should such a collapse occur. The United States could privately offer, for example, not to station American forces in the north—a clear Chinese concern—in order to reassure Beijing over some possible consequences of Pyongyang's collapse. The Kim regime has already lasted decades longer than many expected; it may last decades more. The United States should certainly strengthen its deterrent posture versus North Korea, and work more energetically to pressure the regime against advancing with weapons of mass destruction. An explicit policy of rollback or regime change is not actually necessary. Still, the implicit long-term American goal here can only be the peaceful unification of the Korean peninsula under a democratic and friendly government. There is no other long-term solution.[35]

Jihadist Terrorists

President Obama suggests that al-Qaeda is now on the path to defeat, with only isolated local extremists left outside of a wrecked Pakistani-Afghan core. The most generous thing that can be said of this assessment is that it is seriously flawed. When Obama became president, he inherited an active American war against a transnational network of jihadist terrorists, or more properly, a war declared and waged by these terrorists against the United States several years before 2001. Initially, Obama appeared to believe that declaring this war to be over, or calling it something different—for example, by expunging words like "Islamist" or "jihadist" from key documents including the 2010 Quadrennial Defense Review—would actually help end it successfully.[36] As it turned out, al-Qaeda and likeminded associates felt the war should continue. The president soon shifted toward a counterterror approach more reminiscent of George W. Bush's than anyone would have expected. Still, by his own indication Obama continues to be torn between robust counterterror measures on the one hand, and his incoming assumptions—along with shifting domestic political winds—on the other. As in so many other national security issue areas, this sense of presidential ambivalence has encouraged a number of policy errors, flowing from a misunderstanding of the genuine danger.

Al-Qaeda is and has long been an adaptable, resilient, transnational network of jihadist terrorist groups able to collaborate with one another as well as with local criminals, Islamist nationalists, and tribal leaders. There are certainly multiple doctrinal and organizational disputes within al-Qaeda's decentralized network, but a refusal to admit their common ideology and frequent co-ordination is not especially helpful in grasping the extent of the threat. Documents captured from the 2011 bin Laden raid reveal that al-Qaeda's former leader still provided some practical guidance, inspiration, and direction to regional associates long after his ejection from Afghanistan.[37] The fact that he was often frustrated with these associates hardly means they maintained no connection. Indeed bin Laden sometimes urged local militants not to use al-Qaeda's name, in order to avoid drawing Western attention. This would seem to recommend against an exclusive US focus against only those groups who have openly declared their allegiance to al-Qaeda.[38] Indications are that bin Laden's successor, Ayman al-Zawahiri, tries to play a similar helpful role in relation to allied militants. Al-Qaeda's many affiliates and associates often aid one another in practical ways, for example with weapons, fighters, advice, and funding, and work to win over local Islamists to the cause of transnational jihadist terrorism. The spectacular rise of these regional associates and affiliates means that both the United States and al-Qaeda operate in a different environment than they did a few years ago. If anything, jihadist terrorists have taken advantage of the disorder engendered by the Arab Spring to expand their operations across remarkably large tracts of North Africa and the Middle East. From the group's own point of view, a plausible case can be made that al-Qaeda is gaining rather than losing right now in its long-term struggle against the United States; the jihadist ideology is robust, and its geographic influence wider than ever. Ironically, the single greatest challenge to al-Qaeda today may be ultra-aggressive splinter groups such as the Islamic State of Iraq and Syria (ISIS). With any luck these groups might undermine one another, but this is hardly an excuse for complacency since all of them are violently hostile toward the United States and its allies. Indeed their competition for new recruits may lead jihadist terrorists to engage in ever more dramatic attacks against Western targets.

Working from this more realistic understanding of the continuing threat, the United States should develop strategies of intensified pressure against jihadist terrorists. This need not involve major American combat units or "boots on the ground" all or even most of the time, but it cannot rely so overwhelmingly on drones. An intensified, multidimensional strategy of pressure against al-Qaeda and ISIS must include financial sanctions, advisory and training support to partner governments, technical assistance, special operations, drones, detective work, intelligence capabilities, improved homeland security, cooperation with allies, and on occasion direct military action. To be sure, the Obama administration has done some of this, partly by preserving much of the counterterrorism infrastructure built up during the Bush years, and consequently has had some important operational successes including the strike against bin Laden. But because President Obama still works from a mistaken understanding of jihadist terrorism in its full aspect, he frequently transmits an approach that is halfhearted rather than appropriately Carthaginian. According to their own words, al-Qaeda and like-minded groups seek to violently expunge Western influence from the Muslim world, topple secular governments, establish a series of ministates culminating in a transnational Islamic caliphate, retake historically Muslim lands, acquire weapons of mass destruction, and kill millions of Americans. It is a grave mistake to believe that such deadly and implacable foes can be effectively combated by simply declaring that various wars have ended, blaming previous American presidents, or instructing Muslims on the true nature of their own religion. There is no need for the United States to apologize for past policies in fighting such a murderous and persistent enemy. The disciplining question within each regional context should simply be this: how can the United States work more effectively to undermine, frustrate, and disrupt jihadist terrorists? This would imply, for example, not abandoning Iraq in its counterterror efforts; a clear commitment to a continuing US base presence in Afghanistan; increased security assistance to Libya's new government; aiding whatever moderate forces still exist within Syria's opposition; and greater cooperation with Egypt's government against jihadist militants. It would imply calling terrorist attacks what they are, rather than downplaying their significance or blaming them on Western Internet videos. It would also imply supporting America's intelligence services, rather than castigating and undermining them in their struggle against terrorism when it becomes politically convenient to do so.[39]

President Obama complains that the very counterterror effort he leads risks turning into a "perpetual war."[40] This is a strange statement for an existing commander in chief, since the responsibility is his, and it reveals a backward understanding of the issue. It is the terrorists, not the United States, that desire perpetual war, and that have demonstrated a willingness to wage it. The only answer for Americans is to show members of ISIS and al-Qaeda in the most forceful way that their perpetual war will not succeed. It has become fashionable to say that jihadist terrorism cannot be defeated, it can only be managed or contained. But suicide bombers seeking death cannot really be contained. It was precisely the insight of diplomat George Kennan—the author of containment—that Communism could be contained because Communists were not suicidal. Groups like al-Qaeda are a different sort of challenge, and with them there can truly be no negotiation, compromise, or even containment. If jihadist terrorists are not preempted, they will continue to pursue mass casualty attacks against innocent civilians including Americans. The nature of this particular enemy leaves no superior alternative other than an assertive and determined strategy of rollback. President Clinton's counterterrorism expert Richard Clarke said it best during the late 1990s: "Al Qaeda delenda est."[41]

Defense Spending

Carefully implemented strategies of pressure, along the lines sketched out above, will require some increase in US defense spending. This is not primarily in order to entertain new interventions overseas, but rather to reduce risks, deter a range of adversaries, reassure American allies, and if it comes to that, win any wars the United States must fight as quickly and as capably as possible. In fact, as all four of President Obama's own secretaries of defense have stated, under sequestration American defense expenditures are inadequate to meet existing international commitments—much less any new ones.

US defense spending is sometimes described by its critics as impossibly high and even overwhelming. Of course, from a military point of view, the whole point is to be overwhelming—that is what prevents wars in the first place, and then wins them if necessary. In absolute terms of course, the United States spends a great deal on defense, but the numbers need to be put into proportion, both in relation to America's economy as a whole and to what is gained from defense. US defense spending is on track to drop toward a little over 3% of GDP by 2016.[42] Turned on its head, this means that 97% of America's wealth is spent on goods and services other than national defense. Or to put it another way, Americans spend considerably more on junk food each year than on the US military.

Under President Obama, national defense has already taken more than its share of budget cuts. In 2009–2010, Secretary of Defense Gates implemented a number of cuts in US defense expenditures amounting to hundreds of billions of dollars, even as domestic spending skyrocketed.[43] Beginning in 2011, under the Budget Control Act and subsequent process of sequestration, national defense was cut by roughly one trillion dollars over a period of ten years—half of all the federal spending cuts envisioned, even though defense is now less than 20% of the annual federal budget. Fiscal conservatives agree that defense spending should be scrutinized in the same way as every other category of federal expenditure. But from a conservative point of view, national defense is not quite like every other imaginable category. National defense is and has always been basic to the functioning of a limited and effective government, as specified within the US Constitution. Many other current categories of expenditure do not meet this criterion.

There are certainly specific areas where defense spending can and should be cut. Payroll and benefits, in particular, threaten to eat up the rest of the defense budget if left unaddressed.[44] But in terms of major weapons systems, research and development, modernization, procurement, and the falling numbers of troops within each of the US armed services, overall cuts since 2011 must be reversed. Looking forward, the United States should maintain and spend something closer to 4% than 3% of GDP on defense. Four cents out of every dollar is not too much to spend in order to preserve an international system friendly to US interests. This level of spending is what would be required simply to close the current gap between America's military capabilities and its existing overseas commitments—a gap that if left unaddressed will eventually invite aggression and humiliation.

Current levels of falling US defense expenditure are not inevitable. They are a choice, made for reasons of policy and political priority by members of both major parties. The long-term pattern over the past half-century is that domestic spending rises while defense spending falls as a percentage of both federal expenditure and gross domestic product.[45] To suggest that America's long-term problem of national debt can be solved simply by slashing defense is consequently false. The rising costs of domestic entitlement programs including Social Security, Medicare, and Medicaid will continue to drive up higher levels of debt, even if defense is cut to the very bone. It is domestic spending that has spiraled upward under the Obama administration, and that will continue to rise, as long as domestic entitlement programs are unreformed. There is no sign that the mounting cost of these entitlements will ever be curbed or addressed by President Obama. Indeed, constantly rising domestic expenditures appear to be central to his vision of the federal government's proper role in American life. Any serious attempt to address entitlement spending and to restore national defense will have to await a different president.

Trade Policy

Ever since the 1940s, the United States has pursued a measured overall policy of promoting international trade. Economists confirm that free trade promotes American innovation, jobs, and exports and mutual economic gain between countries. It furthermore reduces poverty overseas, contrary to popular impression. But trade agreements can also promote strategic and geopolitical benefits such as strengthening US allies. The one caveat here is that trade with allies must be distinguished from trade with adversaries. The former has multiple benefits beyond the strictly economic; the latter contains risks that should be factored into any genuinely strategic foreign policy approach. An underlying premise of US trade policy since World War II has been that freer trade internationally not only brings material benefits to Americans, but that it also supports a more open international order friendly to the United States. On this premise, the United States helped create the General Agreement on Tariffs and Trade—later renamed the World Trade Organization (WTO)—to reduce barriers on international trade. In 2001, the WTO began the Doha Round of negotiations, which soon stalled because of intractable differences in position between emerging and established economies. President Bush responded by pursuing a range of bilateral and regional US trade agreements with American allies and partners in the Middle East, Latin America, and the Asia-Pacific. In the abstract, progress on worldwide negotiations through the WTO would be ideal, but in practice because of the stalled Doha Round the true choice for over a decade now has been either an assortment of bilateral and regional trading arrangements, or nothing at all. Bush was therefore quite right to pursue this new course, and Republicans have traditionally provided the lion's share of congressional support for new trade agreements.

Free trade is not an easy sell in domestic political terms. Compared to most foreign policy issues, opposition to free trade tends to be vocal, well organized, and intense. The politics of US trade policy are that export-oriented interest groups organize in favor, while import-competing groups mobilize against. Additionally, organized labor and environmentalist groups at the base of the Democratic Party are today powerful voices against new free trade arrangements. Politically it is always easier to point to the supposed costs of free trade, which tend to be concentrated and dramatic, than to the long-term benefits for American consumers and taxpayers as a whole. Nevertheless, Congress has sometimes shown admirable self-restraint in resisting the temptations of protectionism, for example in approving Trade Promotion Authority, or "fast track," by which the president is empowered to negotiate and present commercial treaties to the legislature for a simple up or down vote. Fast track lapsed in 2007 and will probably be essential to securing passage of any new trade agreements. Senate majority leader Harry Reid (D-NV) clarified his opposition to renewing the president's fast-track authority early in 2014. This left the achievement of fresh US trade initiatives much more difficult by far.

Trade policy under Obama has followed a rather surprising path. When he first ran for president, Obama was distinctly unenthusiastic about numerous free trade agreements. He has never been willing to invest too much political capital in such agreements. Nevertheless, to its credit the Obama administration has in fact completed and initiated some very important free trade initiatives. First, after considerable delay, in 2011 it oversaw the passage through Congress of three US trade agreements— with Panama, Colombia, and South Korea—initially signed and negotiated under President Bush. The latter two agreements, in particular, were hardly uncontroversial, and it took some work to get them ratified. Second, the administration took up the case for two very sweeping regional trade initiatives with US allies and partners in Europe and the Asia-Pacific: the Transatlantic Trade and Investment Partnership (T-TIP) and Trans-Pacific Partnership (TPP), respectively. The latter initiative in particular has the potential to serve American goals in the Asia-Pacific by bolstering US alliances and tugging the region outside of China in an economically liberal direction. Both regional agreements, together with trade promotion authority, serve broad US interests and deserve conservative Republican support. They also deserve an investment of the president's political capital, along with some significant congressional backing from his own party.[46]

The Lessons of Iraq

US foreign policy is now in its post-Iraq era. To be more precise, US grand strategy under President Obama operates under the assumption of several important historical lessons learned from America's wartime experience in Iraq. We know from political psychology that foreign policy decision-makers past and present tend to operate under such assumptions, analogies, or "lessons of history." We also know that such lessons and analogies tend to be overly simplistic, badly drawn, and not infrequently the source of their own distinctive mistakes.[47] For example, when the 1938 Munich conference is compared to every single negotiation internationally, this is not especially helpful. Similarly, the historical pattern is that after very frustrating wartime experiences, Americans say "never again": no more Vietnams, no more Koreas, no more great power wars in Europe, and so on. What this implies, however, is debatable, since events are never quite repeated, and historical lessons are open to competing interpretations. Today, the injunction is clear: no more Iraqs. But what exactly does this imply?

For President Obama, the lessons of the Iraq war are several, even though for the most part they simply confirm his preexisting foreign policy assumptions dating back several years. Obama obviously interprets America's experience in Iraq as overwhelming evidence that the United States should take great care to avoid major military interventions overseas. According to his own words, he feels the United States should focus on domestic needs, avert international confrontation if possible, and wrap up existing wars; it should beware of entangling commitments or slippery slopes that might lead to heavier direct involvement in violent foreign conflict. And if and when the United States must intervene militarily abroad, it should do as lightly, as multilaterally, and as temporarily as possible. This at least is what the president believes. And to be fair, a significant percentage of the American public feels exactly the same way. Even for many Americans skeptical of his overall policy vision, a great number right now share Obama's desire to avoid US involvement in military conflict overseas.

Some of Obama's lessons from Iraq are quite right. A president really should take great care before sending America's armed forces into combat. The question then is whether Obama has actually done this—and whether he has supplemented this sense of care with an also necessary sense of decision and determination. Unfortunately, the answer has often been no. The particular way in which Obama draws lessons from Iraq has encouraged a number of persistent problems in his management of American grand strategy. It has, for example, led him to see multiple new cases of international conflict as very much akin to Iraq, when really they are not. It has frequently blinded him to the many US foreign policy instruments that exist between major ground interventions and doing very little, for fear of "another Iraq." It has more than once allowed the term "multilateralism" to become an excuse for American inaction, since genuinely multilateral solutions to leading international problems are not always possible. It has often prevented him from seeing that retrenchment and accommodation can be taken as signs of weakness rather than benevolent self-restraint. And it has played havoc with several half-hearted efforts to create believable US deterrent threats.

When armed force is used, or even threatened in defense of existing allies, it must be done with sufficient credibility and assertion so as to secure the desired purpose. Anything else is positively irresponsible in relation to such deadly weapons. Successful deterrence requires a believable willingness to fight, and when force is finally employed, however reluctantly, it should be used in a robust and decisive way. Obama seems to have little instinctive feeling for these particular military and strategic realities. Instead, he sincerely interprets his responsibility as being to use as little force as possible, as incrementally as possible, even in support of his own declared international commitments. This is not necessarily the most responsible course. Excessive gradualism, quasi-detachment, and semi-disengagement can actually prolong violent conflict, unnerve US allies, reduce American leverage, and create international power vacuums filled by authoritarian forces. To be sure, Obama is not the only one to have drawn the wrong lessons from Iraq. But since he is currently president, the consequences following from these mistaken lessons loom especially large.

When President George W. Bush authorized the 2003 invasion of Iraq, he did so with far too little preparation toward foreseeable complications of postwar occupation, counterinsurgency, and stability operations. Indeed one of the most compelling arguments made by many of Bush's Democratic Party critics—often made in retrospect—was that the United States should have sent more troops into Iraq from the very start, with better preparation for all possible contingencies. Even many Republicans now admit this mistake in initial Iraq war planning. Now there are two possible "lessons" that might be drawn from this mistake. One is that the United States should never again go to war overseas. The other is that if and when it does go to war, it should do so with much more serious and realistic forethought and preparation. The second lesson is at least as plausible as the first, but many including President Obama seem reluctant to draw and then act upon the obvious policy implication, even when they criticize Bush for the very same error. The obvious policy implication is that when American military intervention is finally deemed necessary, it should be undertaken with adequate determination and seriousness of purpose so as to get it right. Ironically, it was Bush himself that finally demonstrated this kind of determination in 2007, after several years of excruciating frustrations, when he authorized a new surge strategy that helped turn around the course of the war in Iraq. President Obama has never really transmitted this kind of wholehearted commitment to any of the US military engagements he has overseen, even with regard to those he initiated himself.

The lessons of Iraq are powerful, but they are not exactly the ones Obama thinks. As noted by former secretary of defense Gates, the United States has never been especially good at predicting future wars.[48] We cannot simply say, as the Obama administration's 2012 defense guidance says, that America will no longer plan for major stability operations overseas. US adversaries may not be so obliging as to go along with our plans. Unexpected events occur internationally, and the United States needs to be prepared for a variety of possible contingencies. It needs to maintain a robust, balanced range of military capabilities to meet these contingencies. We can hardly assume that counterinsurgency, stability operations, military land campaigns, or "boots on the ground" are practical impossibilities just because they are currently unwanted or unpopular. The United States will not avoid difficult military operations simply because it refuses to plan for them. President Obama, for example, did not plan to attack Libya when he first entered the Oval Office. Similarly, Bush did not expect to invade Iraq when he first ran for president, any more than Bill Clinton expected to forcibly liberate Kosovo from Serbian rule. Clearly, every recent US president has encountered some felt necessity, once in office, to use force abroad in ways he did not originally anticipate. The real question is not whether some future US presidents will engage in military intervention. The odds are, they will. The real question is whether American intervention will be undertaken with the kind of wisdom and competence appropriate to matters of life and death. That—and not an overpowering sense of indecision—would be a good lesson to draw from Iraq.

In sum, a conservative American realism would differ from both the Obama doctrine and the Bush doctrine in significant ways. It would differ from the Obama doctrine in emphasizing credible deterrence and robust strategies of pressure against clearly identified US adversaries, rather than spasmodic retrenchment, ill-fated accommodation, and autobiographical complacency. The United States should distinguish clearly between America's friends and its enemies, supporting its friends and resisting its enemies with a full array of policy tools. Diplomatically, it should work from traditional alliances outward rather than the other way around, and back its warnings with force rather than issuing toothless declarations. There is no reason to be halfhearted in protecting the essence of American primacy, status, and influence internationally. In all of these ways, as well as in its domestic priorities, a strategy based upon conservative American realism would differ from the Obama doctrine. At the same time, a strategy based upon conservative American realism would differ in important ways from the approach pursued by President George W. Bush. Specifically, there is no need for the United States to announce that a doctrine of regime change via preventive warfare lies at the heart of its foreign policy. A president's right to preempt deadly attacks can really be taken for granted. The practical question is when and how to use force wisely. Bungled US interventions only discredit American foreign policy and undermine a president's domestic agenda. In relation to most US adversaries apart from al-Qaeda, the baseline preference should be peace through strength, assertive containment, and strategies of exhaustion and attrition. Direct military intervention should only be undertaken after great care and consideration—and then, with full capability and decision. Here is where an attitude adjustment is in order since the end of the Cold War, of greater skepticism toward supposedly transformational foreign policy approaches of any kind. The great challenge today is not to reorder a US-led international order, but simply to defend it—and this President Obama is not doing with adequate realism or vigilance. Americans should expect to engage in some long-term competition with a variety of bold adversarial forces overseas. These adversaries will not be quickly transformed simply through presidential rhetoric, attempted accommodation, human rights promotion, or American disengagement. But by tapping into its underlying strengths and following tough-minded strategies under effective leadership, the United States will outlast and eventually prevail over these adversaries, just as it always has before.

Presidential Leadership

Both scholarly and journalistic commentary often assumes that the many structural, economic, bureaucratic, and domestic political forces behind American foreign policy are so overwhelming that presidents have no genuine room for maneuver. Certainly this is a common rationale for incoherent, failing, or undesirable policies. Yet close observation reveals that presidents have considerable leeway to make strategic international policy decisions, when they choose to do so. In the modern era, the US foreign policy apparatus is essentially president-centered. It can hardly be otherwise. Presidents are head of state, commander in chief, and party leader. No other individual is truly able or empowered to weigh, judge, and act upon conflicting domestic and international priorities on behalf of the national interest. In bureaucratic terms, when it comes to foreign policy the president is not simply one player among many. Rather, to a great extent it is the president who determines the relative influence of the other bureaucratic players, including the secretary of state. Similarly, while Congress has a vital and constitutional role to play in the formulation of US foreign policy, the reality is that presidents lead in this issue area. Public opinion is clearly a powerful overarching influence as well, as it should be within a democracy, but it is not literally public opinion that makes foreign policy decisions. For one thing, there is considerable uncertainty, inattention, and diffidence among the general public when it comes to most specific international issues. We elect officials, including presidents, and then hold them accountable for this very reason: to make the difficult decisions. The personality, beliefs, and management style of individual presidents therefore really do make a difference.

Obviously the demands on the president are immense, and conflicting pressures are legion. Still, it is the president who decides how these various demands and tensions will be resolved, through specific foreign policy decisions. Choices and alternatives exist. Presidents can lead, bargain, nudge, coordinate, speak out, and set the policy agenda. A key question is one of priorities, including whether a president is willing to spend political capital on behalf of sensible foreign and national security policies. In the end there is simply no substitute for sustained presidential attention in this area. If the president does not impose some sort of order and coherence on the foreign policy process, nobody else either can or will.[49]

President Obama's leadership style in foreign policy should be a puzzle to political scientists. Obama has many of the personal qualities commonly considered essential by scholars: intelligence, adaptability, analytic capacity, personal self-discipline, a deliberate manner, and an appetite for information. Yet his foreign policies have frequently been marked by unexpected failure, pushback, and dysfunction. Is this simply a result of the inevitable complications of world politics—or has it been aggravated by other aspects of Obama's leadership style? Like all presidents, and indeed like the rest of us as well, Obama's better qualities come as part of a package. In his particular case, an admirably deliberate, calm, and confident intellect happens to be joined with other characteristics less helpful to a commander in chief. Specifically, his frequent disinclination to fully commit toward any coherent policy course in one case after another has come across as halfhearted, drifting, and indecisive rather than as genuinely prudent—and that impression has done real damage. Still, it must be conceded that insofar as particular regional or functional US policies are incoherent today, it is largely because the president sees no compelling reason for them to be otherwise. If he wanted to impose greater order on specific policies, he could, but presumably this would involve domestic political risks he does not wish to take—and if his overall course was correct, then history would probably absolve him for a number of lesser failures. The more fundamental problem is the unwisdom of his overarching implicit direction for American grand strategy. Obama entered the White House with little deep international or executive experience, on the confident assumption that he could somehow transcend global differences and retrench US military power without significant cost or risk to American interests. Time and events have proven him basically wrong in this assumption, yet he appears uninterested in empirical disconfirmation. On the contrary, he continues to view himself as highly pragmatic, careful, and internationally effective. This is not prudence—it is a profound complacency.

Prudent political leadership is not simply the public presentation of calm. Nor does it necessarily amount to splitting the difference between opposing choices or to a tactically incremental approach. Rather, the virtue of prudence—in the classical understanding—involves the ability to "calculate well for the attainment of a particular end of a fine sort," so that we may do the right thing at the right time "for the right reason and in the right way."[50] Prudent political leaders are able to translate worthy

ideals into politically feasible policies, through a practical calcula-
tion of appropriate ends and means under specific circumstances.
This sometimes involves taking full responsibility for specific
choices that are bold and decisive rather than gradual or incremental. The unique value of prudence lies in the ability to realize
worthwhile values through the concrete means available within
distinct situations, and then to act effectively upon that realiza-
tion. It is a practical virtue, not an abstract one—and in politics, it
is indispensable.[51]

A genuinely prudent US foreign policy strategy today would
involve a shift toward a different executive decision-making
style, along with a shift in overall direction. In terms of
decision-making: if a president wants to impose greater order and
coherence on US national security strategies, it is certainly possible
to do so. Based on both recent and historical experience, a variety
of tools might be developed. Numerous agencies and departments
including State, Defense, and the National Security Council contain a small number of staff devoted to strategic or policy planning.
The purpose of this effort is not to produce unalterable government plans, but to help senior decision-makers weigh alternative
policy options, assess existing strategies, and anticipate long-term
trends and contingencies sometimes overlooked in the pressure
of the moment. A better coordination and empowerment of these
policy-planning cells could help the president and his principal advisers to achieve a more genuinely strategic approach toward US
foreign policy, whereby words are matched to actions and commitments to capabilities. The bureaucratic impediments to inter-
agency improvements are well understood, and to be fair they
long predate the current administration. The alternative to better
strategic coordination, however, is continued dysfunction at the
highest levels, encouraging regular practical policy failures and
sometimes outright disaster. One option would be for a president

to institute a new strategic planning coordination board, with representatives from policy planning cells within all of the relevant agencies. This approach was used by President Eisenhower with much success. Such a strategic planning board could assist both the president and his leading advisers on the National Security Council to coordinate national security strategy more effectively, if they were truly interested in using it. Alternatively, a president might create a National Security Council strategic planning directorate with enough staff and authority to help bring greater coherence to US foreign policy. The precise organizational flow chart is less important than the fact of genuine interest and trust from the top down. No formal arrangement for strategic planning will avail if it does not fit the personality of the president or if it does not have his confidence. On the other hand, any one of several mechanisms could help considerably if a president decided to get serious about strategic planning in US foreign and national security policy—and since these are literally matters of life and death, getting serious would seem appropriate.[52]

In terms of basic direction, President Obama's overall strategy of accommodation and retrenchment has long since stopped being prudent. A wiser course under today's circumstances would be to adopt intensified strategies of pressure in a differentiated manner against a variety of US competitors overseas. This would involve distinguishing clearly between America's allies and its adversaries, supporting its allies, and pushing back against its adversaries on the understanding that multiple long-term competitions against the United States are already well underway. Hybrid strategies of pressure would aim to impose costs, gain leverage, and wear down major adversaries and competitors, not primarily through direct rollback, but through the attrition and frustration of opposing authoritarian states via peacetime competition. This would still allow for considerable diplomatic and economic interaction in cases such as China. In the case of jihadist terrorists, however, a true strategy of pressure would grasp the full scale of their hostility and aim at their destruction. A conservative American foreign policy realism would build up the US military and avoid ineffectual scolding in favor of focused and believable threats of punishment. It would take great care before committing US forces to combat, and then do so if necessary with decision and determination. It would rest upon a recognition that America's strategic forward presence is fundamentally a keystone of peaceful stability, democracy, and prosperity overseas. It would not necessarily involve major US ground units in new combat interventions; to a greater extent than admitted by President Obama, there are many foreign policy tools between sending in the US Marines and doing nothing at all. But the course proposed here would bolster US deterrent capabilities overseas and take the possible use of force seriously, precisely in order to prevent violent aggression while securing American interests. The overall tone would be protective, vigilant, tenacious, and tough-minded rather than revolutionary. This is what a conservative American realism would look like.

Could a Republican presidential candidate succeed with a foreign policy approach something like this? There is considerable evidence that he or she could. First, with regard to a presidential primary: the GOP's nationalists together with its conservative internationalists agree on a number of foreign and national security fundamentals, including robust counterterrorism, military strength, support for America's allies and resistance to its adversaries. They further agree that President Obama has failed to provide adequate leadership in these areas. A muscular American realism, calling for strategies of intensified pressure against US adversaries overseas, could therefore win support from a majority of interested Republicans in a presidential primary, so long as it is tied to a mainstream conservative domestic platform. To be sure, the most diehard isolationists will never support such a new foreign policy synthesis. But the percentage of GOP primary voters who actively seek to dismantle America's military power and alliances is really very small, and in any case Republican foreign policy cannot be held hostage to it. Most Republicans, like most other Americans, simply and quite rightly want to see greater genuine care exhibited before undertaking any new US interventions abroad. As to what exactly that implies for US foreign policy, the outcome of today's intra-GOP debate is on a knife's edge—and precisely for that reason, there is room to lead on this issue.

In a general election, most Republicans will rally to the GOP nominee, regardless of their foreign policy stance. Their Democratic opponent in 2016 will have no incumbent advantage. Moreover the Democratic Party's presidential nominee will have to answer growing concerns over the consequences of President Obama's foreign policies in the Middle East, Europe, and East Asia. The Republican presidential nominee will certainly need to reassure swing voters of a genuinely prudential approach on military and international matters. But he or she will hardly do so by embracing a neoisolationist foreign policy position. This would only encourage the Democrats to capture the center of political debate, by advertising themselves as stronger and more ready to govern.

A Republican president will find that most GOP conservatives support a robust national security policy if led by a chief executive whose instincts they trust. Indeed a considerable part of conservative opposition to Obama's international approach flows from a deep mistrust of the current president, his management style, and his policy priorities—above all on domestic issues. A GOP president will therefore win back much support from conservatives for a strong, realistic international policy simply by putting an end to the Obama administration's domestic liberal agenda. The Republican Party's current foreign policy debate will not resolve itself until a presidential candidate wins both the nomination and the White House. Republicans will find that the best antidote for current intraparty disputes, on international affairs and on numerous other matters, is to win a presidential election.

Beyond that, any future president will sustain majority backing for a serious foreign policy only by governing successfully. A crucial segment of Democrats and independents will be willing to support the international policy of a Republican president if it is competently managed. To an extent that is underreported today, the Democratic Party is in fact divided between those who still see US foreign policy as overly aggressive, and those who worry that Obama has not done enough to address security threats overseas. This second group is what will allow a Republican president to reach out beyond the GOP base for support, provided both the tone and the policies are right. While the general public is indeed domestically focused right now and averse to major interventions overseas, it is also largely supportive of a leading role in the world including US alliances, robust counterterrorism, and a superior American military. What the general public truly despises are costly, protracted, and bungled interventions that drag on for years, take American lives, and appear to bring no clear conclusion. Precisely to avoid such unhappy outcomes, the next president will have to take control over US foreign policy and impose some coherence on it through better strategic planning. Better policy will have domestic political payoffs as well. Paradoxically, by paying a little less proportionate attention than the Obama White House has to media messaging on a daily basis, a new administration might actually be able to pursue a strong and successful foreign policy with greater popular support over the longer term.

President Obama's successor will have to address the dual imperative of fiscal responsibility and US deterrent capabilities overseas, both currently neglected. The single greatest relevant expense by far is American military spending. The political economy of US grand strategy is often framed as a direct trade-off between military spending and conservative fiscal responsibility. But while America's armed forces are hardly inexpensive, and while certain components of US defense spending such as personnel benefits could certainly be cut or reformed, it is rather misleading to frame the issue as simply a contest between military capabilities on the hand and fiscal conservative priorities, including a domestic system of limited government, on the other. After all, US military power is not only an expense—ultimately, it protects America's system of limited government along with an international order friendly to that system. Conservatives, of all people, understand that a strong national defense is among the genuinely select responsibilities of the US federal government. America's public debt in the Obama era is indeed intolerably high. But it is not defense spending that has skyrocketed on his watch. On the contrary, it is domestic spending that has contributed the lion's share of new debt, consistent with the president's vision of an activist government role for domestic social welfare—and if domestic entitlement programs in particular are not reformed, defense cuts will not help because the nation will become insolvent regardless.

Whatever their other differences, American conservatives of all stripes—including conservative internationalists—agree that President Obama has introduced an unnecessary regimen of higher taxes, hyperregulation, and excessive debt that in combination discourage economic growth and take the country further than ever from distinct US traditions of limited government. The real question is the optimal level of defense spending consistent with a foreign and domestic policy that pursues fiscal responsibility and limited government together with international strength. Some libertarians argue that the answer is significant reductions in taxes, spending, and regulations at home, along with further cuts in defense and the dismantling of America's alliance commitments overseas. On the domestic side at least, these libertarians have the basic direction right: after eight years of President Obama, the country really could use a domestic policy movement in a libertarian direction. On foreign and national security policy, however, the accelerated dismantling of America's military power and alliances would only exacerbate the most worrisome trends under the current administration. Most Republicans appear to understand this instinctively. So while the GOP will always draw heavily upon its libertarian strain, a conservative foreign policy realism cannot and should not embrace any further erosion of US military power and alliances right now beyond the existing damage.

When Obama first entered the White House, there was a reasonable case to be made for a hard-nosed adjustment of American grand strategy. Unfortunately he has not executed any such adjustment. On the contrary, he has simply pursued an implicit overall strategy of American retrenchment and accommodation, in order to focus on domestic policy legacies, and in the hope that this approach would somehow encourage more peaceful and cooperative relations overseas. The strategy was poorly executed and characterized by yawning gaps between words and actions in one case after another. Internationally, it hasn't worked. Both allies and adversaries have interpreted America's current and spasmodic retrenchment in the obvious way, as a sign of US disengagement from international leadership. Multiple security challenges have germinated, and the president's foreign policy rhetoric bears less and less relation to stubborn facts on the ground. Meanwhile

Obama hews to his chosen path, confident that it is the prudent one. Genuine prudence, however, recognizes when circumstances have changed. The true danger today is not an excess of American power overseas, but a lack of it. For all practical purposes, the United States under President Obama has engaged in a fragmentary retreat from international influence. Now the time for retreat is over.

NOTES

Introduction

1. See Robert Singh, *Barack Obama's Post-American Foreign Policy: The Limits of Engagement* (London: Bloomsbury Academic, 2012), 41; Ryan Lizza, "The Consequentialist," *New Yorker*, May 2, 2011; David Rohde, "The Obama Doctrine," *Foreign Policy* 192 (March–April 2012); Robert Weiss, "Imperial Obama: A Kinder, Gentler Empire?" *Social Justice* 37:2–3 (2010–2011), 1–9; and Leslie Gelb, "The Elusive Obama Doctrine," *National Interest* 121 (September–October 2012), 18–28. For other notable efforts to define the Obama Doctrine, see Hal Brands, "Breaking Down Obama's Grand Strategy," *National Interest*, June 23, 2014; Christopher Ford, "Soft on Soft Power," *SAIS Review* 32:1 (Winter–Spring 2012), 89–111; David Sanger, *Confront and Conceal: Obama's Secret Wars and Surprising Use of American Power* (New York: Broadway Books, 2013), xvii; Melvyn Leffler, "Defense on a Diet: How Budget Crises Have Improved U.S. Strategy," *Foreign Affairs* 92:6 (November–December 2013); "The Birth of an Obama Doctrine," *Economist*, March 28, 2011; Nicholas Kitchen, "The Obama Doctrine: Detente or Decline?" *European Political Science* 10 (March 2011), 27–35; Clarence Lusane, "We Must Lead the World: The Obama Doctrine and the Re-branding of American Hegemony," *Black Scholar* 38:1 (Spring 2008), 34–43; Gideon Rachman, "Syria and the Undoing of Obama's Grand Strategy," *Financial Times*, May 3, 2013; Tony Blankley, "Obama the Isolationist?" *National Review*, June 23, 2010; Bruce Thornton, *The Wages of Appeasement: Ancient Athens, Munich, and Obama's America* (New York: Encounter Books, 2011); Charles Krauthammer, "Decline Is a Choice," *Weekly Standard*, October 19, 2009; Daniel Drezner, "Does Obama Have a Grand Strategy?" *Foreign Affairs* 90:4 (July–August 2011), 57–68; Fred Kaplan, "The Realist," *Politico*, February 27, 2014; Erik Owens, "Searching

for an Obama Doctrine: Christian Realism and the Idealist/Realist Tension in Obama's Foreign Policy," *Journal of the Society of Christian Ethics* 32:2 (Fall–Winter 2012), 93–111; Spencer Ackerman, "The Obama Doctrine, Revisited," *American Prospect* 19:4 (March 19, 2008), 12–15; John Podhoretz, "Barack the Neo-con," *New York Post*, September 1, 2010; and Francois Godemont, "The U.S. and Asia in 2009: Public Diplomacy and Strategic Continuity," *Asian Survey* 50:1 (January–February 2010), 8–24.

2. Barack Obama, remarks announcing candidacy for president in Springfield, Illinois, February 10, 2007; and remarks by the president on Afghanistan, June 22, 2011.

3. Richard Betts, *American Force: Dangers, Delusions, and Dilemmas in National Security* (New York: Columbia University Press, 2012), chapter 10; Fareed Zakaria, "Stop Searching for an Obama Doctrine," *Washington Post*, July 6, 2011; Amy Zegart, "A Foreign Policy for the Future," *Defining Ideas*, Hoover Institution, November 20, 2013.

4. Strobe Talbott, *The Russia Hand: A Memoir of Presidential Diplomacy* (New York: Random House, 2002), 133.

5. David Remnick, "Going the Distance," *New Yorker*, January 27, 2014.

6. See especially Hal Brands, *What Good Is Grand Strategy?* (Ithaca, NY: Cornell University Press, 2014).

7. For ample evidence of this, see John Gaddis, *George F. Kennan: An American Life* (New York: Penguin, 2012); George Kennan, *Memoirs, 1925–1950* (New York: Pantheon Books, 1983); and Melvyn Leffler, *A Preponderance of Power: National Security, the Truman Administration, and the Cold War* (Stanford, CA: Stanford University Press, 1993).

8. Further definitions of grand strategy can be found in Robert Art, *A Grand Strategy for America* (Ithaca, NY: Cornell University Press, 2003); Colin Dueck, *Reluctant Crusaders* (Princeton, NJ: Princeton University Press, 2006); Charles Kupchan, *Vulnerability of Empire* (Ithaca, NY: Cornell University Press, 1994); and B. H. Liddell Hart, *Strategy* (New York: Praeger, 1954).

9. For similar efforts to develop a "reform conservatism" for the Republican Party on domestic issues, see Arthur Brooks, "Be Open-Handed toward Your Brothers," *Commentary*, February 2014; David Brooks, "The New Right," *New York Times*, June 9, 2014; Ross Douthat, "What Is Reform Conservatism," *New York Times*, May 30, 2013; Michael Gerson and Peter Wehner, "A Conservative Vision of Government," *National Affairs* 18 (Winter 2014), 78–94; Yuval Levin, "Beyond the Welfare State," *National Affairs* 7 (Spring 2011), 21–38; Ramesh Ponnuru, "Reform Conservatism," *National Review*, February 24, 2014; and the authors of *Room to Grow* (YG Network, 2014).

Chapter 1

1. David Corn, *Showdown: The Inside Story of How Obama Battled the GOP to Set Up the 2012 Election* (New York: William Morrow, 2012), 301.

2. For some definitions of grand strategy, see Robert Art, *A Grand Strategy for America* (Ithaca, NY: Cornell University Press, 2003); Hal Brands, *What Good Is Grand Strategy?* (Ithaca, NY: Cornell University Press, 2014); Colin Dueck, *Reluctant Crusaders* (Princeton, NJ: Princeton University Press, 2006); Charles Kupchan, *Vulnerability of Empire* (Ithaca, NY: Cornell University Press, 1994); and B. H. Liddell Hart, *Strategy* (New York: Praeger, 1954).

3. Peter Trubowitz, *Politics and Strategy: Partisan Ambition and American Statecraft* (Princeton, NJ: Princeton University Press, 2011), 13, 36–37. For a leading scholarly argument favoring US retrenchment today, see Barry Posen, *Restraint: A New Foundation for U.S. Grand Strategy* (Ithaca, NY: Cornell University Press, 2014.)

4. Robert Gilpin, *War and Change in World Politics* (Cambridge University Press, 1983), 194.

5. The most articulate statements of these goals and assumptions were contained in the writings and memoranda of State Department official George Kennan. See especially Kennan to Secretary of State James Byrnes, February 22, 1946, *Foreign Relations of the United States, 1946*, vol. 6 (Washington, DC: GPO, 1969), 696–709 ("Kennan to Byrnes") and "The Sources of Soviet Conduct," *Foreign Affairs*, July 1947.

6. Kennan to Byrnes, 706–8.

7. The most searching arguments in favor of a Cold War strategy of rollback or "liberation" were written by James Burnham. See Burnham, *Containment or Liberation?* (New York: J. Day, 1953), 34–36, 43, 128–40, 251–52.

8. Gordon Craig, "Delbruck: The Military Historian," in Peter Paret, ed., *Makers of Modern Strategy from Machiavelli to the Nuclear Age* (Princeton, NJ: Princeton University Press, 1986), 341–44.

9. Richard Haass and Meghan O'Sullivan, "Terms of Engagement: Alternatives to Punitive Policies," *Survival*, Summer 2000, 114.

10. Daniel Thomas, *The Helsinki Effect: International Norms, Human Rights, and the Demise of Communism* (Princeton, NJ: Princeton University Press, 2001); M. E. Sarotte, *Dealing with the Devil: East Germany, Detente, and Ostpolitik, 1969–1973* (Chapel Hill: University of North Carolina Press, 2001), 169–78; Timothy Garton Ash, *In Europe's Name: Germany and the Divided Continent* (New York: Random House, 1993), 367–68.

11. Some of the most useful modern works on international negotiation, diplomacy, and bargaining include G. R. Berridge, *Diplomacy: Theory and Practice* (New York: Palgrave Macmillan, 2010); Richard Ned Lebow, *The Art of Bargaining* (Baltimore, MD: Johns Hopkins University Press, 1996); Thomas Schelling, *The Strategy of Conflict* (Cambridge, MA: Harvard University Press, 1981); Alexander George, *Forceful Persuasion* (Washington, DC: United States Institute of Peace, 2009); Chas Freeman, *Arts of Power: Statecraft and Diplomacy* (Washington, DC: United States Institute of Peace, 1997); and Henry Kissinger, *Diplomacy* (New York: Simon and Schuster, 1995).

12. Charles Kupchan, *How Enemies Become Friends: The Sources of Stable Peace* (Princeton, NJ: Princeton University Press, 2010), 6, 35–41.

13. John Mearsheimer, *The Tragedy of Great Power Politics* (New York: Norton, 2002), 163–64.

14. See Freeman, *Arts of Power*, 77–79; Gilpin, *War and Change in World Politics*, 193–94; and Stephen Rock, *Appeasement in International Politics* (Lexington: University Press of Kentucky, 2000).

15. Christopher Layne, "From Preponderance to Offshore Balancing," *International Security* 22:1 (Summer 1997), 86–124; "Offshore Balancing Revisited," *Washington Quarterly* 25:2 (Spring 2002), 233–48; *The Peace of Illusions* (Ithaca, NY: Cornell University Press, 2007), 159–203; John Mearsheimer, "Imperial by Design," *National Interest*, January–February 2011, 16–34; *Tragedy of Great Power Politics*, 236–64, 387–90; Robert Pape and James Feldman, *Cutting the Fuse: The Explosion of Global Suicide Terrorism and How to Stop It* (Chicago: University of Chicago Press, 2010), 12–13, 333–35; Stephen Walt, "Offshore Balancing: An Idea Whose Time Has Come," *Foreign Policy*, November 2, 2011.

16. Mearsheimer, "Imperial by Design," 18, 31.

17. Layne, "From Preponderance to Offshore Balancing," 86–87, 112–19; *Peace of Illusions*, 160–90.

18. Layne, *Peace of Illusions*, 190–91; Pape and Feldman, *Cutting the Fuse*, 12–13, 333–35.

19. Mearsheimer, "Imperial by Design," 34.

20. Eric Nordlinger, *Isolationism Reconfigured: American Foreign Policy for a New Century* (Princeton, NJ: Princeton University Press, 1994), 34.

21. Art, *Grand Strategy for America*, 172–222.

22. For more on hybrid US grand strategies, see Colin Dueck, "Hybrid Strategies: The American Experience," *Orbis*, Winter 2011, 30–52.

23. On the previous two paragraphs, see Robert Kaufman, "A Two-Level Interaction: Structure, Stable Liberal Democracy, and U.S. Grand Strategy," *Security Studies* 3:4 (Summer 1994), 688; Alan Lamborn, *The Price of Power* (Boston, MA: Unwin Hyman, 1991), 64; Randall Schweller, "Unanswered Threats: A Neoclassical Realist Theory of Underbalancing,"

International *Security* 29:2 (Fall 2004), 159–201; Jack Snyder, *Myths of Empire: Domestic Politics and International Ambition* (Cornell University Press, 1991), 14–20, 31–48; and Trubowitz, *Politics and Strategy*, 5–6, 23–30.

24. Jonathan Alter, *The Center Holds: Obama and His Enemies* (New York: Simon and Schuster, 2013), 83; Richard Wolffe, *Revival: The Struggle for Survival Inside the Obama White House* (New York: Broadway, 2011), 5.

25. I use the terms "liberal" and "progressive" interchangeably throughout this book, out of deference to liberals who would rather be called progressive.

26. Keith Poole and Howard Rosenthal, *Ideology and Congress* (New Brunswick, NJ: Transaction Publishers, 2007), 3.

27. Alan Abramowitz, *The Polarized Public? Why Our Government Is So Dysfunctional* (Upper Saddle River, NJ: Pearson, 2012); David Leege et al., *The Politics of Cultural Differences: Social Change and Voter Mobilization Strategies in the Post–New Deal Period* (Princeton, NJ: Princeton University Press, 2002); Arthur Paulson, *Electoral Realignment and the Outlook for American Democracy* (Boston, MA: Northeastern University Press, 2007).

28. See Morris Fiorina, *Culture War?* (Boston, MA: Longman, 2011).

29. Some Republican presidents, such as Richard Nixon, have left domestic policy legacies that were as much liberal as conservative. See Joan Hoff, *Nixon Reconsidered* (New York: Basic Books, 1994).

30. Stephen Skowronek, *Presidential Leadership in Political Time: Reprise and Reappraisal*, 2nd ed. (Lawrence: University Press of Kansas, 2011), 12–13, 92–97, 132–33, 172–79.

31. Barack Obama, Remarks Announcing Candidacy for President in Springfield, IL, February 10, 2007.

32. The Editors, "Obama and the Gipper," *Wall Street Journal*, January 19, 2008.

33. Barack Obama, *The Audacity of Hope* (New York: Crown Publishers, 2006), 34–46.

34. Stephen Wayne, "Obama's Personality and Performance," in James Thurber, ed., *Obama in Office* (Boulder, CO: Paradigm Publishers, 2011), 68–71.

35. Daily Kos, "Lifetime Vote Ratings: The Senate," May 27, 2008.

36. Paul Abramson et al., *Change and Continuity in the 2008 and 2010 Elections* (Washington, DC: Congressional Quarterly Press, 2012), 152–68.

37. Janet Box-Steffensmeier and Steven Schier, *The American Elections of 2012* (New York: Routledge, 2013), 184; John Sides and Lynn Vavreck, *The Gamble: Choice and Chance in the 2012 Presidential Election* (Princeton, NJ: Princeton University Press, 2013), 204.

38. Obama, *Audacity of Hope*, 33–42, 57–59.

39. Obama, *Audacity of Hope*, 24.

40. Barack Obama, speech in Osawatomie, KS, December 6, 2011; address to the Democratic National Convention, September 6, 2012; and second inaugural address, January 21, 2013.

41. For a discussion of transformational presidencies in foreign policy, using a very different definition, see Joseph Nye, *Presidential Leadership and the Creation of the American Era* (Princeton, NJ: Princeton University Press, 2014).

42. Michael Grunwald, *The New New Deal: The Hidden Story of Change in the Obama Era* (New York: Simon and Schuster, 2012), 349.

43. Corn, *Showdown*, 10–12, 73; Grunwald, *The New New Deal*, 28–30; and Wolffe, *Revival*, 5, 39, 60–61, 95, 117–18, 194. See also Wayne, "Obama's Personality and Performance," 64–68.

44. Steven Schier, "Obama's 'Big Bang' Presidency," in Schier, ed., *Transforming America: Barack Obama in the White House* (Lanham, MD: Rowman and Littlefield, 2011), 1–15.

45. George Edwards, *Overreach: Leadership in the Obama Presidency* (Princeton, NJ: Princeton University Press, 2012); Gary Jacobson, "The Republican Resurgence in 2010," *Political Science Quarterly* 126:1 (Spring 2011), 27–52.

46. Lyndon Johnson certainly had a clear progressive policy legacy on domestic issues, but he did not serve two full terms as president, nor did he win two presidential elections.

47. For further discussion on this point see Charles Kesler, *I Am the Change: Barack Obama and the Crisis of Liberalism* (New York: Broadside Books, 2012), chapters 1 and 5; and Stanley Renshon, *Barack Obama and the Politics of Redemption* (New York: Routledge, 2011), chapters 3–5, 7.

48. "Lexington," *Economist*, December 1, 2012.

49. Rajiv Chandrasekaran, *Little America: The War within the War for Afghanistan* (New York: Alfred A. Knopf, 2012), chapters 6, 18.

50. Remarks by the President at the Acceptance of the Nobel Peace Prize, Oslo, Norway, December 10, 2009.

51. Barack Obama, Remarks by the President on Afghanistan, June 22, 2011.

52. Ryan Lizza, "The Consequentialist: How the Arab Spring Remade Obama's Foreign Policy," *New Yorker*, May 2, 2011.

Chapter 2

1. Mark Landler, "Lost in Translation: A U.S. Gift to Russia," *New York Times*, March 6, 2009.

2. Barack Obama, *The Audacity of Hope* (New York: Crown Publishers, 2006), 271–80.

3. Ryan Lizza, "The Consequentialist: How the Arab Spring Remade Obama's Foreign Policy," *New Yorker*, May 2, 2011.

4. Obama, *The Audacity of Hope*, 279–80.

5. National Public Radio online, "Transcript: Obama's Speech against the Iraq War," posted January 20, 2009. The speech was delivered in Chicago on October 2, 2002.

6. President Barack Obama's Inaugural Address, January 20, 2009, The White House.

7. Remarks by the President at Cairo University, Cairo, Egypt, June 4, 2009, The White House.

8. Remarks by the President on a New Strategy for Afghanistan and Pakistan, March 27, 2009, The White House.

9. Remarks by President Barack Obama in Prague, Prague, Czech Republic, April 5, 2009, The White House.

10. President Barack Obama's Inaugural Address, January 20, 2009, The White House.

11. Hillary Rodham Clinton, *Hard Choices* (New York: Simon and Schuster, 2014), chapter 11.

12. Jeffrey Bader, *Obama and China's Rise: An Insider's Account of America's Asia Strategy* (Washington, DC: Brookings Institution Press, 2013), 7, 10–11, 21–23.

13. Bader, *Obama and China's Rise*, 6; Council on Foreign Relations Address by Secretary of State Hillary Clinton, Council on Foreign Relations, July 15, 2009.

14. "Barack Obama's Acceptance Speech," *New York Times,* August 28, 2008.

15. Department of Defense, *Quadrennial Defense Review Report,* February 2010. The 2010 QDR was drafted for the most part during 2009, reflecting many of Obama's incoming policy assumptions.

16. "Obama Delivers Berlin Address," *Washington Post,* July 24, 2008.

17. Clinton, *Hard Choices,* chapter 2.

18. "Barack Obama's Acceptance Speech," *New York Times,* August 28, 2008.

19. Barack Obama, "Renewing American Leadership," *Foreign Affairs,* July–August 2007, 2–16.

20. Jack Goldsmith, *Power and Constraint: The Accountable Presidency after 9/11* (New York: Norton, 2012), 4–20, 25–26, 38–44, 210.

21. National Public Radio online, "Transcript: President Obama's Convention Speech," September 6, 2012.

22. Remarks by the President at the National Defense University, Fort McNair, May 23, 2013, The White House.

23. Abdel Bari Atwan, *After Bin Laden: Al Qaeda, the Next Generation* (New York: New Press, 2013), 39–79; Mary Habeck, "Attacking America: Al Qaeda's Grand Strategy in Its War with the World," Foreign Policy Research Institute, February 2014; Seth Jones, *A Persistent Threat: The Evolution of al Qa'ida and Other Salafi Jihadists,* Rand Corporation, June 2014.

24. Atwan, *After Bin Laden,* 8–13; Habeck, "Attacking America;" Jones, *A Persistent Threat.*

25. Liz Sly, "Al-Qaeda Disavows Any Ties with Radical Islamist ISIS Group in Syria, Iraq," *Washington Post,* February 3, 2014; Mark Tran and Matthew Weaver, "ISIS Announces Islamic Caliphate in Area Straddling Iraq and

Syria," *Guardian*, June 30, 2014; Joby Warrick, "ISIS, with Gains in Iraq, Closes in on Founder Zarqawi's Violent Vision," *Washington Post*, June 14, 2014; Clint Watts, "Jihadi Competition after Al Qaeda Hegemony—the 'Old Guard,' Team ISIS and the Battle for Jihadi Hearts and Minds," Foreign Policy Research Institute, February 20, 2014.

26. Pew Research Global Attitudes Project, "Global Opinion of Obama Slips, International Policies Faulted," Pew Research Center, June 13, 2012.

27. Remarks by the President on a New Strategy for Afghanistan and Pakistan, March 27, 2009, The White House.

28. Remarks by the President in Address to the Nation on the Way Forward in Afghanistan and Pakistan, West Point, New York, December 1, 2009, The White House.

29. On the preceding paragraph, see Rajiv Chandrasekaran, *Little America: The War within the War for Afghanistan* (New York: Knopf, 2012), 116–29; Clinton, *Hard Choices*, chapter 7; Robert Gates, *Duty: Memoirs of a Secretary at War* (New York: Alfred A. Knopf, 2014), chapter 10; David Sanger, *Confront and Conceal: Obama's Secret Wars and Surprising Use of American Power* (New York: Broadway Books, 2013), 15–34; and Bob Woodward, *Obama's Wars* (New York: Simon and Schuster, 2010).

30. Remarks by the President on the Way Forward in Afghanistan, June 22, 2011, The White House.

31. David Corn, *Showdown: The Inside Story of How Obama Battled the GOP to Set Up the 2012 Election* (New York: William Morrow, 2012), 296–301; Gates, *Duty*, 492.

32. Gates, *Duty*, 557. Italics removed from original. See also Chandrasekaran, *Little America*, 327–28, 332.

33. Gates, *Duty*, 573; Seth Jones and Keith Crane, *Afghanistan after the Drawdown* (New York: Council on Foreign Relations, November 2013).

34. Frederick Kagan and Kimberly Kagan, "How to Waste a Decade in Afghanistan," *Wall Street Journal*, January 9, 2013.

35. David Remnick, *The Bridge: The Life and Rise of Barack Obama* (New York: Vintage, 2011), 116–17.

36. Richard Wolffe, *Revival: The Struggle for Survival inside the Obama White House* (New York: Broadway Books, 2011), 212.

37. Remarks by President Barack Obama in Prague, Prague, Czech Republic, April 5, 2009, The White House.

38. Remarks by President Obama at the Brandenburg Gate, Berlin, Germany, June 19, 2013, The White House.

39. For an excellent survey of the problem, see Ashley Tellis, "No Escape: Managing the Enduring Reality of Nuclear Weapons," in Tellis, ed., *Strategic Asia, 2013–14: Asia in the Second Nuclear Age* (Seattle, WA: National Bureau of Asian Research, 2013), 3–32.

40. Eric Edelman, Andrew Krepinevich, and Evan Braden Montgomery, "The Dangers of a Nuclear Iran," *Foreign Affairs* 90:1 (January–February 2011); Mitchell Reiss, "A Nuclear-Armed Iran: Possible Security and Diplomatic Implications," Council on Foreign Relations Working Paper, May 2010.

41. For some brief critiques of nuclear zero, see Elbridge Colby, "Nuclear Abolition: A Dangerous Illusion," *Orbis*, Summer 2008, 424–33; Fred Ikle, "Nuclear Abolition: A Reverie," *National Interest*, September–October 2009); Josef Joffe and James Davis, "Less Than Zero," *Foreign Affairs* 90:1 (January–February 2011); Thomas Schelling, "A World without Nuclear Weapons?" *Daedalus* 138:4 (September 2009), 124–29; and Bruno Tertrais, "The Illogic of Zero," *Washington Quarterly* 33:2 (April 2010), 125–38.

42. Clinton, *Hard Choices*, chapter 18; Trita Parsi, *A Single Roll of the Dice: Obama's Diplomacy with Iran* (New Haven, CT: Yale University Press, 2013), chapters 7–8, 10.

43. Sanger, *Confront and Conceal*, chapter 8.

44. Gregory Jones, "Facing the Reality of Iran as a De Facto Nuclear State," Nonproliferation Policy Education Center, March 22, 2012.

45. Ray Takeyh, "A Kinder, Gentler Iran?" *Los Angeles Times*, September 20, 2013.

46. Adam Gabbatt, "Obama Sends Letter to Kim Jong-Il," *Guardian*, December 16, 2009.

47. Victor Cha, *The Impossible State: North Korea, Past and Future* (New York: Ecco, 2013), 271–74, 295–97, 313–14, 465–66.

48. Jeffrey Mankoff, *Russian Foreign Policy: The Return of Great Power Politics*, 2nd ed. (Lanham, MD: Rowman and Littlefield, 2011), 114, 116, 128.

49. Mankoff, *Russian Foreign Policy*, 116, 120, 129.

50. J. David Goodman, "Microphone Catches a Candid Obama," *New York Times*, March 26, 2012.

51. Luke Harding, "Wikileaks Cables: Dmitry Medvedev 'Plays Robin to Putin's Batman,'" *Guardian*, December 1, 2010.

52. Vladimir Putin, "A New Integration Project for Eurasia—a Future Being Born Today," *Izvestiya*, October 4, 2011 (Johnson's Russia List, No. 180, October 6, Item 30).

53. James Sherr, *Hard Diplomacy and Soft Coercion: Russia's Influence Abroad* (London: Chatham House, 2013), chapters 4–5.

54. Michael Gordon, "Russia Displays a New Military Prowess in Ukraine's East," *New York Times*, April 21, 2014; David Herszenhorn, "Facing Russian Threat, Ukraine Halts Plans for Deals with E.U.," *New York Times*, November 21, 2013; Neil MacFarquhar, "Russia and 2 Neighbors Form Economic Union That Has a Ukraine-Size Hole," *New York Times*, May 29, 2014; Halia Pavliva, Natasha Doff and Ksenia Galouchko, "Obama

Sanctions Underwhelm Russian Stock Traders as Market Jumps," *Business Week*, April 29, 2014.

55. Leon Aron, "The Putin Doctrine," *Foreign Affairs*, March 8, 2013; Ariel Cohen, "Putin's New 'Fortress Russia,' " *New York Times*, October 19, 2012; Nikolas Gvosdev, "As U.S. Influence Recedes, Russia Finds Openings in Egypt, Saudi Arabia," *World Politics Review*, November 15, 2013.

56. Martin Indyk, Kenneth Lieberthal, and Michael O'Hanlon, *Bending History: Barack Obama's Foreign Policy* (Washington, DC: Brookings Institution Press, 2012), 26; James Mann, *The Obamians: The Struggle inside the White House to Redefine American Power* (New York: Penguin, 2012), 72.

57. Bader, *Obama and China's Rise*, 7–25.

58. Mark Landler, "Clinton Paints China Policy with a Green Hue," *New York Times*, February 21, 2009.

59. Daniel Drezner, *The System Worked: How the World Stopped Another Great Depression* (New York: Oxford University Press, 2014), 136–40.

60. John Vidal, Allegra Stratton, and Suzanne Goldenberg, "Low Targets, Goals Dropped: Copenhagen Ends in Failure," *Guardian*, December 18, 2009.

61. Of course the Chinese simultaneously find their North Korean allies to be a tiresome burden. See Andrei Lankov, *The Real North Korea* (New York: Oxford University Press, 2013).

62. On the preceding paragraph, see Clinton, *Hard Choices*, chapter 3; and Robert Sutter, *Foreign Relations of the PRC* (Lanham, MD: Rowman and Littlefield, 2013), 121, 139, 142–43, 207–8.

63. Hillary Clinton, "America's Pacific Century," *Foreign Policy*, November 2011, 56–63; Remarks by President Obama to the Australian Parliament, Canberra, Australia, November 17, 2011, The White House.

64. Nguyen Manh Hung, "Could Conflict in the South China Sea Lead to a 'New Cold War'?" *Asia Society*, October 2, 2012.

65. Regarding the last point especially, see Edward Luttwak, *The Rise of China vs. the Logic of Strategy* (Cambridge, MA: Belknap Press of Harvard University Press, 2012).

66. Vali Nasr, *The Dispensable Nation: American Foreign Policy in Retreat* (New York: Doubleday, 2013), 164, 170.

67. Remarks by the President on the Situation in Egypt, February 1, 2011, The White House.

68. Mann, *The Obamians*, 263, 266.

69. Indyk, Lieberthal, and O'Hanlon, *Bending History*, 148–50.

70. Mann, *The Obamians*, 265. See also Mark Landler and Helene Cooper, "Allies Press U.S. to Go Slow on Egypt," *New York Times*, February 8, 2011.

71. Nasr, *Dispensable Nation*, 169–70. See also Sanger, *Confront and Conceal*, 319–20.

72. Mann, *The Obamians*, 326; Sanger, *Confront and Conceal*, 333.

73. Ana Belen Soage and Jorge Fuentelsaz Franganillo, "The Muslim Brothers in Egypt," in Barry Rubin, ed., *The Muslim Brotherhood: The Organization and Policies of a Global Islamist Movement* (New York: Palgrave Macmillan, 2010), 39–55; Eric Trager, "The Unbreakable Muslim Brotherhood: Grim Prospects for a Liberal Egypt," *Foreign Affairs* 90:5 (September–October 2011), 114–26.

74. David Kirkpatrick, "Morsi's Slurs against Jews Stir Concern," *New York Times*, January 14, 2013.

75. On Obama's decision to support Egypt's Muslim Brotherhood, see Henry Kissinger, "Idealism and Pragmatism in the Middle East," *Washington Post*, August 5, 2012.

76. Charlie Wells, "U.S. Embassy in Cairo Confronts Muslim Brotherhood over Mixed Messages Sent via Twitter," *New York Daily News*, September 14, 2012.

77. Atwan, *After Bin Laden*, 222–25.

78. Massimo Calabresi, "Why the U.S. Went to War: Inside the White House Debate on Libya," *Time*, March 20, 2011; Clinton, *Hard Choices*, chapter 16; Gates, *Duty*, 510–23; Sanger, *Confront and Conceal*, 340–42.

79. Ryan Lizza, "The Consequentialist."

80. See, for example, Remarks by the President to the UN General Assembly, New York, September 25, 2012, The White House.

81. "Accountability Review Board [ARB] Report on the September 11th attack in Benghazi," U.S. Department of State, December 18, 2012, 1–39.

82. Charles Dunne et al., "Letter Urges Secretary Kerry to Bolster Support for Democracy in Libya One Year after Benghazi Attacks," Freedom House, September 10, 2013; David Ignatius, "U.S. Inattention to Libya Breeds Chaos," *Washington Post*, October 25, 2013.

83. Alan Kuperman, "A Model Humanitarian Intervention? Reassessing NATO's Libya Campaign," *International Security* 38:1 (Summer 2013), 105–36.

84. Indyk, Lieberthal, and O'Hanlon, *Bending History*, 168–69.

85. For background on the Syrian civil war, see Fouad Ajami, *The Syrian Rebellion* (Stanford, CA: Hoover Institution Press, 2012); and Emile Hokayem, *Syria's Uprising and the Fracturing of the Levant* (London: Routledge, 2013).

86. Statement by President Obama on the Situation in Syria, August 18, 2011, The White House.

87. Mark Landler, "Obama Threatens Force against Syria," *New York Times*, August 21, 2012.

88. Jonathan Alter, *The Center Holds: Obama and His Enemies* (New York: Simon and Schuster, 2013), 285.

89. Clinton, *Hard Choices*, 461–64; Mark Mazzetti, Robert Worth, and Michael Gordon, "Obama's Uncertain Path Amid Syria Bloodshed," *New York*

Times, October 22, 2013; Leon Panetta, *Worthy Fights: A Memoir of Leadership in War and Peace* (New York: Penguin Press, 2014), 449–50.

90. Seth Jones, "Syria's Growing Jihad," *Survival* 55:4 (August–September 2013), 53–72.

91. Aaron Blake, "Kerry: Military Action in Syria Would Be 'Unbelievably Small,'" *Washington Post*, September 9, 2013.

92. Loveday Morris, "Seven Syrian Islamist Rebel Groups Form New Islamic Front," *Washington Post*, November 22, 2013; Liz Sly and Karen DeYoung, "Largest Syrian Rebel Groups Form Islamic Alliance, in Possible Blow to U.S. influence," *Washington Post*, September 25, 2013.

93. Mark Landler, "Rice Offers a More Modest Strategy for Mideast," *New York Times*, October 26, 2013.

94. Remarks by President Obama in Address to the United Nations General Assembly, New York, September 24, 2013, The White House.

95. Panetta, *Worthy Fights*, 450–51.

96. For a balanced assessment of the relative importance of the U.S. surge in altering Iraqi political and military conditions by 2008–2009, see Stephen Biddle, Jeffrey Friedman, and Jacob Shapiro, "Testing the Surge: Why Did Violence Decline in Iraq in 2007?" *International Security* 37:1 (Summer 2012), 7–40.

97. Indyk, Lieberthal, and O'Hanlon, *Bending History*, 75–80.

98. Mann, *The Obamians*, 331–32.

99. Nasr, *Dispensable Nation*, 149–150. See also Gates, *Duty*, 555.

100. National Public Radio online, "Transcript: President Obama's Convention Speech," September 6, 2012.

101. Michael Gordon and Bernard Trainor, *The Endgame: The Inside Story of the Struggle for Iraq, from George W. Bush to Barack Obama* (New York: Pantheon, 2012), 523–683, 688–91; Panetta, *Worthy Fights*, 392–94.

102. Peter Baker, "White House Scraps Bush's Approach to Missile Shield," *New York Times*, September 17, 2009.

103. A. Wess Mitchell and Jakub Grygiel, "The Vulnerability of Peripheries," *American Interest*, Spring 2011, 5–16.

104. Office of Management and Budget (OMB), *Historical Tables: Budget of the U.S. Government, Fiscal Year 2014* (Washington, DC, April 2013), 151–52, 155–56.

105. Gates, *Duty*, 303–22, 453–65, 546–51; Thom Shanker, "Gates Warns against Big Cuts in Military Spending," *New York Times*, May 22, 2011.

106. Department of Defense, *Quadrennial Defense Review Report*, February 2010. For a useful critique, see Roy Godson and Richard Shultz, "A QDR for All Seasons?" *Joint Force Quarterly* 59 (4th Quarter 2010), 52–56.

107. Department of Defense, *Sustaining U.S. Global Leadership: Priorities for 21st Century Defense*, January 2012, 4.

108. Department of Defense, *Sustaining U.S. Global Leadership*, 3, 6.

109. OMB, *Historical Tables*, 104–7.

110. Catherine Dale and Pat Towell, *In Brief: Assessing DOD's New Strategic Guidance*, Congressional Research Service, January 12, 2012. The 2014 Quadrennial Defense Review was more explicit regarding assumptions of risk. See U.S. Department of Defense, *Quadrennial Defense Review* (March 2014).

111. On this point, and on the assumption of increased risk, see the stark assessment from a bipartisan panel led by William Perry and John Abizaid, co-chairs, *Ensuring a Strong U.S. National Defense: The National Defense Panel Review of the 2014 Quadrennial Defense Review* (Washington, DC: United States Institute of Peace, July 31, 2014.)

112. Michael O'Hanlon, *The Wounded Giant: America's Armed Forces in an Age of Austerity* (New York: Penguin, 2011), xv.

113. Colin Clark, "U.S. Military Could Not Handle One Major Theater Operation If Sequestration Sticks," *Breaking Defense*, September 18, 2013.

114. International Institute for Strategic Studies, *The Military Balance 2013* (London: Routledge, 2013), 54.

115. Ibid., 32–33, 42. See also the essays by Andrew Erickson and Roy Kamphausen in Ashley Tellis, ed., *Strategic Asia 2012–13: China's Military Challenge* (Seattle, WA: National Bureau of Asian Research, 2012).

116. Peter Beinart, "Obama's Foreign Policy Doctrine Finally Emerges with 'Offshore Balancing,'" *Daily Beast*, November 28, 2011.

117. Christopher Layne, "The (Almost) Triumph of Offshore Balancing," *National Interest*, January 27, 2012.

118. See John Mearsheimer, "Imperial by Design," *National Interest* 111 (January–February 2011), 16–34.

119. See Drezner, *The System Worked*.

120. Robert Gilpin, *War and Change in World Politics* (New York: Cambridge University Press, 1983), 194.

121. See especially John Gaddis, *Strategies of Containment: A Critical Appraisal of American National Security Policy during the Cold War*, rev. ed. (New York: Oxford University Press, 2005).

122. Secretary of Defense Chuck Hagel, "Statement on Strategic Choices and Management Review," U.S. Department of Defense, July 31, 2013.

Chapter 3

1. Alexis de Tocqueville, *Democracy in America*, ed. J. P. Mayer and Max Lerner, trans. George Lawrence (New York: Harper and Row, 1966), 229.

2. Ole Holsti, *Public Opinion and American Foreign Policy*, rev. ed. (Ann Arbor: University of Michigan Press, 2004); Benjamin Page and Robert Shapiro, *The Rational Public* (Chicago: University of Chicago Press, 1992), chapters 5 and 6.

3. See for example *Foreign Policy in the New Millennium* (Chicago: Chicago Council on Global Affairs, 2012); and Andrew Kohut, "American International Engagement on the Rocks," Pew Research Global Attitudes Project, July 11, 2013.

4. *Beyond Red vs. Blue: The Political Typology* (Pew Research Center for the People and the Press, 2011), 89.

5. Jeffrey Jones, "Americans Oppose U.S. Military Involvement in Syria," Gallup, May 31, 2013.

6. Karen DeYoung and Scott Clement, "Many Americans Say Afghan War Isn't Worth Fighting," *Washington Post*, July 26, 2013.

7. The remainder say they have no opinion. See Rebecca Ballhaus, "WSJ/NBC Poll: Drone Attacks Have Broad Support," *Wall Street Journal*, June 5, 2013.

8. Dan Balz and Peyton Craighill, "Poll: Public Supports Strikes in Iraq, Syria; Obama's Ratings Hover Near His All-Time Lows," *Washington Post*, September 9, 2014.

9. Jeff Mason, "Most Americans Would Back U.S. Strike over Iran Nuclear Weapon: Poll," Reuters, March 13, 2012; Chemi Shalev, "Poll: 64% of Americans Would Support U.S. Strike to Prevent Iran's Nuclear Program," *Haaretz*, March 19, 2013.

10. Jeffrey Jones, "Americans Divided in Views of U.S. Defense Spending," Gallup, February 21, 2013.

11. "U.S. Public, Experts Differ on China Policies: Public Deeply Concerned about China's Economic Power," Pew Research Global Attitudes Project, September 18, 2012.

12. *Constrained Internationalism: Adapting to New Realities* (Chicago: Chicago Council on Global Affairs, 2010), 4, 41.

13. "Survey on Foreign Policy and American Overseas Commitments," *YouGov*, April 26–May 2, 2012.

14. Frank Newport, "Obama Rated Highest on Foreign Affairs, Lowest on Deficit," Gallup, February 11, 2013.

15. Tal Kopan, "Poll: Obama's Approval on Syria Sinks," *Politico*, September 10, 2013.

16. Patrick O'Connor, "Poll Shows Erosion in President's Support," *Wall Street Journal*, June 18, 2014. See also Robert Kagan, "President Obama's Foreign Policy Paradox," *Washington Post*, March 26, 2014.

17. Page and Shapiro, *The Rational Public*, 348–50.

18. Holsti, *Public Opinion*, 51–54, 130–61.

19. Peter Liberman, "An Eye for an Eye," *International Organization* 60:3 (July 2006), 687–722; Shoon Murray, *Anchors against Change: American Opinion Leaders' Beliefs after the Cold War* (Ann Arbor: University of Michigan Press, 2002), 4–8, 79–89. See also Brian Rathbun, *Trust in International*

Cooperation: *International Security Institutions, Domestic Politics and American Multilateralism* (New York: Cambridge University Press, 2012).

20. Eugene Wittkopf, *Faces of Internationalism: Public Opinion and American Foreign Policy* (Durham, NC: Duke University Press, 1990).

21. Thomas Edsall, "The Future of the Obama Coalition," *New York Times,* November 27, 2011; John Judis, *The Emerging Democratic Majority* (New York: Scribner, 2002), 37–67; James Lindsay, "National Security, the Electoral Connection, and Policy Choice," in Martin Levin, Daniel DiSalvo, and Martin Shapiro, eds., *Building Coalitions* (Baltimore, MD: Johns Hopkins University Press, 2012), 278.

22. Pew Research Center, *2012 American Values Survey* (Pew Research Center for the People and the Press, 2012), 79.

23. Thomas Frank, *What's the Matter with Kansas* (New York: Metropolitan Books, 2004), 7.

24. Pew Research Center, "In Shift from Bush Era, More Conservatives Say 'Come Home, America,'" June 16, 2011.

25. Jones, "Americans Divided in Views of Defense Spending."

26. Kohut, "American International Engagement on the Rocks."

27. Mason, "Most Americans Would Back U.S. Strike over Iran Nuclear Weapon."

28. Ballhaus, "WSJ/NBC Poll: Drone Attacks Have Broad Support."

29. Newport, "Obama Rated Highest on Foreign Affairs, Lowest on Deficit."

30. See, for example, the jump in support among Democrats for arming Syrian rebels, with no similar jump among Republicans or independents, after President Obama announced his decision in favor of it: Frank Newport, "Americans Disapprove of U.S. Decision to Arm Syrian Rebels," Gallup, June 17, 2013.

31. See, for example, Michael Tomasky, "GOP Goes Isolationist," *Daily Beast,* June 14, 2011.

32. See, for example, Patrick Buchanan, *A Republic, Not an Empire* (Washington, DC: Regnery Publishing, 2013); Benjamin Friedman and Justin Logan, "Why the U.S. Military Budget Is 'Foolish and Sustainable,'" *Orbis* 56:2 (Spring 2012), 177–91; Daniel Larison, "Forget Reagan," *American Conservative,* May–June 2013; and Ron Paul, *The Revolution* (New York: Grand Central Publishing, 2009).

33. Pew Research Center, *2012 American Values Survey* (Pew Research Center for the People and the Press, 2012), 79.

34. Jeffrey Jones, "Americans Divided in Views of U.S. Defense Spending," Gallup, February 21, 2013.

35. Mason, "Most Americans Would Back U.S. Strike over Iran Nuclear Weapon"; Shalev, "Poll: 64% of Americans Would Support U.S. Strike to Prevent Iran's Nuclear Program."

36. Ballhaus, "WSJ/NBC Poll: Drone Attacks Have Broad Support."

37. Gary Jacobson, "A Tale of Two Wars: Public Opinion on the U.S. Military Interventions in Afghanistan and Iraq," *Presidential Studies Quarterly* 40 (December 2010), 585–610.

38. Sebastian Payne and Robert Costa, "Islamic State Prompts GOP to Strike More Hawkish Tone," *Washington Post*, September 4, 2014.

39. Pew Research Center, "Strong on Defense and Israel, Tough on China: Tea Party and Foreign Policy," Pew Research Center for the People and the Press, October 7, 2011.

40. Brian Rathbun, "Steeped in International Affairs? The Foreign Policy Views of the Tea Party," *Foreign Policy Analysis* 9 (2013), 21–37.

41. Theda Skocpol and Vanessa Williamson, *The Tea Party and the Remaking of Republican Conservatism* (New York: Oxford University Press, 2012), 64.

42. Chicago Council, *Foreign Policy in the New Millennium*, chapter 5.

43. Kurt Taylor Gaubatz, *Elections and War* (Stanford, CA: Stanford University Press, 1999), 49–50, 78–79, 126–27, 142–45.

44. Paul Abramson et al., *Change and Continuity in the 2008 and 2010 Elections* (Washington, DC: Congressional Quarterly Press, 2012), 152–68, 191; James Ceaser, Andrew Busch, and John Pitney, *Epic Journey: The 2012 Elections and American Politics* (Lanham, MD: Rowman and Littlefield, 2013), 131–62; Gary Jacobson, "The 2008 Presidential and Congressional Elections," *Political Science Quarterly* 124:1 (Spring 2009), 1–30; Dalia Sussman, "Poll Finds McCain Edge on Security," *New York Times*, September 25, 2008.

45. Lydia Saad, "Americans Still Prefer Republicans for Combating Terrorism," Gallup, September 11, 2009; Jeffrey Jones, "Americans Give GOP Edge on Most Election Issues: Greatest Republican Advantages on Terrorism, Immigration, Federal Spending," Gallup, September 1, 2010.

46. Rajiv Chandrasekaran, *Little America: The War within the War for Afghanistan* (New York: Alfred A. Knopf, 2012), 116–29; Richard Wolffe, *Revival: The Struggle for Survival inside the Obama White House* (New York: Broadway Paperbacks, 2011), 239–43; Bob Woodward, *Obama's Wars* (New York: Simon and Schuster, 2011), 336.

47. William McGurn, "Bin Laden's Last Challenge—to Republicans," *Wall Street Journal*, May 3, 2011.

48. Barack Obama, "Remarks by the President on the Way Forward in Afghanistan," June 22, 2011.

49. Pew Research Center, "Views of Obama's Approach for Afghanistan Troop Withdrawal Little Changed," June 23, 2011.

50. Kasie Hunt, "Huntsman Focuses on Foreign Policy," *Politico*, June 3, 2011.

51. James Lindsay, "Campaign 2012 Roundup: Is Foreign Policy a Problem for Ron Paul?" Council on Foreign Relations, November 28, 2011.

52. Gary Jacobson, "How the Economy and Partisanship Shaped the 2012 Presidential and Congressional Elections," *Political Science Quarterly*

128:1 (Spring 2013), 15; Larry Sabato, "The Obama Encore That Broke Some Rules," in Sabato, ed., *Barack Obama and the New America* (Lanham, MD: Rowman and Littlefield, 2013), 33.

53. Dan Balz, *Collision 2012: Obama vs. Romney and the Future of Elections in America* (New York: Viking, 2013), 316; The Institute of Politics, John F. Kennedy School of Government, *Campaign for President: The Managers Look at 2012* (Lanham, MD: Rowman and Littlefield, 2013), 234–35.

54. Ceaser, Busch, and Pitney, *After Hope and Change*, 24, 107–14; John Sides and Lynn Vavreck, *The Gamble: Choice and Chance in the 2012 Presidential Election* (Princeton, NJ: Princeton University Press), 148–50, 163–64, 224–25.

55. President Obama, Second Inaugural Address, January 21, 2013.

56. For contemporary assessments of Hagel's nomination from a variety of perspectives, see Peter Beinart, "Why Hagel Matters," *Daily Beast,* January 7, 2013; David Brooks, "Why Hagel Was Picked," *New York Times,* January 7, 2013; Ross Douthat, "The Obama Synthesis," *New York Times,* January 12, 2013; and William Kristol, "There's No Case for Hagel," *Weekly Standard,* January 4, 2013.

57. James Lindsay, *Congress and the Politics of U.S. Foreign Policy* (Baltimore, MD: Johns Hopkins University Press, 1994); Marie Henehan, *Foreign Policy and Congress* (Ann Arbor: University of Michigan Press, 2000).

58. George Edwards, *Overreach: Leadership in the Obama Presidency* (Princeton, NJ: Princeton University Press, 2012); Gary Jacobson, "The Republican Resurgence in 2010," *Political Science Quarterly* 126:1 (Spring 2011), 27–52.

59. Bob Woodward, *The Price of Politics* (New York: Simon and Schuster, 2012), 127–28, 142, 203–4, 222–23, 326, 339, 344, 348–56, 360, 378–80.

60. David Rogers, "House Democrats Unite on Afghanistan Exit," *Politico,* May 30, 2011.

61. Stephen Dinan, "Bipartisan Congress Rebuffs Obama on Libya Mission," *Washington Times,* June 3, 2011.

62. Art Swift, "Americans Evenly Divided on Russia's Plan for Syria," Gallup, September 13, 2013.

63. Chris Cillizza and Aaron Blake, "Majority of House Leaning 'No' on Syria Resolution," *Washington Post,* September 6, 2013.

64. ABC News / *Washington Post* poll, "With Poor Ratings on Handling Syria, Obama's Approval Worst in Over a Year," September 17, 2013.

65. Payne and Costa, "Islamic State Prompts GOP to Strike More Hawkish Tone."

66. Thomas Preston, *The President and His Inner Circle: Leadership Style and the Advisory Process in Foreign Affairs* (New York: Columbia University Press, 2001), 9–31; Peter Rodman, *Presidential Command: Power, Leadership, and the Making of Foreign Policy from Richard Nixon to George W. Bush* (New York: Vintage Books, 2010), 289.

67. Gates, *Duty*, 585–86, 587.

68. Martin Indyk, Kenneth Lieberthal, and Michael O'Hanlon, *Bending History: Barack Obama's Foreign Policy* (Washington, DC: Brookings Institution Press, 2012), 16–20; James Mann, *The Obamians* (New York: Penguin, 2012), 66–75.

69. Mann, *The Obamians*, 224–25.

70. For Gates's own description of his relationship with Obama, see Gates, *Duty*, 268–303, 584–88.

71. Kim Ghattas, *The Secretary: A Journey with Hillary Clinton from Beirut to the Heart of American Power* (New York: Times Books, 2013), 18–19, 119–21. Clinton's account of her selection as secretary of state is in her memoir, *Hard Choices* (New York: Simon and Schuster, 2014), chapter 1. For a useful description of Clinton's political rehabilitation while in that office, see Jonathan Allen and Amie Parnes, *HRC: State Secrets and the Rebirth of Hillary Clinton* (New York: Crown, 2014).

72. Zbigniew Brzezinski, "From Hope to Audacity: Appraising Obama's Foreign Policy," *Foreign Affairs* 89:1 (January–February 2010), 18; Michael Crowley, "The Decider," *New Republic*, August 12, 2009; Indyk, Lieberthal, and O'Hanlon, *Bending History*, 20–21; Edward Luce and Daniel Dombey, "Waiting on a Sun King," *Financial Times*, March 30, 2010; Mann, *The Obamians*, xx–xxi; David Plouffe, *The Audacity to Win* (New York: Viking, 2009), 8.

73. Indyk, Lieberthal, and O'Hanlon, *Bending History*, 4, 6–7, 20–21; Mann, *The Obamians*, 166; Stephen Wayne, "Obama's Personality and Performance," in James Thurber, ed., *Obama in Office* (Boulder, CO: Paradigm Publishers, 2011), 69–70.

74. On the previous paragraph, see Adam Garfinkle, "An Innocent Abroad," *American Interest* 6:2 (November–December 2010); Indyk, Lieberthal, and O'Hanlon, *Bending History*, 270; Luce and Dombey, "Waiting on a Sun King;" and Wolffe, *Revival*, 319.

75. Brzezinski, *Foreign Affairs*, 18–19; Gates, *Duty*, 584.

76. Indyk, Lieberthal, and O'Hanlon, *Bending History*, 20.

77. Mann, *The Obamians*, 69.

78. Gates, *Duty*, 588.

79. Vali Nasr, *The Dispensable Nation* (New York: Doubleday, 2013), 2. For an even more withering assessment of the foreign policy decision-making process from a former Obama administration official, see Rosa Brooks, "The Case for Intervention," *Foreign Policy*, October 18, 2012. From April 2009 to July 2011, Brooks served as counselor to the under secretary of defense for policy.

80. ABC News / *Washington Post* poll, "With Poor Ratings on Handling Syria, Obama's Approval Worst in Over a Year."

81. Andrew Dugan, "Democrats Lack Advantage on Three Key U.S. Issue Areas," Gallup, September 16, 2013.

Chapter 4

1. Nicol Rae, "Be Careful What You Wish For: The Rise of Responsible Parties in American National Politics," *Annual Review of Political Science* 10 (2007), 169–91.

2. See Arthur Brooks, "Be Open-Handed toward Your Brothers," *Commentary*, February 2014; David Brooks, "The New Right," *New York Times*, June 9, 2014; Ross Douthat, "What Is Reform Conservatism," *New York Times*, May 30, 2013; Michael Gerson and Peter Wehner, "A Conservative Vision of Government," *National Affairs* 18 (Winter 2014), 78–94; Yuval Levin, "Beyond the Welfare State," *National Affairs* 7 (Spring 2011), 21–38; Ramesh Ponnuru, "Reform Conservatism," *National Review*, February 24, 2014; and the authors of *Room to Grow* (YG Network, 2014).

3. Andrew Kohut, *Trends in American Values: 1987–2012* (Pew Research Center for the People and the Press, 2012).

4. Andrew Kohut, "American International Engagement on the Rocks," Pew Research Global Attitudes Project, July 11, 2013.

5. Rasmussen Reports, "28% Say Libya Important to U.S. National Security Interests, 42% Disagree," March 25, 2011.

6. Jeffrey Jones, "Americans Oppose U.S. Military Involvement in Syria," Gallup, May 31, 2013.

7. Pew Research Center, "In Shift from Bush Era, More Conservatives Say 'Come Home, America,'" June 16, 2011.

8. Pew Research Center, *Public Sees U.S. Power Declining as Support for Global Engagement Slips*, December 2013, 32.

9. Robert Taft, *A Foreign Policy for Americans* (Garden City, NY: Doubleday, 1951).

10. Kim Holmes, *Rebound* (Lanham, MD: Rowman and Littlefield, 2013), 201.

11. Michael Barone, "Not So Hawkish: Republicans after the Iraq War," *National Review*, March 28, 2013.

12. Alex Altman, "The Rebel," *Time*, April 15, 2013; W. James Antle III, "Rand Plan: Will the Tea Parties Turn Antiwar?" *American Conservative*, August 1, 2010; Sam Tanenhaus and Jim Rutenberg, "Rand Paul's Mixed Inheritance," *New York Times*, January 25, 2014.

13. This paragraph is based upon the following sources: Julia Ioffe, "President Rand Paul," *New Republic*, June 17, 2013; Daniel Larison, "Rand Paul: Foreign Policy Is Congress's Business," *American Conservative*, February 4, 2013; Ryan Lizza, "The Revenge of Rand Paul," *New Yorker*, October 6, 2014; Rand Paul, "Containment and Radical Islam," address at the Heritage Foundation, February 6, 2013; Rand Paul, "Obama's

Unconstitutional Libyan War," *Washington Times*, June 15, 2011; Rand Paul, "Rand Paul on Diplomacy," *National Interest*, January 16, 2014; Stuart Reid, "The Education of Rand Paul," *Washington Monthly*, July–August 2013.

14. Ioffe, "President Rand Paul."

15. David Boaz, ed., *Cato Handbook for Policymakers*, 7th ed. (Washington, DC: Cato Institute, 2009), 201.

16. Boaz, *Cato Handbook for Policymakers*, 201.

17. Boaz, *Cato Handbook for Policymakers*, 201.

18. Boaz, *Cato Handbook for Policymakers*, 201.

19. Boaz, *Cato Handbook for Policymakers*, 507.

20. Boaz, *Cato Handbook for Policymakers*, 561.

21. Boaz, *Cato Handbook for Policymakers*, 561.

22. Boaz, *Cato Handbook for Policymakers*, 561.

23. Boaz, *Cato Handbook for Policymakers*, 655.

24. Justin Logan, "Should the NATO Alliance Continue?" *Congressional Quarterly Researcher*, March 23, 2012, 293.

25. My definition draws on Ole Holsti, *Public Opinion and American Foreign Policy* (Ann Arbor: University of Michigan Press, 2004), 51–54, 130–37, 130–61, and Eugene Wittkopf, *Faces of Internationalism* (Durham, NC: Duke University Press, 1990), 9–49. For a somewhat different definition, see Henry Nau, *Conservative Internationalism* (Princeton, NJ: Princeton University Press, 2013), 51–52.

26. Nau, *Conservative Internationalism*, 55–57.

27. *Foreign Policy in the New Millennium* (Chicago: Chicago Council on Global Affairs, 2012), chapter 5.

28. Holsti, *Public Opinion and American Foreign Policy*, 155, 176; *Beyond Red vs. Blue: The Political Typology* (Pew Research Center for the People and the Press, 2011), 100.

29. Jeane Kirkpatrick, "Dictatorships and Double Standards," *Commentary*, November 1979, 35–45.

30. Michele Dunne and Robert Kagan, "Egypt's Transition to Democracy," Brookings Institution, February 7, 2011; Charles Krauthammer, "Toward a Soft Landing in Egypt," *Washington Post*, February 4, 2011.

31. For a convincing account on this point, see Peter Baker, *Days of Fire: Bush and Cheney in the White House* (New York: Doubleday, 2013).

32. "Survey on Foreign Policy and American Overseas Commitments," *YouGov*, April 26–May 2, 2012.

33. "Survey on Foreign Policy and American Overseas Commitments."

34. Pew Research Center for the People and the Press, "Support for U.S. Airstrikes in Iraq; Concern about Getting Too Involved," August 18, 2014.

35. *Beyond Red vs. Blue*, 92.

36. Jeff Mason, "Most Americans Would Back U.S. Strike over Iran Nuclear Weapon Program: Poll," Reuters, March 13, 2012.
37. Jeffrey Jones, "Americans Divided in Views of U.S. Defense Spending," Gallup, February 21, 2013.
38. *Public Sees U.S. Power Declining as Support for Global Engagement Slips*, 33; Rebecca Ballhaus, "WSJ/NBC Poll: Drone Attacks Have Broad Support," *Wall Street Journal*, June 5, 2013.
39. *Foreign Policy in the New Millennium*, 44.
40. "Survey on Foreign Policy and American Overseas Commitments."
41. For some useful discussion, see Charles Dunn, *The Conservative Tradition in America* (Lanham, MD: Rowman and Littlefield, 1996), 35–36; Holsti, *Public Opinion and American Foreign Policy*, 52–54, 130–37, 157; Peter Liberman, "An Eye for an Eye," *International Organization* 60:3 (July 2006), 687–722; and Brian Rathbun, "Does One Right Make a Realist? Conservatism, Neo-conservatism, and Isolationism in the Foreign Policy Ideology of American Elites," *Political Science Quarterly* 123:2 (Summer 2008), 271–300.
42. Walter Russell Mead, *Special Providence* (New York: Alfred A. Knopf, 2001), chapter 7.
43. Holsti, *Public Opinion and American Foreign Policy*, 155, 176.
44. Taft, *A Foreign Policy for Americans*.
45. On this paragraph and the two that follow, see Colin Dueck, *Hard Line: The Republican Party and U.S. Foreign Policy since World War II* (Princeton, NJ: Princeton University Press, 2010).
46. See, for example, Stanley Kurtz, "Libya, War Powers, and Hawkish Conservatives," *National Review*, June 15, 2011.
47. Ted Cruz, "The Vital Role of the Senate in Foreign Policy," Heritage Foundation, September 11, 2013.
48. Scott Conroy, "Palin's Foreign Policy Embraces Instinct, Shuns Doctrine," *RealClearPolitics*, May 6, 2011.
49. Elizabeth Price Foley, *The Tea Party: Three Principles* (New York: Cambridge University Press, 2012), chapter 3.
50. Pew Research Center, "Strong on Defense and Israel, Tough on China: Tea Party and Foreign Policy," October 7, 2011.
51. Brian Rathbun, "Steeped in International Affairs? The Foreign Policy Views of the Tea Party," *Foreign Policy Analysis* 9 (2013), 21–37. Rathbun thereby confirms Walter Russell Mead's own impressions in "The Tea Party and Foreign Policy: What Populism Means for Globalism," *Foreign Affairs*, March–April 2011.
52. Rand Paul, "Rand Paul on Diplomacy," *National Interest*, January 16, 2014.
53. The Brookings Institution, "2013 American Values Survey: In Search of Libertarians in America" (Washington, DC: Brookings Institution, 2013).
54. Henry Olsen, "A GOP Dark Horse?" *National Affairs* 8 (Summer 2011); John Sides and Lynn Vavreck, *The Gamble: Choice and Continuity in the*

2012 Presidential Election (Princeton, NJ: Princeton University Press, 2013), chapter 3.

55. Sides and Vavreck, *The Gamble*, 235–38.
56. Kurt Taylor Gaubatz, *Elections and War* (Stanford, CA: Stanford University Press, 1999), 49–50, 78–79, 126–27, 142–45.
57. Andrew Dugan, "Democrats Lack Advantage on Three Key U.S. Issue Areas," Gallup, September 16, 2013.
58. Morris Fiorina, *Retrospective Voting in American National Elections* (New Haven, CT: Yale University Press, 1981).
59. Patrick O'Connor, "WSJ/NBC News Poll: Obama's Approval Rating Hits New Low," *Wall Street Journal*, March 12, 2014.
60. Pew Research Center, *Public Sees U.S. Power Declining as Support for Global Engagement Slips*, December 2013.
61. Daniel Larison, "Forget Reagan," *American Conservative*, May–June 2013.

Chapter 5

1. American grand strategy under Reagan was laid out in key documents including NSDD-32, "U.S. National Security Strategy," May 20, 1982, and NSDD-75, "U.S. Relations with the USSR," January 17, 1983, Ronald Reagan Library, Simi Valley, California. Some of the most useful secondary commentary includes John Arquilla, *The Reagan Imprint* (Chicago: Ivan R Dee, 2006); Alan Dobson, "The Reagan Administration, Economic Warfare, and Starting to Close Down the Cold War," *Diplomatic History*, June 2005, 531–56; and Paul Lettow, *Ronald Reagan and His Quest to Abolish Nuclear Weapons* (New York: Random House, 2005).
2. Fred Kaplan, "The Realist," *Politico*, February 27, 2014.
3. Jeffrey Bader, *Obama and China's Rise* (Washington, DC: Brookings Institution Press, 2013), 6.
4. Hans Morgenthau, *Politics among Nations: The Struggle for Power and Peace*, 7th ed. (New York: McGraw Hill, 2006).
5. Morgenthau, *Politics among Nations*; E. H. Carr, *The Twenty Year's Crisis* (New York: Palgrave Macmillan, 2001); Reinhold Niebuhr, *The Children of Light and the Children of Darkness* (Chicago: University of Chicago Press, 2011); Nicholas Spykman, *America's Strategy in World Politics* (Edison, NJ: Transaction Publishers, 2007); George Kennan, *American Diplomacy*, 60th anniversary expanded ed. (Chicago: University of Chicago Press, 2012); Henry Kissinger, *Diplomacy* (New York: Simon and Schuster, 1995); Kenneth Waltz, *Theory of International Politics* (Long

Grove, IL: Waveland Press, 2010); Robert Gilpin, *War and Change in World Politics* (New York: Cambridge University Press, 1983); Stephen Walt, *Taming American Power* (New York: Norton, 2006); John Mearsheimer, *The Tragedy of Great Power Politics*, updated ed. (New York: Norton, 2014); and Robert Art, *A Grand Strategy for America* (Ithaca, NY: Cornell University Press, 2004).

6. Colin Dueck, *Hard Line: The Republican Party and U.S. Foreign Policy since World War II* (Princeton, NJ: Princeton University Press, 2010), chapters 3, 5–7.

7. Samuel Huntington, "Why International Primacy Matters," *International Security* 17:4 (Spring 1993), 68–83; Robert Jervis, "International Primacy: Is the Game Worth the Candle?" *International Security* 17:4 (Spring 1993), 52–67.

8. Charles Krauthammer, "The Unipolar Moment," *Foreign Affairs* 70:1 (1990–91), 23–33.

9. Stephen Brooks and William Wohlforth, *World out of Balance: International Relations and the Challenge of American Primacy* (Princeton, NJ: Princeton University Press, 2008).

10. Samuel Huntington, "The Lonely Superpower," *Foreign Affairs* 78:2 (March–April 1999), 35–49.

11. Barry Buzan and Ole Waever, *Regions and Powers: The Structure of International Security* (New York: Cambridge University Press, 2004), 34–35.

12. Huntington, "Why International Primacy Matters," 83.

13. See, for example, Christopher Layne, *Peace of Illusions* (Ithaca: Cornell University Press, 2007).

14. On the previous two paragraphs, see in particular Stephen Brooks, John Ikenberry, and William Wohlforth, "Don't Come Home, America," *International Security* 37:3 (Winter 2012–13), 7–51; and Art, *A Grand Strategy for America*, 8–9, 42–43, 136–145, 172–222.

15. Regarding the continued and relative extent of US capabilities and resources from a comparative international perspective, see Michael Beckley, "China's Century? Why America's Edge Will Endure," *International Security* 36:3 (Winter 2011–12), 41–78; Brooks and Wohlforth, *World out of Balance*; Eric Edelman, *Understanding America's Contested Primacy* (Washington, DC: Center for Strategic and Budgetary Assessments, 2010); Lawrence Freedman, "A Subversive on a Hill," *National Interest*, May–June 2009, 39–48; Aaron Friedberg, *The Weary Titan* (Princeton, NJ: Princeton University Press, 2010), 305–18; John Ikenberry, *Liberal Leviathan: The Origins, Crisis, and Transformation of the American World Order* (Princeton, NJ: Princeton University Press, 2012), chapter 4; John Ikenberry, Michael Mastanduno, and William Wohlforth, eds., *International Relations Theory and the Consequences of Unipolarity* (New York: Cambridge University

Press, 2011); Josef Joffe, *The Myth of America's Decline* (New York: Liveright, 2013); Robert Lieber, *Power and Willpower in the American Future* (New York: Cambridge University Press, 2012); Kati Suominen, *Peerless and Periled: The Paradox of American Leadership in the World Economic Order* (Stanford, CA: Stanford Economics and Finance, 2012); and Susan Yoshihara and Douglas Sylva, eds., *Population Decline and the Remaking of Great Power Politics* (Washington, DC: Potomac Books, 2011).

16. US Department of Defense, *Quadrennial Defense Review*, March 2014.

17. Francis Fukuyama, *The End of History and the Last Man* (New York: Free Press, 1992).

18. See the report by Freedom House, *Freedom in the World 2014*.

19. For some useful related commentary, see Azar Gat, "The Return of Authoritarian Great Powers," *Foreign Affairs* 86:4 (July–August 2007), 59–69; Jakub Grygiel, *Great Powers and Geopolitical Change* (Baltimore, MD: Johns Hopkins University Press, 2006), chapter 7; Robert Kagan, *The Return of History and the End of Dreams* (New York: Vintage, 2009); Robert Kaplan, *The Revenge of Geography* (New York: Random House, 2012); Walter Russell Mead, "The Return of Geopolitics," *Foreign Affairs* 93:3 (May–June 2014), 69–79; Alexandros Petersen, *The World Island: Geopolitics and the Fate of the West* (Santa Barbara, CA: Praeger, 2011); and Dale Walton, *Geopolitics and the Great Powers in the 21st Century* (New York: Routledge, 2007).

20. Glenn Snyder, *Alliance Politics* (Ithaca, NY: Cornell University Press, 2007), 181–86.

21. A. Wess Mitchell, Jakub Grygiel, and Robert Kron, "Hingepoint Allies: Bolstering U.S. Alliances with Exposed States in Central Europe, East Asia and the Middle East," Center for European Policy Analysis, October 8, 2010.

22. Daniel Goldhagen, *The Devil That Never Dies: The Rise and Threat of Global Antisemitism* (New York: Little, Brown, 2013), 131–33, 219–20, 236–37.

23. Some of the most useful and enduring works on deterrence and compellence include Robert Art and Patrick Cronin, eds., *The United States and Coercive Diplomacy* (Washington, DC: United States Institute of Peace, 2003); Lawrence Freedman, *Deterrence* (Cambridge: Polity, 2004); Alexander George, *Forceful Persuasion* (Washington, DC: United States Institute of Peace, 2009); Alexander George and Richard Smoke, *Deterrence in American Foreign Policy* (New York: Columbia University Press, 1974); Paul Huth, *Extended Deterrence and the Prevention of War* (New Haven, CT: Yale University Press, 1991); Patrick Morgan, *Deterrence Now* (New York: Cambridge University Press, 2003); Thomas Schelling, *Arms and Influence* (New Haven, CT: Yale University Press, 1967); and Thomas Schelling, *The Strategy of Conflict* (Cambridge, MA: Harvard University Press, 1981).

24. Ian Brzezinski, "Three Ways NATO Can Bolster Ukraine's Security," *Washington Post*, March 24, 2014; Edward Lucas, A. Wess Mitchell, et al., "Report No. 35: Central European Security After Crimea," Center for European Policy Analysis, March 25, 2014.

25. Peter Baker, "In Cold War Echo, Obama Strategy Writes Off Putin," *New York Times*, April 19, 2014.

26. James Sherr, *Hard Diplomacy and Soft Coercion: Russia's Influence Abroad* (London: Chatham House, 2013), 113.

27. For some useful discussion, see Dan Blumenthal, "The U.S. Response to China's Military Modernization," in Ashley Tellis, ed., *Strategic Asia, 2012–13: China's Military Challenge* (Seattle, WA: National Bureau of Asian Research, 2012), 309–40; Elbridge Colby and Ely Ratner, "Roiling the Waters: Why the United States Needs to Stop Playing Peacemaker and Start Making China Feel Uncomfortable," *Foreign Policy*, January 21, 2014; Jacqueline Newmyer Deal, "Chinese Dominance Isn't Certain," *National Interest*, May–June 2014; Aaron Friedberg, *A Contest for Supremacy: China, America, and the Struggle for Mastery in Asia* (New York: Norton: 2012); Avery Goldstein, "China's Real and Present Danger," *Foreign Affairs*, September–October 2013; Michael Green, "Negotiating Asia's Troubled Waters," *New York Times*, April 23, 2014; Sebastian Heilmann and Dirk Schmidt, *China's Foreign Political and Economic Relations* (Lanham, MD: Rowman and Littlefield, 2014); Edward Luttwak, *The Rise of China vs. the Logic of Strategy* (Cambridge, MA: Belknap Press of Harvard University Press, 2012); Thomas Mahnken, ed., *Competitive Strategies for the 21st Century: Theory, History, and Practice* (Stanford, CA: Stanford University Press, 2012); and Ashley Tellis, "Balancing without Containment: A U.S. Strategy for Confronting China's Rise," *Washington Quarterly* 36:4 (Fall 2013), 109–24.

28. Matthew Kroenig, *A Time to Attack: The Looming Iranian Nuclear Threat* (New York: Palgrave Macmillan, 2014); Kenneth Pollack, *Unthinkable: Iran, the Bomb, and American Strategy* (New York: Simon and Schuster, 2013).

29. For some interesting recommendations on the subject of "political warfare," see Max Boot and Michael Doran, "Policy Innovation Memorandum No. 33," Council on Foreign Relations, June 7, 2013.

30. David Sanger, "U.S. Confronts Consequences of Underestimating North Korean Leader," *New York Times*, April 24, 2014.

31. Patrick Cronin, "If Deterrence Fails: Rethinking Conflict on the Korean Peninsula," Center for a New American Security, March 2014.

32. Victor Cha, *The Impossible State: North Korea, Past and Future* (New York: Ecco, 2013), 297–305.

33. Peter Walker, "North Korea Human Rights Abuses Resemble Those of the Nazis, Says UN Inquiry," *Guardian*, February 17, 2014.

34. On North Korea's system of work camps, see Blaine Harden, *Escape from Camp 14* (New York: Penguin, 2013); and Melanie Kirkpatrick, *Escape from North Korea: The Untold Story of Asia's Underground Railroad* (New York: Encounter Books, 2014).

35. Sue Mi Terry, "A Korea Whole and Free," *Foreign Affairs* 93:4 (July–August 2014), 153–62.

36. US Department of Defense, *Quadrennial Defense Review Report,* February 2010.

37. Don Rassler et al., "Letters from Abbottabad: Bin Ladin Sidelined?" The Combating Terrorism Center at West Point, May 3, 2012.

38. Katherine Zimmerman, "The Al Qaeda Network: A New Framework for Defining the Enemy," American Enterprise Institute, September 2013.

39. Michael Hayden, "American Intelligence and the 'High Noon' Scenario," *Wall Street Journal,* October 30, 2013.

40. Remarks by the President at the National Defense University, Fort McNair, May 23, 2013, The White House.

41. Al-qaeda must be destroyed. Richard Clarke, *Against All Enemies* (New York: Free Press, 2004), chapter 8.

42. Office of Management and Budget (OMB), *Historical Tables: Budget of the U.S. Government, Fiscal Year 2014* (Washington, DC: April 2013), 155–56.

43. Gates, *Duty,* 303–22, 453–65, 546–51.

44. Gordon Adams et al., "Defense Reform Consensus," *The Hill,* June 3, 2013.

45. OMB, *Historical Tables,* 155–56.

46. Robert Zoellick, "Leading from the Front on Free Trade," *Wall Street Journal,* January 12, 2014.

47. Some of the classic works on this topic include Yuen Khong, *Analogies at War: Korea, Munich, Dien Bien Phu, and the Vietnam Decisions of 1965* (Princeton, NJ: Princeton University Press, 1992); Ernest May, *"Lessons" of the Past: The Use and Misuse of History in American Foreign Policy* (New York: Oxford University Press, 1975); Richard Neustadt and Ernest May, *Thinking in Time: The Uses of History for Decision-Makers* (New York: Free Press, 1988).

48. Gates, *Duty,* 590.

49. John Burke and Fred Greenstein, *How Presidents Test Reality* (New York: Russell Sage Foundation, 1991); William Newmann, *Managing National Security Policy: The President and the Process* (Pittsburgh, PA: University of Pittsburgh Press, 2003); Thomas Preston, *The President and His Inner Circle: Leadership Style and the Advisory Process in Foreign Affairs* (New York: Columbia University Press, 2001); Peter Rodman, *Presidential Command: Power, Leadership, and the Making of Foreign Policy from Richard Nixon to George W. Bush* (New York: Vintage Books, 2010); Elizabeth Saunders, *Leaders at War: How Presidents Shape Military Interventions* (Ithaca, NY: Cornell University Press, 2011); Steve Yetiv, *Explaining Foreign*

Policy: U.S. Decision-Making in the Gulf Wars, 2nd ed. (Baltimore, MD: Johns Hopkins University Press, 2011).

50. Aristotle, *The Ethics* (Baltimore, MD: Penguin, 1966 edition), 65, 176.

51. For a fine application to the study of US presidents, see Ethan Fishman, *The Prudential Presidency: An Aristotelian Approach to Presidential Leadership* (Westport, CT: Praeger, 2001).

52. See Aaron Friedberg, "Strengthening U.S. Strategic Planning," *Washington Quarterly* 31:1 (Winter 2007–8), 47–60; Paul Lettow and Tom Mahnken, "Toolbox: Getting Serious about Strategic Planning," *American Interest*, September–October 2009; and the essays by Richard Haass, Peter Feaver and William Inboden, and Andrew Erdmann, in Daniel Drezner, ed., *Avoiding Trivia: The Role of Strategic Planning in American Foreign Policy* (Washington, DC: Brookings Institution Press, 2009).

BIBLIOGRAPHY

Selected Addresses and Works by Barack Obama

Dreams from My Father: A Story of Race and Inheritance. New York: Times Books, 1995.

Speech against the Iraq war, delivered in Chicago on October 2, 2002.

The Audacity of Hope. New York: Crown Publishers, 2006.

Remarks announcing candidacy for president in Springfield, IL, February 10, 2007.

"Renewing American Leadership." *Foreign Affairs*, July–August 2007, 2–16.

"Obama Delivers Berlin Address." *Washington Post*, July 24, 2008.

"Barack Obama's Acceptance Speech." *New York Times*, August 28, 2008.

Inaugural Address, Washington, DC, January 20, 2009.

Remarks on a New Strategy for Afghanistan and Pakistan, White House, March 27, 2009.

Remarks in Prague, Czech Republic, April 5, 2009.

Remarks at Cairo University, Cairo, Egypt, June 4, 2009.

Address to the Nation on the Way Forward in Afghanistan and Pakistan, West Point, New York, December 1, 2009.

Remarks at the Acceptance of the Nobel Peace Prize, Oslo, Norway, December 10, 2009.

Remarks on the Situation in Egypt, White House, February 1, 2011.

Remarks on the Way Forward in Afghanistan, White House, June 22, 2011.

Statement on the Situation in Syria, White House, August 18, 2011.

Remarks to the Australian Parliament, Canberra, Australia, November 17, 2011.

Speech in Osawatomie, Kansas, December 6, 2011.

Address to the Democratic National Convention, September 6, 2012.

Remarks to the UN General Assembly, New York, September 25, 2012.

Second Inaugural Address, Washington, DC, January 21, 2013.

Remarks at the National Defense University, Fort McNair, Washington, DC, May 23, 2013.

Remarks at the Brandenburg Gate, Berlin, Germany, June 19, 2013.

Address to the United Nations General Assembly, New York, September 24, 2013.

Remarks on Review of Signals Intelligence, Department of Justice, Washington, DC, January 17, 2014.

Address to European Youth, Brussels, Belgium, March 26, 2014.

Remarks at the United States Military Academy Commencement Ceremony, West Point, NY, May 28, 2014.

Address to the United Nations General Assembly, New York, September 24, 2014.

The Obama Era

Abramson, Paul, et al. *Change and Continuity in the 2008 and 2010 Elections.* Washington, DC: Congressional Quarterly Press, 2012.

Alter, Jonathan. *The Center Holds: Obama and His Enemies.* New York: Simon and Schuster, 2013.

Balz, Dan. *Collision 2012: Obama vs. Romney and the Future of Elections in America.* New York: Viking, 2013.

Boaz, David, ed. *Cato Handbook for Policymakers.* 7th ed. Washington, DC: Cato Institute, 2009.

Box-Steffensmeier, Janet, and Steven Schier, eds. *The American Elections of 2012.* New York: Routledge, 2013.

Brookings Institution. "2013 American Values Survey: In Search of Libertarians in America." Washington, DC: Brookings Institution, 2013.

Ceaser, James, Andrew Busch, and John Pitney. *After Hope and Change: The 2012 Elections and American Politics.* Lanham, MD: Rowman and Littlefield, 2013.

———. *Epic Journey: The 2008 Elections and American Politics.* Lanham, MD: Rowman and Littlefield, 2011.

Codevilla, Angelo. "The Chosen One." *Claremont Review of Books* 11:3 (Summer 2011).

Corn, David. *Showdown: The Inside Story of How Obama Battled the GOP to Set Up the 2012 Election.* New York: William Morrow, 2012.

Eberstadt, Nicholas. *A Nation of Takers: America's Entitlement Epidemic.* West Conshohocken, PA: Templeton Press, 2012.

Edsall, Thomas. "The Future of the Obama Coalition." *New York Times,* November 27, 2011.

Edwards, George. *Overreach: Leadership in the Obama Presidency.* Princeton, NJ: Princeton University Press, 2012.

Fallows, James. "Obama, Explained." *Atlantic,* March 2012.

Ferguson, Niall. *The Great Degeneration.* New York: Penguin, 2013.

Fiorina, Morris. *Culture War?* Boston, MA: Longman, 2011.

Foley, Elizabeth Price. *The Tea Party: Three Principles.* New York: Cambridge University Press, 2012.

Gelman, Andrew. *Red State, Blue State, Rich State, Poor State*. Princeton, NJ: Princeton University Press, 2010.

Goldsmith, Jack. *Power and Constraint: The Accountable Presidency after 9/11*. New York: Norton, 2012.

Grunwald, Michael. *The New New Deal: The Hidden Story of Change in the Obama Era*. New York: Simon and Schuster, 2012.

Holmes, Kim. *Rebound*. Lanham, MD: Rowman and Littlefield, 2013.

Institute of Politics, John F. Kennedy School of Government. *Campaign for President: The Managers Look at 2012*. Lanham, MD: Rowman and Littlefield, 2013.

Jacobson, Gary. "The 2008 Presidential and Congressional Elections." *Political Science Quarterly* 124:1 (Spring 2009), 1–30.

———. "How the Economy and Partisanship Shaped the 2012 Presidential and Congressional Elections." *Political Science Quarterly* 128:1 (Spring 2013), 1–38.

———. "The Republican Resurgence in 2010." *Political Science Quarterly* 126:1 (Spring 2011), 27–52.

Judis, John. *The Emerging Democratic Majority*. New York: Scribner, 2002.

Kesler, Charles. *I Am the Change: Barack Obama and the Crisis of Liberalism*. New York: Broadside Books, 2012.

Kimball, Roger, ed. *The New Leviathan: The State versus the Individual in the 21st Century*. New York: Encounter Books, 2012.

Kloppenberg, James. *Reading Obama: Dreams, Hope, and the American Political Tradition*. Princeton, NJ: Princeton University Press, 2010.

Kohut, Andrew. *Trends in American Values: 1987–2012*. Pew Research Center for the People and the Press, 2012.

Maraniss, David. *Barack Obama: The Story*. New York: Simon and Schuster, 2013.

Office of Management and Budget. *Historical Tables: Budget of the U.S. Government, Fiscal Year 2014*. Washington, DC, April 2013.

Olsen, Henry. "A GOP Dark Horse?" *National Affairs* 8 (Summer 2011), 106–20.

Pew Research Center. *2012 American Values Survey*. 2012.

———. *Beyond Red vs. Blue: The Political Typology*. 2014.

———. *Political Polarization in the American Public*. 2014.

Plouffe, David. *The Audacity to Win*. New York: Viking, 2009.

Rae, Nicol. "Be Careful What You Wish For: The Rise of Responsible Parties in American National Politics." *Annual Review of Political Science* 10 (2007), 169–91.

Remnick, David. *The Bridge: The Life and Rise of Barack Obama*. New York: Vintage, 2011.

———. "Going the Distance." *New Yorker*, January 27, 2014.

Renshon, Stanley. *Barack Obama and the Politics of Redemption*. New York: Routledge, 2011.

Sabato, Larry, ed. *Barack Obama and the New America*. Lanham, MD: Rowman and Littlefield, 2013.

Schier, Steven, ed. *Transforming America: Barack Obama in the White House*. Lanham, MD: Rowman and Littlefield, 2011.

Sides, John, and Lynn Vavreck. *The Gamble: Choice and Chance in the 2012 Presidential Election*. Princeton, NJ: Princeton University Press, 2013.

Skocpol, Theda. *Obama and America's Political Future*. Cambridge, MA: Harvard University Press, 2012.

Skocpol, Theda, and Vanessa Williamson. *The Tea Party and the Remaking of Republican Conservatism*. New York: Oxford University Press, 2012.

Skowronek, Stephen. *Presidential Leadership in Political Time: Reprise and Reappraisal*. 2nd ed. Lawrence: University Press of Kansas, 2011.

Tanenhaus, Sam. *The Death of Conservatism: A Movement and Its Consequences*. New York: Random House, 2010.

Thurber, James, ed. *Obama in Office*. Boulder, CO: Paradigm Publishers, 2011.

Voegeli, William. *Never Enough: America's Limitless Welfare State*. New York: Encounter Books, 2012.

Wolffe, Richard. *Revival: The Struggle for Survival inside the Obama White House*. New York: Broadway, 2011.

Woodward, Bob. *The Price of Politics*. New York: Simon and Schuster, 2012.

Grand Strategy

Aron, Raymond. *Peace and War: A Theory of International Relations*. New Brunswick, NJ: Transaction Publishers, 2003.

Art, Robert. *A Grand Strategy for America*. Ithaca, NY: Cornell University Press, 2003.

Art, Robert, and Patrick Cronin, eds. *The United States and Coercive Diplomacy*. Washington, DC: United States Institute of Peace, 2003.

Baldwin, David. *Economic Statecraft*. Princeton, NJ: Princeton University Press, 1985.

Betts, Richard. *American Force: Dangers, Delusions, and Dilemmas in National Security*. New York: Columbia University Press, 2012.

Brands, Hal. *What Good Is Grand Strategy?* Ithaca, NY: Cornell University Press, 2014.

Brooks, Stephen, John Ikenberry, and William Wohlforth. "Don't Come Home, America." *International Security* 37:3 (Winter 2012–13), 7–51.

Deibel, Terry. *Foreign Affairs Strategy: Logic for American Statecraft*. New York: Cambridge University Press, 2007.

Dueck, Colin. "Hybrid Strategies: The American Experience." *Orbis* (Winter 2011), 30–52.

———. *Reluctant Crusaders*. Princeton, NJ: Princeton University Press, 2006.

Feaver, Peter. "American Grand Strategy at the Crossroads." In Richard Fontaine and Kristin Lord, eds., *America's Path: Grand Strategy for the Next Administration*. Washington, DC: Center for a New American Security, 2012.

Freedman, Lawrence. *Strategy: A History*. New York: Oxford University Press, 2013.

Freeman, Chas. *Arts of Power: Statecraft and Diplomacy*. Washington, DC: United States Institute of Peace, 1997.

Gaddis, John. *Strategies of Containment: A Critical Appraisal of American National Security Policy during the Cold War*. Rev. ed. New York: Oxford University Press, 2005.

George, Alexander. *Forceful Persuasion: Coercive Diplomacy as an Alternative to War*. Washington, DC: United States Institute of Peace, 2009.

Gilpin, Robert. *War and Change in World Politics*. New York: Cambridge University Press, 1983.

Gray, Colin. *Modern Strategy*. New York: Oxford University Press, 1999.

Grygiel, Jakub. *Great Powers and Geopolitical Change*. Baltimore, MD: Johns Hopkins University Press, 2006.

Hill, Charles. *Grand Strategies: Literature, Statecraft, and World Order*. New Haven, CT: Yale University Press, 2011.

Huntington, Samuel. "Why International Primacy Matters." *International Security* 17:4 (Spring 1993), 68–83.

Ikenberry, John. *Liberal Leviathan: The Origins, Crisis, and Transformation of the American World Order*. Princeton, NJ: Princeton University Press, 2012.

Johnston, Alastair Iain. *Cultural Realism: Strategic Culture and Grand Strategy in Chinese History*. Princeton, NJ: Princeton University Press, 1998.

Kennan, George. *American Diplomacy*. 60th anniversary expanded ed. Chicago: University of Chicago Press, 2012.

Kennedy, Paul. *The Rise and Fall of the Great Powers*. New York: Vintage, 1989.

Kissinger, Henry. *Diplomacy*. New York: Simon and Schuster, 1995.

Kupchan, Charles. *How Enemies Become Friends: The Sources of Stable Peace*. Princeton, NJ: Princeton University Press, 2010.

———. *Vulnerability of Empire*. New York: Cornell University Press, 1994.

Lamborn, Alan. *The Price of Power*. Boston, MA: Unwin Hyman, 1991.

Layne, Christopher. "From Preponderance to Offshore Balancing." *International Security* 22:1 (Summer 1997), 86–124.

———. *The Peace of Illusions*. Ithaca, NY: Cornell University Press, 2007.

Liddell Hart, B. H. *Strategy*. New York: Praeger, 1954.

Luttwak, Edward. *The Grand Strategy of the Byzantine Empire*. Cambridge, MA: Belknap Press of Harvard University Press, 2011.

———. *The Grand Strategy of the Roman Empire*. Baltimore, MD: Johns Hopkins University Press, 1979.

Luttwak, Edward. *Strategy: The Logic of War and Peace.* Rev. ed. Cambridge, MA: Belknap Press of Harvard University Press, 2001.

Mahnken, Thomas, ed. *Competitive Strategies for the 21st Century: Theory, History, and Practice.* Stanford, CA: Stanford University Press, 2012.

Mearsheimer, John. "Imperial by Design." *National Interest,* January–February 2011, 16–34.

———. *The Tragedy of Great Power Politics.* Updated ed. New York: Norton, 2014.

Miller, Paul. "Five Pillars of American Grand Strategy." *Survival* 54:5 (October–November 2012), 7–44.

Morgenthau, Hans. *Politics among Nations: The Struggle for Power and Peace.* 7th ed. New York: McGraw Hill, 2006.

Murray, Williamson, Richard Hart Sinnreich, and James Lacey, eds. *The Shaping of Grand Strategy: Policy, Diplomacy, and War.* New York: Cambridge University Press, 2011.

Narizny, Kevin. *The Political Economy of Grand Strategy.* Ithaca, NY: Cornell University Press, 2007.

Owens, Mac. "Principle and Prudence in American Foreign Policy." Foreign Policy Research Institute, January 2014.

Paret, Peter, ed. *Makers of Modern Strategy from Machiavelli to the Nuclear Age.* Princeton, NJ: Princeton University Press, 1986.

Platias, Athanassioss, and Constantinios Koliopoulos. *Thucydides on Strategy.* New York: Oxford University Press, 2009.

Posen, Barry. *Restraint: A New Foundation for U.S. Grand Strategy.* Ithaca, NY: Cornell University Press, 2014.

Powell, Robert. *In the Shadow of Power: States and Strategies in International Politics.* Princeton, NJ: Princeton University Press, 1999.

Preble, Christopher. *The Power Problem.* Ithaca, NY: Cornell University Press, 2009.

Rock, Stephen. *Appeasement in International Politics.* Lawrence: University Press of Kansas, 2000.

Rosecrance, Richard, and Arthur Stein, eds. *The Domestic Bases of Grand Strategy.* Ithaca, NY: Cornell University Press, 1993.

Schelling, Thomas. *Arms and Influence.* New Haven, CT: Yale University Press, 1967.

———. *The Strategy of Conflict.* Cambridge, MA: Harvard University Press, 1981.

Schweller, Randall. "Unanswered Threats: A Neoclassical Realist Theory of Underbalancing." *International Security* 29:2 (Fall 2004), 159–201.

Snyder, Glenn. *Alliance Politics.* Ithaca, NY: Cornell University Press, 2007.

Snyder, Jack. *Myths of Empire: Domestic Politics and International Ambition.* Ithaca, NY: Cornell University Press, 1991.

Spykman, Nicholas. *America's Strategy in World Politics.* New Brunswick, NJ: Transaction Publishers, 2007.

Taliaferro, Jeffrey, Norrin Ripsman, and Steven Lobell, eds. *The Challenge of Grand Strategy*. New York: Cambridge University Press, 2013.

Walt, Stephen. "Offshore Balancing: An Idea Whose Time Has Come." *Foreign Policy*, November 2, 2011.

———. *Taming American Power*. New York: Norton, 2006.

Zegart, Amy. "A Foreign Policy for the Future." Defining Ideas. Hoover Institution, November 20, 2013.

Presidential Leadership and Foreign Policy Decision-Making

Burke, John, and Fred Greenstein. *How Presidents Test Reality*. New York: Russell Sage Foundation, 1991.

Cohen, Eliot. *Supreme Command: Soldiers, Statesmen, and Leadership in Wartime*. New York: Free Press, 2002.

Drezner, Daniel, ed. *Avoiding Trivia: The Role of Strategic Planning in American Foreign Policy*. Washington, DC: Brookings Institution Press, 2009.

Durant, Robert, and Paul Diehl. "Agendas, Alternatives, and Public Policy: Lessons from the U.S. Foreign Policy Arena." *Journal of Public Policy* 9:2 (1989), 179–205.

Friedberg, Aaron. "Strengthening U.S. Strategic Planning." *Washington Quarterly* 31:1 (Winter 2007–8), 47–60.

Gelb, Leslie. *Power Rules*. New York: Harper Perennial, 2009.

George, Alexander. *Presidential Decisionmaking in Foreign Policy: The Effective Use of Information and Advice*. Boulder, CO: Westview Press, 1980.

Halperin, Morton, and Priscilla Clapp. *Bureaucratic Politics and Foreign Policy*. 2nd ed. Washington, DC: Brookings Institution Press, 2006.

Khong, Yuen. *Analogies at War: Korea, Munich, Dien Bien Phu, and the Vietnam Decisions of 1965*. Princeton, NJ: Princeton University Press, 1992.

Kowert, Paul. *Groupthink or Deadlock: When Do Leaders Learn from Their Advisors?* Albany: SUNY Press, 2002.

Krasner, Stephen. "Are Bureaucracies Important? Or Allison Wonderland." *Foreign Policy* 7 (1972), 159–79.

Lettow, Paul, and Tom Mahnken. "Toolbox: Getting Serious about Strategic Planning." *American Interest*, September–October 2009.

May, Ernest. *"Lessons" of the Past: The Use and Misuse of History in American Foreign Policy*. New York: Oxford University Press, 1975.

McDermott, Rose. *Risk-Taking in International Politics: Prospect Theory in American Foreign Policy*. Ann Arbor: University of Michigan Press, 2001.

Mintz, Alex, and Karl DeRouen. *Understanding Foreign Policy Decision Making*. New York: Cambridge University Press, 2010.

Newmann, William. *Managing National Security Policy: The President and the Process*. Pittsburgh, PA: University of Pittsburgh Press, 2003.

Nye, Joseph. *Presidential Leadership and the Creation of the American Era*. Princeton, NJ: Princeton University Press, 2014.

Preston, Thomas. *The President and His Inner Circle: Leadership Style and the Advisory Process in Foreign Affairs*. New York: Columbia University Press, 2001.

Renshon, Stanley, and Deborah Welch Larson, eds. *Good Judgment in Foreign Policy*. Lanham, MD: Rowman and Littlefield, 2003.

Rodman, Peter. *Presidential Command: Power, Leadership, and the Making of Foreign Policy from Richard Nixon to George W. Bush*. New York: Vintage Books, 2010.

Saunders, Elizabeth. *Leaders at War: How Presidents Shape Military Interventions*. Ithaca, NY: Cornell University Press, 2011.

Sestanovich, Stephen. *Maximalist: America in the World from Truman to Obama*. New York: Knopf, 2014.

Snyder, Richard, H. W. Bruck, and Burton Sapin. *Foreign Policy Decision Making*. New York: Palgrave Macmillan, 2002.

t'Hart, Paul, Eric Stern, and Bengt Sundelius, eds. *Beyond Groupthink: Political Group Dynamics and Foreign Policy-making*. Ann Arbor: University of Michigan Press, 1997.

Walton, Dale. *Grand Strategy and the Presidency*. New York: Routledge, 2013.

Western, Jon. "Sources of Humanitarian Intervention: Beliefs, Information, and Advocacy in the U.S. Decisions on Somalia and Bosnia." *International Security* 26:4 (Spring 2002), 112–42.

Yetiv, Steve. *Explaining Foreign Policy: U.S. Decision-Making in the Gulf Wars*. 2nd ed. Baltimore, MD: Johns Hopkins University Press, 2011.

Domestic Politics and US Foreign Policy

General

Auerswald, David, and Colton Campbell, eds. *Congress and the Politics of National Security*. New York: Cambridge University Press, 2011.

Bueno de Mequita, Bruce, Alastair Smith, Randolph Siverson, and James Morrow. *The Logic of Political Survival*. Cambridge, MA: MIT Press, 2004.

Destler, I. M. *American Trade Politics*. 4th ed. Washington, DC: Institute for International Economics, 2005.

Dueck, Colin. *Hard Line: The Republican Party and U.S. Foreign Policy since World War II*. Princeton, NJ: Princeton University Press, 2010.

Fiorina, Morris. *Retrospective Voting in American National Elections*. New Haven, CT: Yale University Press, 1981.

Gaubatz, Kurt Taylor. *Elections and War*. Stanford, CA: Stanford University Press, 1999.

Gelpi, Christopher, Peter Feaver, and Jason Reifler. *Paying the Human Costs of War: American Public Opinion and Casualties in Military Conflicts*. Princeton, NJ: Princeton University Press, 2009.

Henehan, Marie. *Foreign Policy and Congress*. Ann Arbor: University of Michigan Press, 2000.

Holsti, Ole. *Public Opinion and American Foreign Policy*. Rev. ed. Ann Arbor: University of Michigan Press, 2004.

Kaufman, Robert. "A Two-Level Interaction: Structure, Stable Liberal Democracy, and U.S. Grand Strategy." *Security Studies* 3:4 (Summer 1994), 678–717.

Levin, Martin, Daniel DiSalvo, and Martin Shapiro, eds. *Building Coalitions, Making Policy*. Baltimore, MD: Johns Hopkins University Press, 2012.

Levy, Jack, and William Mabe. "Politically Motivated Opposition to War." *International Studies Review* 6:4 (December 2004), 65–84.

Liberman, Peter. "An Eye for an Eye." *International Organization* 60:3 (July 2006), 687–722.

Lindsay, James. *Congress and the Politics of U.S. Foreign Policy*. Baltimore, MD: Johns Hopkins University Press, 1994.

McCormick, James, ed. *The Domestic Sources of Foreign Policy*. 6th ed. Lanham, MD: Rowman and Littlefield, 2012.

Mead, Walter Russell. *Special Providence*. New York: Alfred A. Knopf, 2001.

Mueller, John. *War, Presidents, and Public Opinion*. New York: John Wiley and Sons, 1973.

Nau, Henry. *Conservative Internationalism*. Princeton, NJ: Princeton University Press, 2013.

Nincic, Miroslav. *Democracy and Foreign Policy*. New York: Columbia University Press, 1992.

Page, Benjamin, and Robert Shapiro. *The Rational Public*. Chicago: University of Chicago Press, 1992.

Putnam, Robert. "Diplomacy and Domestic Politics: The Logic of Two-Level Games." *International Organization* 42:3 (June 1988), 427–60.

Quandt, William. "The Electoral Cycle and the Conduct of Foreign Policy." *Political Science Quarterly* 101:5 (1986), 825–37.

Rathbun, Brian. "Does One Right Make a Realist? Conservatism, Neo-conservatism, and Isolationism in the Foreign Policy Ideology of American Elites." *Political Science Quarterly* 123:2 (Summer 2008), 271–300.

———. *Trust in International Cooperation: International Security Institutions, Domestic Politics and American Multilateralism*. New York: Cambridge University Press, 2012.

Rhodes, Edward. "Sea Change: Interest-Based vs. Cultural-Cognitive Accounts of Strategic Choice in the 1890s." *Security Studies* 5:4 (Summer 1996), 73–124.

Russett, Bruce. *Controlling the Sword: The Democratic Governance of National Security*. Cambridge, MA: Harvard University Press, 1990.

Tocqueville, Alexis de. *Democracy in America*. Ed. J. P. Mayer and Max Lerner. Trans. George Lawrence. New York: Harper and Row, 1966.

Trubowitz, Peter. *Politics and Strategy: Partisan Ambition and American Statecraft.* Princeton, NJ: Princeton University Press, 2011.

Contemporary

Antle, W. James, III. "Rand Plan: Will the Tea Parties Turn Antiwar?" *American Conservative*, August 1, 2010.

Ballhaus, Rebecca. "WSJ/NBC Poll: Drone Attacks Have Broad Support." *Wall Street Journal*, June 5, 2013.

Balz, Dan, and Peyton Craighill. "Poll: Public Supports Strikes in Iraq, Syria; Obama's Ratings Hover Near His All-Time Lows." *Washington Post*, September 9, 2014.

Barone, Michael. "Not So Hawkish: Republicans after the Iraq War." *National Review*, March 28, 2013.

Chicago Council on Global Affairs. *Constrained Internationalism: Adapting to New Realities.* Chicago Council on Global Affairs, 2010.

———. *Foreign Policy in the New Millennium.* Chicago: Chicago Council on Global Affairs, 2012.

Cillizza, Chris, and Aaron Blake. "Majority of House Leaning 'No' on Syria Resolution." *Washington Post*, September 6, 2013.

Clement, Scott. "Majority of Americans Say Afghan War Has Not Been Worth Fighting." *Washington Post*, December 19, 2013.

Cruz, Ted. "The Vital Role of the Senate in Foreign Policy." Heritage Foundation, September 11, 2013.

Dinan, Stephen. "Bipartisan Congress Rebuffs Obama on Libya Mission." *Washington Times*, June 3, 2011.

Douthat, Ross. "The Obama Synthesis." *New York Times*, January 12, 2013.

Dugan, Andrew. "Democrats Lack Advantage on Three Key U.S. Issue Areas." Gallup, September 16, 2013.

Eilperin, Juliet. "Obama Lays Out His Foreign Policy Doctrine: Singles, Doubles, and the Occasional Home Run." *Washington Post*, April 28, 2014.

Frank, Barney. "The New Mandate on Defense." *Democracy: A Journal of Ideas* 27 (Winter 2013), 50–56.

Gerson, Michael. "1952 All Over Again." *National Journal*, June 21, 2014.

Haass, Richard. *Foreign Policy Begins at Home.* New York: Basic Books, 2013.

Hunt, Kasie. "Huntsman Focuses on Foreign Policy." *Politico*, June 3, 2011.

Jacobson, Gary. "A Tale of Two Wars: Public Opinion on the U.S. Military Interventions in Afghanistan and Iraq." *Presidential Studies Quarterly* 40 (December 2010), 585–610.

Jones, Jeffrey. "Americans Divided in Views of U.S. Defense Spending." Gallup, February 21, 2013.

———. "Americans Give GOP Edge on Most Election Issues: Greatest Republican Advantages on Terrorism, Immigration, Federal Spending." Gallup, September 1, 2010.

———. "Americans Oppose U.S. Military Involvement in Syria." Gallup, May 31, 2013.

Kagan, Robert. "President Obama's Foreign Policy Paradox." *Washington Post*, March 26, 2014.

Kohut, Andrew. "American International Engagement on the Rocks." Pew Research Global Attitudes Project, July 11, 2013.

Kurtz, Stanley. "Libya, War Powers, and Hawkish Conservatives." *National Review*, June 15, 2011.

Lindsay, James. "Campaign 2012 Roundup: Is Foreign Policy a Problem for Ron Paul?" Council on Foreign Relations, November 28, 2011.

Mandelbaum, Michael. *The Frugal Superpower*. New York: PublicAffairs, 2010.

Mason, Jeff. "Most Americans Would Back U.S. Strike over Iran Nuclear Weapon: Poll." Reuters, March 13, 2012.

McGurn, William. "Bin Laden's Last Challenge—to Republicans." *Wall Street Journal*, May 3, 2011.

Mead, Walter Russell. "The Tea Party and Foreign Policy: What Populism Means for Globalism." *Foreign Affairs*, March–April 2011, 28–44.

Newport, Frank. "Americans Disapprove of U.S. Decision to Arm Syrian Rebels." Gallup, June 17, 2013.

———. "Obama Rated Highest on Foreign Affairs, Lowest on Deficit." Gallup, February 11, 2013.

O'Connor, Patrick. "WSJ/NBC News Poll: Obama's Approval Rating Hits New Low." *Wall Street Journal*, March 12, 2014.

Paul, Rand. "Containment and Radical Islam." Address at the Heritage Foundation, February 6, 2013.

———. "Obama's Unconstitutional Libyan War." *Washington Times*, June 15, 2011.

———. "Rand Paul on Diplomacy." *National Interest*, January 16, 2014.

Payne, Sebastian, and Robert Costa. "Islamic State Prompts GOP to Strike More Hawkish Tone." *Washington Post*, September 4, 2014.

Pew Research Center. "In Shift from Bush Era, More Conservatives Say 'Come Home, America.'" June 16, 2011.

———. *Public Sees U.S. Power Declining as Support for Global Engagement Slips.* December 2013.

———. "Strong on Defense and Israel, Tough on China: Tea Party and Foreign Policy." October 7, 2011.

———. "Support for U.S. Airstrikes in Iraq; Concern About Getting Too Involved." August 18, 2014.

———. "Views of Obama's Approach for Afghanistan Troop Withdrawal Little Changed." June 23, 2011.

Pew Research Global Attitudes Project. "U.S. Public, Experts Differ on China Policies: Public Deeply Concerned about China's Economic Power." September 18, 2012.

Ponnuru, Ramesh. "The Angry Republican Foreign-Policy Mess." *Bloomberg View*, April 21, 2014.

Rasmussen Reports. "28% Say Libya Important to U.S. National Security Interests, 42% Disagree." March 25, 2011.

Rathbun, Brian. "Steeped in International Affairs? The Foreign Policy Views of the Tea Party." *Foreign Policy Analysis* 9 (2013), 21–37.

Rogers, David. "House Democrats Unite on Afghanistan Exit." *Politico,* May 30, 2011.

Rosen, Stephen. "The National Security Generation Gap." *Wall Street Journal,* March 30, 2014.

Saad, Lydia. "Americans Still Prefer Republicans for Combating Terrorism." Gallup, September 11, 2009.

Shalev, Chemi. "Poll: 64% of Americans Would Support U.S. Strike to Prevent Iran's Nuclear Program." *Haaretz,* March 19, 2013.

Shear, Michael, and Dalia Sussman. "Poll Finds Dissatisfaction over Iraq." *New York Times,* June 23, 2014.

Stephens, Bret. "Getting the GOP's Groove Back: How to Bridge the Republican Foreign Policy Divide." *Foreign Affairs* 92:2 (March–April 2013), 130–40.

Sussman, Dalia. "Poll Finds McCain Edge on Security." *New York Times,* September 25, 2008.

Swift, Art. "Americans Evenly Divided on Russia's Plan for Syria." Gallup, September 13, 2013.

Tanenhaus, Sam, and Jim Rutenberg. "Rand Paul's Mixed Inheritance." *New York Times,* January 25, 2014.

YouGov. "Survey on Foreign Policy and American Overseas Commitments." April 26–May 2, 2012.

US Foreign and National Security Policy under President Obama

Ackerman, Spencer. "The Obama Doctrine." *American Prospect* 19:4 (March 19, 2008), 12–15.

———. "The Obama Doctrine, Revisited." *American Prospect* 21:4 (March 24, 2010), 12–15.

Adams, Gordon, et al. "Defense Reform Consensus." *The Hill,* June 3, 2013.

Ali, Tariq. *The Obama Syndrome.* London: Verso, 2011.

Allen, Jonathan, and Amie Parnes. *HRC: State Secrets and the Rebirth of Hillary Clinton.* New York: Crown, 2014.

Aslund, Anders. "Moscow Is in No Economic Shape to Fight a War." *Moscow Times,* April 22, 2014.

Bader, Jeffrey. *Obama and China's Rise: An Insider's Account of America's Asia Strategy.* Washington, DC: Brookings Institution Press, 2013.

Baker, Peter. "In Cold War Echo, Obama Strategy Writes Off Putin." *New York Times,* April 19, 2014.

———. "White House Scraps Bush's Approach to Missile Shield." *New York Times,* September 17, 2009.

Baker, Pete, and Steven Lee Myers. "Ties Fraying, Obama Drops Putin Meeting." *New York Times*, August 7, 2013.

Beinart, Peter. "Obama's Foreign Policy Doctrine Finally Emerges with 'Offshore Balancing.'" *Daily Beast*, November 28, 2011.

Bergen, Peter. *Manhunt: The Ten-Year Search for Bin Laden from 9/11 to Abbottabad*. New York: Crown, 2012.

Blake, Aaron. "Kerry: Military Action in Syria Would Be 'Unbelievably Small.'" *Washington Post*, September 9, 2013.

Bradley, John. *After the Arab Spring*. New York: Palgrave Macmillan, 2012.

Brands, Hal. "Breaking Down Obama's Grand Strategy." *National Interest*, June 23, 2014.

Brooks, David. "Why Hagel Was Picked." *New York Times*, January 7, 2013.

Brooks, Rosa. "The Case for Intervention." *Foreign Policy*, October 18, 2012.

Brzezinski, Zbigniew. "From Hope to Audacity: Appraising Obama's Foreign Policy." *Foreign Affairs* 89:1 (January–February 2010), 16–30.

Calabresi, Massimo. "Why the U.S. Went to War: Inside the White House Debate on Libya." *Time*, March 20, 2011.

Chandrasekaran, Rajiv. *Little America: The War within the War for Afghanistan*. New York: Alfred A. Knopf, 2012.

Chivvis, Christopher. *Toppling Qaddafi: Libya and the Limits of Liberal Intervention*. New York: Cambridge University Press, 2014.

Clark, Colin. "U.S. Military Could Not Handle One Major Theater Operation If Sequestration Sticks." *Breaking Defense*, September 18, 2013.

Clinton, Hillary. Address at the Council on Foreign Relations, July 15, 2009.

———. "America's Pacific Century." *Foreign Policy*, November 2011, 56–63.

———. *Hard Choices*. New York: Simon and Schuster, 2014.

Cohen, Ariel. "Putin's New 'Fortress Russia.'" *New York Times*, October 19, 2012.

Colby, Elbridge, and Ely Ratner. "Roiling the Waters: Why the United States Needs to Stop Playing Peacemaker and Start Making China Feel Uncomfortable." *Foreign Policy*, January 21, 2014.

Crocker, Ryan. "It's Not Too Late to Reengage with Iraq." *Washington Post*, June 19, 2014.

Crowley, Michael. "The Decider." *New Republic*, August 12, 2009.

Dale, Catherine, and Pat Towell. *In Brief: Assessing DOD's New Strategic Guidance*. Congressional Research Service, January 12, 2012.

Donnelly, Thomas, and Gary Schmitt. "Reverse the Defense Cuts." *National Review*, March 27, 2014.

Doran, Michael, and Max Boot. "Obama's Losing Bet on Iran." *New York Times*, January 15, 2014.

Drezner, Daniel. "Does Obama Have a Grand Strategy?" *Foreign Affairs* 90:4 (July–August 2011), 57–68.

———. *The System Worked: How the World Stopped Another Great Depression*. New York: Oxford University Press, 2014.

Dunne, Charles, et al. "Letter Urges Secretary Kerry to Bolster Support for Democracy in Libya One Year after Benghazi Attacks." Freedom House, September 10, 2013.

Eaglen, Mackenzie, and Roger Zakheim. "Rethinking the Quadrennial Defense Review." *Defense News*, March 19, 2014.

Economist. "The Birth of an Obama Doctrine." March 28, 2011.

────. "The State of Al Qaeda: The Unquenchable Fire." September 28, 2013.

Ferguson, Niall. "Obama's Egypt and Foreign-Policy Failures." *Newsweek*, February 15, 2011.

Ford, Christopher. "Soft on Soft Power." *SAIS Review* 32:1 (Winter–Spring 2012), 89–111.

Fravel, Taylor. "The Dangerous Math of Chinese Island Disputes." *Wall Street Journal*, October 28, 2012.

Freedman, Lawrence. "A Subversive on a Hill." *National Interest*, May–June 2009, 39–48.

Friedberg, Aaron. *Beyond Air-Sea Battle: The Debate over U.S. Military Strategy in Asia*. London: International Institute for Strategic Studies, 2014.

Gabbatt, Adam. "Obama Sends Letter to Kim Jong-Il." *Guardian*, December 16, 2009.

Garfinkle, Adam. "An Innocent Abroad." *American Interest*, November–December 2010.

Gates, Robert. *Duty: Memoirs of a Secretary at War*. New York: Knopf, 2014.

Gelb, Leslie. "The Elusive Obama Doctrine." *National Interest* 121 (September–October 2012), 18–28.

Ghattas, Kim. *The Secretary: A Journey with Hillary Clinton from Beirut to the Heart of American Power*. New York: Times Books, 2013.

Godemont, Francois. "The U.S. and Asia in 2009: Public Diplomacy and Strategic Continuity." *Asian Survey* 50:1 (January–February 2010), 8–24.

Godson, Roy, and Richard Shultz. "A QDR for All Seasons?" *Joint Force Quarterly* 59 (4th Quarter 2010), 52–56.

Goodman, J. David. "Microphone Catches a Candid Obama." *New York Times*, March 26, 2012.

Gordon, Michael. "Russia Displays a New Military Prowess in Ukraine's East." *New York Times*, April 21, 2014.

Gordon, Michael, and Bernard Trainor. *The Endgame: The Inside Story of the Struggle for Iraq, from George W. Bush to Barack Obama*. New York: Pantheon, 2012.

Green, Michael. "Negotiating Asia's Troubled Waters." *New York Times*, April 23, 2014.

Gvosdev, Nikolas. "As U.S. Influence Recedes, Russia Finds Openings in Egypt, Saudi Arabia." *World Politics Review*, November 15, 2013.

Hagel, Chuck. "Statement on Strategic Choices and Management Review." U.S. Department of Defense, July 31, 2013.

Harding, Luke. "Wikileaks Cables: Dmitry Medvedev 'Plays Robin to Putin's Batman.'" *Guardian*, December 1, 2010.

Hayden, Michael. "American Intelligence and the 'High Noon' Scenario." *Wall Street Journal*, October 30, 2013.

Heisbourg, Francois. "A Surprising Little War: First Lessons of Mali." *Survival* 55:2 (April–May 2013), 7–18.

Herszenhorn, David. "Facing Russian Threat, Ukraine Halts Plans for Deals with E.U." *New York Times*, November 21, 2013.

Holmes, Kim, and James Jay Carafano. "Defining the Obama Doctrine." Heritage Foundation, September 1, 2010.

Hung, Nguyen Manh. "Could Conflict in the South China Sea Lead to a 'New Cold War'?" *Asia Society*, October 2, 2012.

Ignatius, David. "U.S. Inattention to Libya Breeds Chaos." *Washington Post*, October 25, 2013.

Inboden, Will. "The Obama Administration's Diplomatic Deficit." *Foreign Policy*, August 8, 2013.

Indyk, Martin, Kenneth Lieberthal, and Michael O'Hanlon. *Bending History: Barack Obama's Foreign Policy*. Washington, DC: Brookings Institution Press, 2012.

Jones, Seth. *Hunting in the Shadows: The Pursuit of Al Qaeda since 9/11*. New York: Norton, 2013.

———. "Syria's Growing Jihad." *Survival* 55:4 (August–September 2013), 53–72.

Kagan, Frederick, and Kimberly Kagan. "How to Waste a Decade in Afghanistan." *Wall Street Journal*, January 9, 2013.

Kass, John. "Secret Drone Strikes Simplify Obama Doctrine." *Chicago Tribune*, February 7, 2013.

Katz, Mark. "Mutual Frustration: The State of Russian-American Relations." *Georgetown Journal of International Affairs*, August 9, 2013.

Kirchick, James. "Treason Chic." *Commentary*, October 2013.

Kirkpatrick, David. "Morsi's Slurs against Jews Stir Concern." *New York Times*, January 14, 2013.

Kissinger, Henry. "Idealism and Pragmatism in the Middle East." *Washington Post*, August 5, 2012.

Kitchen, Nicholas. "The Obama Doctrine: Detente or Decline?" *European Political Science* 10 (March 2011), 27–35.

Krauthammer, Charles. "Decline Is a Choice." *Weekly Standard*, October 19, 2009.

Krepinevich, Andrew. *Why Air-Sea Battle?* Center for Strategic and Budgetary Assessments, February 2010.

Kuperman, Alan. "A Model Humanitarian Intervention? Reassessing NATO's Libya Campaign." *International Security* 38:1 (Summer 2013), 105–36.

Lagon, Mark. "The Value of Values: Soft Power under Obama." *World Affairs* (September–October 2011), 69–77.

Laidi, Zaki. *Limited Achievements: Obama's Foreign Policy.* New York: Palgrave Macmillan, 2012.

Landler, Mark. "Clinton Paints China Policy with a Green Hue." *New York Times,* February 21, 2009.

———. "Obama Threatens Force against Syria." *New York Times,* August 21, 2012.

———. "Rice Offers a More Modest Strategy for Mideast." *New York Times,* October 26, 2013.

Landler, Mark, and Helene Cooper. "Allies Press U.S. to Go Slow on Egypt." *New York Times,* February 8, 2011.

Layne, Christopher. "The (Almost) Triumph of Offshore Balancing." *National Interest,* January 27, 2012.

Lelyveld, Joseph. "Obama Abroad: The Report Card." *New York Review of Books,* August 16, 2012.

Lindberg, Tod. "The Depressed Hyperpower." *Commentary,* July 2013.

Lizza, Ryan. "The Consequentialist: How the Arab Spring Remade Obama's Foreign Policy." *New Yorker,* May 2, 2011.

Luce, Edward, and Daniel Dombey. "Waiting on a Sun King." *Financial Times,* March 30, 2010.

Lusane, Clarence. "We Must Lead the World: The Obama Doctrine and the Re-branding of American Hegemony." *Black Scholar* 38:1 (Spring 2008), 34–43.

Lynch, Marc. *The Arab Uprisings.* New York: PublicAffairs, 2013.

MacFarquhar, Neil. "Russia and 2 Neighbors Form Economic Union That Has a Ukraine-Size Hole." *New York Times,* May 29, 2014.

Mann, James. *The Obamians: The Struggle inside the White House to Redefine American Power.* New York: Penguin, 2012.

Mazzetti, Mark. *The Way of the Knife.* New York: Penguin, 2014.

Mazzetti, Mark, Robert Worth, and Michael Gordon. "Obama's Uncertain Path amid Syria Bloodshed." *New York Times,* October 22, 2013.

McCarthy, Andrew. *Spring Fever: The Illusion of Islamic Democracy.* New York: Encounter Books, 2013.

McGrath, Bryan. "This Is What Assumption of Additional Risk Looks Like." *Information Dissemination,* March 25, 2014.

Michta, Andrew. "America the Hesitant." *American Interest,* July 1, 2014.

Morris, Loveday. "Seven Syrian Islamist Rebel Groups Form New Islamic Front." *Washington Post,* November 22, 2013.

Nasr, Vali. *The Dispensable Nation: American Foreign Policy in Retreat.* New York: Doubleday, 2013.

Owens, Erik. "Searching for an Obama Doctrine: Christian Realism and the Idealist/Realist Tension in Obama's Foreign Policy." *Journal of the Society of Christian Ethics* 32:2 (Fall–Winter 2012), 93–111.

Panetta, Leon. *Worthy Fights: A Memoir of Leadership in War and Peace.* New York: Penguin, 2014.

Parsi, Trita. *A Single Roll of the Dice: Obama's Diplomacy with Iran.* New Haven, CT: Yale University Press, 2013.

Pavliva, Halia, Natasha Doff, and Ksenia Galouchko. "Obama Sanctions Underwhelm Russian Stock Traders as Market Jumps." *Business Week*, April 29, 2014.

Perry, William, and John Abizaid, co-chairs. *Ensuring a Strong U.S. Defense for the Future: The National Defense Panel Review of the 2014 Quadrennial Defense Review.* Washington, DC: United States Institute of Peace, July 31, 2014.

Pew Research Global Attitudes Project. "Global Opinion of Obama Slips, International Policies Faulted." Pew Research Center, June 13, 2012.

Podhoretz, John. "Barack the Neo-con." *New York Post*, September 1, 2010.

Rabkin, Jeremy. "Libya: Our First Cosmopolitan War?" Foreign Policy Research Institute, May 2011.

Rachman, Gideon. "Syria and the Undoing of Obama's Grand Strategy." *Financial Times*, May 3, 2013.

Rassler, Don, et al. "Letters from Abbottabad: Bin Ladin Sidelined?" Combating Terrorism Center at West Point, May 3, 2012.

Renshon, Stanley. *National Security in the Obama Administration: Reassessing the Bush Doctrine.* New York: Routledge, 2009.

Rohde, David. "The Obama Doctrine." *Foreign Policy*, March–April 2012.

Rovner, Joshua, and Austin Long. "Reckless Reforms: Why the Obama Administration Should Ignore Recommendations from the Panel It Established to Review NSA Surveillance." *Foreign Policy*, January 2, 2014.

Sanger, David. *Confront and Conceal: Obama's Secret Wars and Surprising Use of American Power.* New York: Broadway Books, 2013.

———. "U.S. Confronts Consequences of Underestimating North Korean Leader." *New York Times*, April 24, 2014.

Schake, Kori. "How to Lose Friends and Alienate Allies." *Foreign Policy*, June 30, 2014.

Shanker, Thom. "Gates Warns against Big Cuts in Military Spending." *New York Times*, May 22, 2011.

Simes, Dimitri, and Paul Saunders. "Leading Blindly across a Minefield." *National Interest*, January–February 2013, 5–10.

Singh, Robert. *Barack Obama's Post-American Foreign Policy: The Limits of Engagement.* London: Bloomsbury Academic, 2012.

Sly, Liz. "Al-Qaeda Disavows Any Ties with Radical Islamist ISIS Group in Syria, Iraq." *Washington Post*, February 3, 2014.

Sly, Liz, and Karen De Young. "Largest Syrian Rebel Groups Form Islamic Alliance, in Possible Blow to U.S. Influence." *Washington Post*, September 25, 2013.

Star, Alexander, ed. *Open Secrets: Wikileaks, War, and American Diplomacy.* New York: Grove Press, 2011.

Takeyh, Ray. "A Kinder, Gentler Iran?" *Los Angeles Times*, September 20, 2013.

Trager, Eric. "The Unbreakable Muslim Brotherhood: Grim Prospects for a Liberal Egypt." *Foreign Affairs* 90:5 (September–October 2011), 114–26.

Tran, Mark, and Matthew Weaver. "ISIS Announces Islamic Caliphate in Area Straddling Iraq and Syria." *Guardian*, June 30, 2014.

US Department of Defense. *Quadrennial Defense Review*. February 2010.

———. *Quadrennial Defense Review*. March 2014.

———. *Sustaining U.S. Global Leadership: Priorities for 21st Century Defense*. January 2012.

US Department of State. "Accountability Review Board Report on the September 11th Attack in Benghazi." December 18, 2012, 1–39.

———. *Leading through Civilian Power: The First Quadrennial Diplomacy and Development Review*. December 2010.

Vidal, John, Allegra Stratton, and Suzanne Goldenberg. "Low Targets, Goals Dropped: Copenhagen Ends in Failure." *Guardian*, December 18, 2009.

Walker, Peter. "North Korea Human Rights Abuses Resemble Those of the Nazis, Says UN Inquiry." *Guardian*, February 17, 2014.

Weiss, Robert. "Imperial Obama: A Kinder, Gentler Empire?" *Social Justice* 37:2–3 (2010–11), 1–9.

Wells, Charlie. "U.S. Embassy in Cairo Confronts Muslim Brotherhood over Mixed Messages Sent via Twitter." *New York Daily News*, September 14, 2012.

Warrick, Joby. "ISIS, with Gains in Iraq, Closes in on Founder Zarqawi's Violent Vision." *Washington Post*, June 14, 2014.

West, Bing. *The Wrong War: Grit, Strategy, and the Way Out of Afghanistan*. New York: Random House, 2011.

White House, The. *National Security Strategy*. May 2010.

Wieseltier, Leon. "The Inconvenience of History." *New Republic*, April 23, 2014.

Woodward, Bob. *Obama's Wars*. New York: Simon and Schuster, 2010.

Zakaria, Fareed. "Stop Searching for an Obama Doctrine." *Washington Post*, July 6, 2011.

Zakheim, Dov. "Barack Obama's Legacy Problem." *National Interest*, May 13, 2014.

Zoellick, Robert. "Leading from the Front on Free Trade." *Wall Street Journal*, January 12, 2014.

International Challenges

Ajami, Fouad. *The Syrian Rebellion*. Stanford, CA: Hoover Institution Press, 2012.

Aron, Leon. "The Putin Doctrine." *Foreign Affairs* online, March 8, 2013.

Atwan, Abdel Bari. *After Bin Laden: Al Qaeda, the Next Generation*. New York: New Press, 2013.

Bacevich, Andrew. *Breach of Trust*. New York: Metropolitan Books, 2013.

Beckley, Michael. "China's Century? Why America's Edge Will Endure." *International Security* 36:3 (Winter 2011–12), 41–78.

Blackwill, Robert, and Meghan O'Sullivan. "America's Energy Edge: The Geopolitical Consequences of the Shale Revolution." *Foreign Affairs* 93:2 (March–April 2014), 102–14.

Blumenthal, Dan, and Phillip Swagel. *Awkward Embrace: The United States and China in the 21st Century.* Washington, DC: AEI Press, 2012.

Boot, Max, and Michael Doran. "Policy Innovation Memorandum No. 33." Council on Foreign Relations, June 7, 2013.

Bracken, Paul. *The Second Nuclear Age: Strategy, Danger, and the New Power Politics.* New York: St. Martin's Griffin, 2013.

Brooks, Stephen, and William Wohlforth. *World out of Balance: International Relations and the Challenge of American Primacy.* Princeton, NJ: Princeton University Press, 2008.

Brown, Michael, et al., eds. *Contending with Terrorism: Roots, Strategies, and Responses.* Cambridge, MA: MIT Press, 2010.

Brzezinski, Ian. "Three Ways NATO Can Bolster Ukraine's Security." *Washington Post*, March 24, 2014.

Brzezinski, Zbigniew. *Strategic Vision: America and the Crisis of Global Power.* New York: Basic Books, 2013.

Cha, Victor. *The Impossible State: North Korea, Past and Future.* New York: Ecco, 2013.

Chan, Steve. *Looking for Balance: China, the United States, and Power Balancing in East Asia.* Stanford, CA: Stanford University Press, 2012.

Colby, Elbridge. "Nuclear Abolition: A Dangerous Illusion." *Orbis*, Summer 2008, 424–33.

Cronin, Audrey. *How Terrorism Ends: Understanding the Decline and Demise of Terrorist Campaigns.* Princeton, NJ: Princeton University Press, 2011.

Cronin, Patrick. "If Deterrence Fails: Rethinking Conflict on the Korean Peninsula." Center for a New American Security, March 2014.

Cropsey, Seth. *Mayday: The Decline of American Naval Supremacy.* New York: Overlook, 2014.

Deal, Jacqueline Newmyer. "Chinese Dominance Isn't Certain." *National Interest*, May–June 2014.

Edelman, Eric. *Understanding America's Contested Primacy.* Washington, DC: Center for Strategic and Budgetary Assessments, 2010.

Edelman, Eric, Andrew Krepinevich, and Evan Braden Montgomery. "The Dangers of a Nuclear Iran." *Foreign Affairs* 90:1 (January–February 2011).

Freedom House. *Freedom in the World 2014.*

Friedberg, Aaron. *A Contest for Supremacy: China, America, and the Struggle for Mastery in Asia.* New York: Norton, 2012.

Gat, Azar. "The Return of Authoritarian Great Powers." *Foreign Affairs* 86:4 (July–August 2007), 59–69.

Goldhagen, Daniel. *The Devil That Never Dies: The Rise and Threat of Global Antisemitism.* New York: Little, Brown, 2013.

Goldstein, Avery. "China's Real and Present Danger." *Foreign Affairs,* September–October 2013, 136–44.

Grygiel, Jakub. "Europe: Strategic Drifter." *National Interest,* July–August 2013, 31–38.

Habeck, Mary. *Knowing the Enemy: Jihadist Ideology and the War on Terror.* New Haven, CT: Yale University Press, 2007.

———. "Attacking America: Al Qaeda's Grand Strategy in Its War with the World." Foreign Policy Research Institute, February 2014.

Heilmann, Sebastian, and Dirk Schmidt. *China's Foreign Political and Economic Relations.* Lanham, MD: Rowman and Littlefield, 2014.

Henriksen, Thomas. *America and the Rogue States.* New York: Palgrave Macmillan, 2012.

Hoffman, Frank. "Forward Partnership: A Sustainable American Strategy." *Orbis* 57:1 (Winter 2013), 20–40.

Hokayem, Emile. *Syria's Uprising and the Fracturing of the Levant.* London: International Institute for Strategic Studies, 2013.

Ikenberry, John, Michael Mastanduno, and William Wohlforth, eds. *International Relations Theory and the Consequences of Unipolarity.* New York: Cambridge University Press, 2011.

International Institute for Strategic Studies. *The Military Balance 2013.* London: Routledge, 2013.

———. *The Military Balance 2014.* London: Routledge, 2014.

Irwin, Douglas. *Free Trade under Fire.* Princeton, NJ: Princeton University Press, 2009.

Joffe, Josef. *The Myth of America's Decline.* New York: Liveright, 2013.

Joffe, Josef, and James Davis. "Less Than Zero." *Foreign Affairs* 90:1 (January–February 2011).

Jones, Bruce. *Still Ours to Lead.* Washington, DC: Brookings Institution Press, 2014.

Jones, Gregory. "Facing the Reality of Iran as a De Facto Nuclear State." Nonproliferation Policy Education Center, March 22, 2012.

Jones, Seth. *A Persistent Threat: The Evolution of al Qa'ida and Other Salafi Jihadists.* Rand Corporation, June 2014.

Jones, Seth, and Keith Crane. *Afghanistan after the Drawdown.* New York: Council on Foreign Relations, November 2013.

Kagan, Robert. *The Return of History and the End of Dreams.* New York: Vintage, 2009.

———. *The World America Made.* New York: Knopf, 2012.

Kaplan, Robert. *The Revenge of Geography.* New York: Random House, 2012.

Katz, Mark. *Leaving without Losing: The War on Terror after Iraq and Afghanistan.* Baltimore, MD: Johns Hopkins University Press, 2012.

Kepel, Gilles, and Jean-Pierre Milelli, eds. *Al Qaeda in Its Own Words*. Cambridge, MA: Belknap Press of Harvard University Press, 2008.

Kilcullen, David. *Counterinsurgency*. New York: Oxford University Press, 2010.

———. *Out of the Mountains: The Coming Age of the Urban Guerrilla*. New York: Oxford University Press, 2013.

Kroenig, Matthew. *A Time to Attack: The Looming Iranian Nuclear Threat*. New York: Palgrave Macmillan, 2014.

Kupchan, Charles. *No One's World*. New York: Oxford University Press, 2013.

Leffler, Melvyn. "Defense on a Diet: How Budget Crises Have Improved U.S. Strategy." *Foreign Affairs* 92:6 (November/December 2013), 65–76.

Lieber, Robert. *Power and Willpower in the American Future*. New York: Cambridge University Press, 2012.

Litwak, Robert. *Outlier States: American Strategies to Change, Contain, or Engage Regimes*. Washington, DC: Woodrow Wilson Center Press, 2012.

Lo, Bobo. *Axis of Convenience: Moscow, Beijing, and the New Geopolitics*. London: Chatham House, 2008.

Lucas, Edward, A. Wess Mitchell, et al. "Report No. 35: Central European Security After Crimea." Center for European Policy Analysis, March 25, 2014.

Luttwak, Edward. *The Rise of China vs. the Logic of Strategy*. Cambridge, MA: Belknap Press, 2012.

Mandaville, Peter. *Islam and Politics*. New York: Routledge, 2014.

Mankoff, Jeffrey. *Russian Foreign Policy: The Return of Great Power Politics*. 2nd ed. Lanham, MD: Rowman and Littlefield, 2011.

Markey, Daniel. *No Exit from Pakistan: America's Tortured Relationship with Islamabad*. New York: Cambridge University Press, 2013.

Mead, Walter Russell. "The Return of Geopolitics." *Foreign Affairs* 93:3 (May–June 2014), 69–79.

Menon, Rajan. *The End of Alliances*. New York: Oxford University Press, 2007.

Mitchell, A. Wess, and Jakub Grygiel. "The Vulnerability of Peripheries." *American Interest*, Spring 2011, 5–16.

Mitchell, A. Wess, Jakub Grygiel, and Robert Kron. "Hingepoint Allies: Bolstering U.S. Alliances with Exposed States in Central Europe, East Asia and the Middle East." Center for European Policy Analysis, October 8, 2010.

Nathan, Andrew, and Andrew Scobell. *China's Search for Security*. New York: Columbia University Press, 2012.

National Intelligence Council. *Global Trends 2030: Alternative Worlds*. December 2012.

Nau, Henry, and Deepa Ollapally, eds. *Worldviews of Aspiring Powers*. New York: Oxford University Press, 2012.

Nye, Joseph. *The Future of Power*. New York: PublicAffairs, 2011.

O'Hanlon, Michael. *Healing the Wounded Giant: Maintaining Military Preeminence While Cutting the Defense Budget.* Washington, DC: Brookings Institution Press, 2013.

———. *The Wounded Giant: America's Armed Forces in an Age of Austerity.* New York: Penguin, 2011.

Pape, Robert, and James Feldman. *Cutting the Fuse: The Explosion of Global Suicide Terrorism and How to Stop It.* Chicago: University of Chicago Press, 2010.

Patrick, Stewart. *Weak Links: Fragile States, Global Threats, and International Security.* New York: Oxford University Press, 2011.

Petersen, Alexandros. *The World Island: Geopolitics and the Fate of the West.* Santa Barbara, CA: Praeger, 2011.

Pollack, Kenneth. *Unthinkable: Iran, the Bomb, and American Strategy.* New York: Simon and Schuster, 2013.

Potter, William, and Gaukhar Mukhatzanova, eds. *Forecasting Nuclear Proliferation in the 21st Century.* 2 vols. Stanford, CA: Stanford Security Studies, 2010.

Putin, Vladimir. "A New Integration Project for Eurasia—a Future Being Born Today." *Izvestiya,* October 4, 2011. (Johnson's Russia List, No. 180, October 6, Item 30.)

Rachman, Gideon. *Zero-Sum Future: American Power in an Age of Anxiety.* New York: Simon and Schuster, 2011.

Ravich, Samantha. "Playing the Long Game." *American Interest,* March 1, 2011.

Reiss, Mitchell. "A Nuclear-Armed Iran: Possible Security and Diplomatic Implications." Council on Foreign Relations Working Paper, May 2010.

Ross, Robert, and Zhu Feng, eds. *China's Ascent: Power, Security, and the Future of International Politics.* Ithaca, NY: Cornell University Press, 2008.

Rothstein, Hy, and John Arquilla, eds. *Afghan Endgames: Strategy and Policy Choices for America's Longest War.* Washington, DC: Georgetown University Press, 2012.

Rubin, Barry, ed. *The Muslim Brotherhood: The Organization and Policies of a Global Islamist Movement.* New York: Palgrave Macmillan, 2010.

Rubin, Michael. *Dancing with the Devil: The Perils of Engaging Rogue Regimes.* New York: Encounter Books, 2014.

Ryan, Michael. *Decoding Al Qaeda's Strategy.* New York: Columbia University Press, 2013.

Schadlow, Nadia. "Competitive Engagement: Upgrading America's Influence." *Orbis* 57:4 (Autumn 2013), 501–15.

Schelling, Thomas. "A World without Nuclear Weapons?" *Daedalus* 138:4 (September 2009), 124–29.

Shambaugh, David. *China Goes Global: The Partial Power.* New York: Oxford University Press, 2013.

Sherr, James. *Hard Diplomacy and Soft Coercion: Russia's Influence Abroad.* London: Chatham House, 2013.

Smith, Lee. *The Consequences of Syria.* Stanford, CA: Hoover Institution Press, 2014.

Sokolski, Henry, ed. *The Next Arms Race.* Washington, DC: Nonproliferation Policy Education Center, 2012.

Springer, Devin, James Regens, and David Edger. *Islamic Radicalism and Global Jihad.* Washington, DC: Georgetown University Press, 2009.

Suominen, Kati. *Peerless and Periled: The Paradox of American Leadership in the World Economic Order.* Stanford, CA: Stanford Economics and Finance, 2012.

Sutter, Robert. *Foreign Relations of the PRC.* Lanham, MD: Rowman and Littlefield, 2013.

Takeyh, Ray. *Guardians of the Revolution: Iran and the World in the Age of the Ayatollahs.* New York: Oxford University Press, 2009.

Talent, Jim, and Jon Kyl. *A Strong and Focused National Security Strategy.* Heritage Foundation, October 31, 2013.

Tellis, Ashley. "Balancing without Containment: A U.S. Strategy for Confronting China's Rise." *Washington Quarterly* 36:4 (Fall 2013), 109–24.

———, ed. *Strategic Asia, 2012–13: China's Military Challenge.* Seattle, WA: National Bureau of Asian Research, 2012.

———. *Strategic Asia, 2013–14: Asia in the Second Nuclear Age.* Seattle, WA: National Bureau of Asian Research, 2013.

Terry, Sue Mi. "A Korea Whole and Free." *Foreign Affairs* 93:4 (July–August 2014), 153–62.

Tertrais, Bruno. "The Illogic of Zero." *Washington Quarterly* 33:2 (April 2010), 125–38.

Thomas, Jim. "From Protectorates to Partnerships." *American Interest* 6:5 (May–June 2011), 37–44.

Walton, Dale. *Geopolitics and the Great Powers in the 21st Century.* New York: Routledge, 2007.

Waltz, Kenneth. "Why Iran Should Get the Bomb." *Foreign Affairs* 91:4 (July–August 2012).

Watts, Barry. *The Evolution of Precision Strike.* Center for Strategic and Budgetary Assessments, August 2013.

Watts, Clint. "Jihadi Competition after Al Qaeda Hegemony: The 'Old Guard,' Team ISIS and the Battle for Jihadi Hearts and Minds." Foreign Policy Research Institute, February 20, 2014.

Yergin, Daniel. *The Quest: Energy, Security, and the Remaking of the Modern World.* New York: Penguin, 2012.

Yoshihara, Susan, and Douglas Sylva, eds. *Population Decline and the Remaking of Great Power Politics.* Washington, DC: Potomac Books, 2011.

Yoshihara, Toshi, and James Holmes. *Red Star over the Pacific: China's Rise and the Challenge to U.S. Maritime Strategy.* Annapolis, MD: Naval Institute Press, 2013.

Zakaria, Fareed. *The Post-American World: Release 2.0.* New York: Norton, 2012.

Zimmerman, Katherine. "The Al Qaeda Network: A New Framework for Defining the Enemy." American Enterprise Institute, September 2013.

SUBJECT INDEX

Buchanan, Pat, 121, 124, 162, 186, 189
Budget Control Act of 2011, 94, 140–141, 238
Budget deficit, 11, 140
Bush, George H. W., 17, 168
Bush, George W.: 2008 election, effect on,
193; American realism compared to, 246;
and conservative nationalists, 180–181;
effectiveness within Republican Party,
123, 127; freedom agenda of, 213; Iraq
security agreement of, 88; Iraq surge
strategy of, 130–131, 244; and mistakes
of Iraq war, 244; North Korea relations
with, 64; public opinion on strategic
activism of, 112; regime change tactics
of, 17, 23, 36; September 11, 2001, attacks,
effect on, 169; unpopularity of, 131
Bush, Jeb, 173
Buzan, Barry, 203–204

Carr, E. H., 200
Cato Handbook for Policymakers, 167
Cato Institute, 9, 124, 159, 166–168
Center for the National Interest, 200
Cha, Victor, 230
Chechnya, 51
Chemical weapons: nonproliferation
agreement, 58, 165; in Syria, 85–87, 143
Chicago Council on Global Affairs, 111, 113
China: competitive policies of, 217;
containment policy toward, 37, 72, 74,
225; diplomacy policy toward, 37, 74,
151; hybrid strategies toward, 72–73, 252;
maritime territorial disputes, 74, 224;
and North Korea, 73, 232, 268n61; and
nuclear nonproliferation, 59, 73; Open
Door policy toward, 19; public opinion
on rise of, 113; rise to great power
status, 210–211, 212, 221–222, 224–226.
See also Great powers
Christie, Chris, 173
Clarke, Richard, 237
Climate change, 73, 151, 213
Clinton, Bill: containment policy of, 16;
on democratic enlargement, 213;
foreign policy as low priority for, 111;
internationalist policies of, 180; Obama
on presidency of, 28, 31; on presidential
grand strategy, 4–5
Clinton, Hillary: as possible 2016
Democratic candidate, 166, 194–195;
as secretary of state, 41, 55, 73, 85,
146, 276n71
Coercive diplomacy, 219

Cold War: and conservative
anti-interventionists, 118–119, 161; and
conservative internationalists, 168;
and conservative nationalists, 179;
containment policy during, 16–17, 23;
and hawkish internationalism, 119;
hybrid strategies during, 23; Obama's
criticism of arms race of, 43; power of
transnational contact in, 19; and public
opinion, 111. *See also* Soviet Union
Communism. *See* Cold War; Soviet Union
Comprehensive Test Ban Treaty, 58
Congressional politics, 138–144; and
Afghanistan war, 141–142; deference
toward White House, 138–139; and
Libya situation, 142; recommended
strategies for, 247–248; Republican
control during Obama's second term,
139; and Syria crisis, 142–143; voting
along single ideological continuum, 26
Conservative American realism, 11, 196,
197–257; and adversaries, 217–218; and
allies, 215–217; as alternative to Obama
doctrine, 197, 246; benefits of, 11, 204,
206; and defense spending, 237–239;
disagreement among realists, 201;
foreign policy assumptions, 213–215;
foreign policy realism, 198–202; and
great power competition, 220–226;
Iraq war, lessons from, 241–247; and
jihadist terrorists, 233–237; as mindset,
201; and national security challenges
and threats, 212–213; and presidential
leadership, 247–257; recommended
approach for, 250–252; and rogue state
adversaries, 226–233; skepticism of, 199;
and strategies of pressure, 218–220; and
trade policy, 239–241; US capabilities
and resources in, 208–212; US forward
strategic presence in, 205–208; US
interests and primacy in, 202–205
Conservative anti-interventionists/
noninterventionists, 9–10, 22–23, 118,
159–168; in 2016 election, 187, 195; and
Cold War, 118–119; distinguished from
nationalists, 182–183; and election
(2012), 134; goals of, 159; historical
precedent for, 160–162; minority of
Republicans as, 158, 159; reasons for rise
of, 162–163; Republicans as, 121, 124–125,
157; as significant political force and
faction of today's Republicans, 163–164.
See also Paul, Rand

Conservative internationalists, 157, 168–176; in 2016 election, 187–188; agreement with conservative nationalists, 158, 182; distinguished from liberal internationalists, 170–171; goals of, 169–170; as hawks, 118; historical precedent for, 168–169; as leaders of Republican Party, 168, 173; major force in today's Republican Party, 176; Republican voters favoring, 174; strengths of, 173–174; types of, 171–172. *See also* Neoconservatives

Conservative nationalists, 10, 157, 176–185; in 2010 House of Representatives, 183; in 2016 election, as influential faction, 187; agreement with conservative internationalists, 158, 182; base of support for, 176, 178; distinguished from anti-interventionists, 182–183; goals of, 176–178; historical precedent for, 177–179; and Jacksonian tradition, 178–182; overall opposition to Obama policies, 182; as representative of average Republican voter, 183

Conservatives: national security views of, 9–10; Republican Party alignment with, 26, 124, 155–156. *See also specific types above*

Constitutionality issues, 32, 124, 127, 138, 163, 164, 166, 238

Containment policy: with China, 37, 72, 74, 225; as foreign policy option, 14, 16, 23; with jihadist terrorists, 236; with North Korea, 37, 65, 103

Corn, David, 13–14

Counterterrorism, 48–57, 113–114; and change from Bush to Obama administration, 131–132, 233, 235; conservative internationalists on, 175; conservative nationalists on, 181; and offshore balancing, 100; and perpetual war, 236

Credibility, 75, 88, 96, 205, 218, 219, 243, 246

Cruz, Ted, 126, 184

Cuba, 18

Czech Republic, 92

Dagestan, 51

Defense spending, 47, 94–100; budget cuts, 94–96, 141; conservative anti-interventionists on, 160, 164; conservative internationalists on, 170, 175; and offshore balancing, 21; Rand Paul's views on, 166, 188; as percent of GDP, 94; public opinion on, 113,

121; recommended US strategy for, 237–239, 255; Republicans on, 125; and sequestration, 94–95, 97, 98, 141, 237, 238. *See also* Retrenchment

Delbruck, Hans, 18

Democracy promotion, 35, 127, 140, 169, 170, 171, 172, 181, 182, 213, 214, 225, 229

Democrats: 2016 election issues for, 9; and Afghanistan war, 55–56; base of support for, 240; characterization of voting blocs of, 120; divisiveness of foreign policy among, 121–122; dovish internationalism of, 119, 120, 179; liberal stance of, 26, 155; and New Deal hawkish policies, 120; support for Obama foreign policy, 122–123

Detention and interrogation policies, 54

Deterrence policies, 60, 72–73, 75, 101, 103, 171, 196, 197, 218–219, 221–232, 243, 246, 252

Diplomacy: with China, 37, 74, 151; coercive diplomacy, 219; and conservative American realism, 199; conservative internationalists on, 170; conservative nationalists on, 182; as foreign policy option, 19–20; in Middle East, 87–88, 228; as Obama choice of strategy, 47, 92, 105; Rand Paul's views on, 188; with Russia, 37, 67, 71

Disengagement, policy of: arguments for, 205–208; dangers of, 7, 66, 207, 216; in Iraq, 90–91; in Libya, 82. *See also* Diplomacy; Retrenchment

Disentanglement. *See* Conservative anti-interventionists/ noninterventionists

Doha Round, 240

Domestic policies: conservative anti-interventionists/ noninterventionists on, 163; conservative nationalists on, 177, 182; economic policies, 114, 156, 211; government spending linked to, 239, 255; as priority for Obama, 3, 6, 14, 33–34, 107, 148–150, 242; as priority in public opinion, 112; Tea Party on, 184–185

Domestic politics, 109–153; and congressional politics, 138–144; and electoral politics, 129–138; incorporated into foreign policy, 2–3, 148–150; and party politics, 116–129; trade-offs with international policy, 25. *See also* Grand strategy; Presidential leadership; Public opinion

Donilon, Thomas, 145
Dovish internationalism, 117–120, 166, 179
Drone strikes, 35, 49, 55, 94, 101, 151;
    conservative anti-interventionist
    opposition to, 160, 188; conservative
    internationalist support for, 175; public
    support for, 112, 113, 122; Republican
    support for, 125

East Asia policy, 93–94, 98, 103. *See also* Asia
    pivot; *specific countries*
East Germany, 19
Economic stimulus package (2009), 32
Economist on Obama's domestic legacy, 33
Egypt, 50–51, 75–82, 92, 103, 236
Eikenberry, Karl, 55
Eisenhower, Dwight: decision-making
    process of, 251; election of (1952),
    161, 168; marginalization of
    anti-interventionists under, 186; regime
    change tactics of, 17
Election of 1952, 161, 168
Election of 2008, 130–131
Election of 2012, 32, 39, 50, 90, 134–137;
    Benghazi attack, effect of, 136; bin
    Laden strike, effect of, 133, 136, 152, 192;
    domestic politics as winning issue for
    Obama in, 152; foreign policy as winning
    issue for Obama in, 8, 110; Republicans
    seeking nomination, 134–135
Election of 2016, 10, 152–153, 186–196, 253;
    Hillary Clinton as possible Democratic
    candidate, 166, 194–195; influence of
    conservative nationalists, 187
Electoral politics, 129–138; swing voters, 116,
    129, 130, 136, 156, 191, 194, 195, 253; war
    as factor in, 129–130. *See also specific
    election years above*
Elite opinion-makers, 117
Emanuel, Rahm, 55
Engagement, strategy of: bargaining as,
    19–20; with China, 73; as foreign policy
    option, 18; in incoming Obama policy,
    46; integration as, 18–19; with Iraq, 88;
    with Russia, 66–67; with traditional
    allies, 91–92
Entrapment fears, 215–216, 242
Eurasian Economic Union, 71
European Union, 70, 210, 222
Evangelicals, 173

Financial crisis (2008–2009), 101
Foreign aid, 175, 182

Foreign policy: in 2016 elections, 186–196;
    public opinion on, 110–111, 115;
    trade-offs with domestic policy, 25. *See
    also* Grand strategy; Obama doctrine;
    headings starting with "Conservative"
Fort Hood, Texas, attack (2009), 51, 132
France, 59, 82
Free Syrian Army, 87
Free trade, 170
Fukuyama, Francis, 213

Gaddafi, Mu'ammer, 82, 103–104, 142
Gadsden flag as Tea Party symbol, 185
Gallup polls, 111, 113, 114, 121, 153, 160
Gates, Robert, 55, 56, 65, 94, 145, 146, 149,
    237, 245
Gelb, Leslie, 1, 2
Geopolitics, 199
Georgia, Russian invasion of, 67, 71
Ghani, Ashraf, 57
Gilpin, Robert, 16, 200
Gingrich, Newt, 135
Goldwater, Barry, 119, 180
Graham, Lindsey, 133, 173
Grand strategy, 13–39; assumptions of,
    5; Clinton on, 4; complexity and
    contentiousness of, 5; defined, 2, 14–15;
    and diplomacy, 19; hybrid strategies of,
    23–24, 36–37, 46, 47, 100–101; matched
    to public opinion, 113, 115–116, 135, 150;
    misalignment of defense posture under,
    97; Obama's approach to, 2, 33–39;
    options in, 6, 15–25, 220; in Syria, 87;
    trade-offs associated with, 104; types of
    US strategies, 14–25. *See also* Containment
    policy; Engagement; Obama doctrine;
    Regime change; Retrenchment
Great powers: and American unipolar
    moment, 203–204; bargaining strategy
    used with, 37; diplomacy used with, 37;
    realism of US role as stabilizing force,
    207; rivalry and cooperation with,
    65–75, 220–226. *See also* China; Russia
Guantánamo Bay, 132
Guatemala, 17

Hagel, Chuck, 104, 137, 146
Hamas, 64, 80
Haqqani, 57
Hawkish internationalism, 117–118; of New
    Deal Democrats, 120; of Republican
    Party, 119, 120–121, 125, 128, 158; of Tea
    Party, 126

Layne, Christopher, 20, 99
Liberal policies, 8; classic liberal tradition in
    American foreign policy, 213–214; and
    dovish internationalism, 118, 119; liberal
    internationalism, 170–171, 176, 185
Libertarians, 9, 159, 161, 162, 164, 166,
    189–190, 256
Libya, US intervention in, 17, 35, 37, 50, 82–84,
    103–104, 112, 151; Hillary Clinton on,
    195; and congressional politics, 141,
    142; conservative anti-interventionist
    views on, 160, 162; conservative
    internationalist views on, 174;
    conservative nationalist views on, 182;
    continuing US role in, 236
Lizza, Ryan, 1, 43
Logan, Justin, 167

al-Maliki, Nouri, 89–91
Mankoff, Jeffrey, 68
Mann, James, 77, 149
Marshall, George, 5
McCain, John, 29, 131, 171, 173, 193
McDonough, Denis, 145
McGovern, George, 119–120
Mead, Walter Russell, 178
Mearsheimer, John, 20, 21, 200
Medvedev, Dmitry, 67, 69, 71
Middle East policy: conservative
    internationalists on, 175–176; diplomacy
    in, 87–88, 151, 228; and traditional allies,
    92. See also specific countries
Military presence: desirability of, 205–208;
    recommendations for, 256. See also
    Defense spending; Retrenchment
Missile defense plans, 92
Mohammed, Khalid Sheikh, 132
Morgenthau, Hans, 200
Morsi, Mohamed, 77, 79–81
Mubarak, Hosni, 76–77, 81, 92
Multilateral institutions, 170–171, 213
Multipolarity, 203, 208–211
Muslim Brotherhood, 50–51, 76–82, 218

Nasr, Vali, 76, 78, 149–150
Nationalists. See Conservative nationalists
National Review, 183
National security: challenges and threats,
    34, 212–213; and Clinton administration,
    111; Republican stance on, 158. See also
    Military presence
National Security Council, 251
NATO, 67, 161, 165, 175–176, 216, 221–222

Neoconservatives, 9, 10, 123, 127, 128–129,
    156, 158, 172
Neoisolationists, 158, 194, 195–196, 253
New Deal, 120, 179
New START Treaty, 58, 66, 69
Niebuhr, Reinhold, 200
Nigeria, 51, 102
Nixon, Richard, 16, 145, 168, 263n29
Nonentanglement. See Conservative
    anti-interventionists/
    noninterventionists
Noninterventionists. See Conservative
    anti-interventionists/
    noninterventionists
Non-Proliferation Treaty (NPT), 58
North Korea, 18, 22, 59, 63, 64–65, 101; and
    China, 73, 232, 268n61; containment
    policy toward, 37, 65, 103; as rogue state,
    212, 229–233
Nuclear proliferation and disarmament, 43,
    57–65, 66, 73, 102–103, 213. See also specific
    countries
Nuclear Security Summit (Washington,
    DC), 58
Nuclear Weapons Posture Review, 58

Obama, Barack: and 2016 election, 192, 193,
    253; and American creed, 30–31; on
    G. W. Bush, 48, 67, 106; character of,
    6, 14, 25, 28–29, 31, 145, 147, 151, 249;
    comparing Clinton's and Reagan's
    presidencies, 28; decision-making
    process of, 6, 29, 109, 145–148; domestic
    expenditures of, 239; effectiveness
    within Democratic Party, 122–123;
    election of (2008), 130; grand strategy
    of, 33–39; incoming foreign policy of,
    42–47; liberal leanings of, 26, 29–30,
    137; on nuclear disarmament, 57–58;
    overseas upbringing of, 42; place in
    American politics, 25–33; on Putin,
    41; on Reagan's foreign policy, 43;
    re-election of (2012), 8, 32, 39, 69,
    90, 101, 137; Republican antagonism
    toward, 128; as senator, 29, 43, 88, 130;
    as transformational president, 28,
    32–33, 38, 105–106; unpopularity of, 8–9,
    192–193. See also headings below starting
    with "Obama"
Obama doctrine: and 2016 elections,
    152–153; ambiguity of, 1–2; and Arab
    Spring, 75–91; conservative American
    realism as alternative to, 197; and

Republicans, 155–196; and 2016 elections, 10, 153, 186–196, 253–254; cohesive foreign policy of (pre-Obama), 121; congressional control during Obama's second term, 139; conservative internationalists, 168–176; conservative nationalists, 10, 176–185; conservative noninterventionists, 9–10, 159–168; conservative stance of, 26, 124, 155–156, 189; division over international issues, 9–10, 156–158, 186, 254; hawkish internationalism of, 119, 120–121, 125, 128, 158; and Jacksonian tradition, 178–182, 185, 186; national security views of, 9–10, 253; opposition to Obama's domestic policies, 8; opposition to Obama's foreign policies, 109–110; overview of major schools of thought on foreign policy among, 157–158. *See also* Conservative anti-interventionists/ noninterventionists; Conservative internationalists; Conservative nationalists

Retrenchment: arguments for, 205–208; in Asia-Pacific, 75; as basic strategy option, 15–16; conservative anti-interventionist support for, 159; conservative internationalist opposition to, 175; as election issue (2012), 134; goals of, 38; negative results of, 207, 251; Obama's strategy of, 14, 34, 36, 46–47, 49, 93–96, 102, 151, 251, 256; Rand Paul's views on, 165–166; public opinion on, 113; Tea Party view of, 126; traditional allies, effect on, 92, 104. *See also* Defense spending

Rhodes, Benjamin, 145
Rice, Susan, 82, 137, 145
Rogue state adversaries, 57–65, 226–233
Rollback. *See* Regime change
Romney, Mitt, 29, 83, 135, 136, 173
Roosevelt, Franklin, 16, 27
Roosevelt, Theodore, 16
Rouhani, Hassan, 60, 61–62, 226–227
Rubio, Marco, 173, 185
Russia: diplomacy with, 37, 67, 71; in Eurasian Economic Union, 71; great power status of, 211, 212, 221–223; influence rebuilding of, 103; and nuclear nonproliferation, 58, 59, 66, 67, 69, 72; reset of US relations with, 41, 67–69, 71, 151, 222; Snowden granted asylum

in, 72; in Syrian crisis, 72, 85, 86, 143; Ukraine annexation by, 70–71, 221. *See also* Great powers

Ryan, Paul, 173

Santorum, Rick, 135, 173
Separation of powers, 138
September 11, 2001 terrorist attacks, 111, 139, 169
Sherr, James, 223
Singh, Robert, 1
Six-Party Talks (North Korea, South Korea, Russia, Japan, China, and United States), 64
Skowronek, Stephen, 27
Snowden, Edward, 72, 160
Somalia, 51
South Korea, 175, 231, 241
Soviet Union: aversion to waging war, 18; containment policy toward, 16–17, 119; invasion of Afghanistan, 111; US detente with, 19. *See also* Cold War
Spykman, Nicholas, 200
Sunni vs. Shia: in Iraq, 91; in Syria, 85
Superpowers, 203–204, 210–212
Swing voters, 116, 129, 130, 136, 156, 169, 191, 194, 195, 253
Syria: chemical weapons in, 86; civil war in, 8, 50, 84–88, 103; and congressional policy, 141, 143–144; conservative anti-inventionalist opposition to airstrikes against, 160, 162; conservative internationalist support for airstrikes against, 174; conservative nationalist opposition to airstrikes against, 182; public opinion on Obama's handling of, 112, 115, 122, 143, 150, 273n30; Republican support for airstrikes against, 126; as rogue state, 212; Russian role in, 72, 85, 86, 143; US policy toward, 84–88, 92, 103. *See also* Islamic State of Iraq and Syria (ISIS)

Taft, Robert, 119, 124, 125, 161, 179
Taliban, 54–57, 69, 102, 130, 132
Tea Party, 10, 123, 124, 125, 126, 139, 156, 157–158, 160, 164, 176, 183–185, 189
Terrorism: attacks in United States since 2009, 54; Iran in support of, 64; Libya as terrorist haven, 84; and offshore balancing, 21; waging of transnational war, 212. *See also* al-Qaeda; Counterterrorism; Islamic State of Iraq and Syria (ISIS)